PRAXIS PARAPRO ASSESSMENT 0755
TEACHER CERTIFICATION EXAM

By: Sharon Wynne, M.S.

XAMonline, INC.
Boston

Copyright © 2010 XAMonline, Inc.
All rights reserved. No part of the material protected by this copyright notice may be reproduced or utilized in any form or by any means, electronic or mechanical, including photocopying, recording or by any information storage and retrievable system, without written permission from the copyright holder.

To obtain permission(s) to use the material from this work for any purpose including workshops or seminars, please submit a written request to:

XAMonline, Inc.
25 First Street, Suite 106
Cambridge, MA 02141
Toll Free 1-800-509-4128
Email: info@xamonline.com
Web: www.xamonline.com
Fax: 1-617-583-5552

Library of Congress Cataloging-in-Publication Data

Wynne, Sharon A.
    PRAXIS ParaPro Assessment 0755 / Sharon A. Wynne. 3rd ed
    ISBN 978-1-60787-052-4
    1. ParaPro Assessment 0755
    2. Study Guides
    3. PRAXIS
    4. Teachers' Certification & Licensure
    5. Careers

Disclaimer:
The opinions expressed in this publication are the sole works of XAMonline and were created independently from the National Education Association, Educational Testing Service, or any State Department of Education, National Evaluation Systems or other testing affiliates.

Between the time of publication and printing, state specific standards as well as testing formats and Web site information may change and therefore would not be included in part or in whole within this product. Sample test questions are developed by XAMonline and reflect content similar to that on real tests; however, they are not former test questions. XAMonline assembles content that aligns with state standards but makes no claims nor guarantees teacher candidates a passing score. Numerical scores are determined by testing companies such as NES or ETS and then are compared with individual state standards. A passing score varies from state to state.

Printed in the United States of America

PRAXIS ParaPro Assessment 0755
ISBN: 978-1-60787-052-4

Table of Contents

DOMAIN I
READING 1

COMPETENCY 1
READING SKILLS AND KNOWLEDGE 3

Skill 1.1: Identify the main idea or primary purpose 3
Skill 1.2: Identify supporting ideas 5
Skill 1.3: Identify how a reading selection is organized 6
Skill 1.4: Determine the meanings of words or phrases in context 7
Skill 1.5: Draw inferences or implications from directly stated content 11
Skill 1.6: Determine whether information is presented as fact or opinion 14
Skill 1.7: Interpret information from tables, diagrams, charts, and graphs 15

COMPETENCY 2
APPLICATION OF READING SKILLS AND KNOWLEDGE TO CLASSROOM INSTRUCTION 16

Skill 2.1: Understand how to help students sound out words *(e.g., recognize long and short vowels, consonant sounds, rhymes)* 16
Skill 2.2: Understand how to help students break down words into parts *(e.g., recognize syllables, root words, prefixes, and suffixes)* ... 20
Skill 2.3: Understand how to help students decode words or phrases using context clues 29
Skill 2.4: Understand how to help students distinguish among synonyms, antonyms, and homonyms 40
Skill 2.5: Understand how to help students alphabetize words 41
Skill 2.6: Understand how to help students use prereading strategies, such as skimming or making predictions 47
Skill 2.7: Understand how to ask questions about a reading selection to help students understand the selection 48
Skill 2.8: Understand how to make accurate observations about students' ability to understand and interpret text 61
Skill 2.9: Understand how to help students use a dictionary 67
Skill 2.10: Understand how to help students interpret written directions 69

SAMPLE TEST
READING 74
Answer Key 79
Rigor Table 79

DOMAIN II
MATHEMATICS 81

COMPETENCY 3
NUMBER SENSE AND BASIC ALGEBRA 83

Skill 3.1: Perform basic addition, subtraction, multiplication, and division of whole numbers, fractions, and decimals 83

Skill 3.2: Recognize multiplication as repeated addition and division as repeated subtraction 95

Skill 3.3: Recognize and interpret mathematical symbols 95

Skill 3.4: Understand the definitions of basic terms such as sum, difference, product, quotient, numerator, and denominator 96

Skill 3.5: Recognize the position of numbers in relation to one another 96

Skill 3.6: Recognize equivalent forms of a number 97

Skill 3.7: Demonstrate knowledge of place value for whole numbers and decimal numbers 100

Skill 3.8: Compute percentages 102

Skill 3.9: Demonstrate knowledge of basic concepts of exponents 105

Skill 3.10: Demonstrate knowledge of order of operations *(parentheses, exponents, multiplication, division, addition, and subtraction)* 107

Skill 3.11: Use mental math to solve problems by estimation 107

Skill 3.12: Solve word problems 111

Skill 3.13: Solve one-step, single-variable linear equations *(find x if $x + 4 = 2$)* 115

Skill 3.14: Identify what comes next in a sequence of numbers 116

COMPETENCY 4
GEOMETRY AND MEASUREMENT 117

Skill 4.1: Represent time and money in more than one way *(e.g., 30 minutes = hour; 10:15 = quarter after 10; $0.50 = 50 cents = half dollar)* 117

Skill 4.2: Convert between units of measure in the same system *(e.g., inches to feet, centimeters to meters)* 119

Skill 4.3: Identify basic geometrical shapes *(e.g., isosceles triangle, right triangle, polygon)* 123

Skill 4.4: Perform computations related to area, volume, and perimeter for basic shapes 128

Skill 4.5: Graph data on an xy-coordinate plane 134

COMPETENCY 5
DATA ANALYSIS 136

Skill 5.1: Interpret information from tables, charts, and graphs 136

Skill 5.2: Interpret trends over time given a table, chart, or graph with time-related data 140

Skill 5.3: Create basic tables, charts, and graphs 142

Skill 5.4: Compute means, medians, and modes 142

COMPETENCY 6
APPLICATION OF MATHEMATICS SKILLS AND KNOWLEDGE TO CLASSROOM INSTRUCTION 143

SAMPLE TEST
MATHEMATICS 144
Answer Key 149
Rigor Table 149

DOMAIN III
WRITING 151

COMPETENCY 7
WRITING SKILLS AND KNOWLEDGE 153
Skill 7.1: Basic grammatical errors in standard written English 153
Skill 7.2: Errors in word usage *(e.g., their/they're/there, then/than)* 153
Skill 7.3: Errors in punctuation 157
Skill 7.4: Parts of a sentence *(e.g., subject and verb/predicate)* 162
Skill 7.5: Parts of speech *(nouns, verbs, pronouns, adjectives, adverbs, and prepositions)* 169
Skill 7.6: Errors in spelling 194

COMPETENCY 8
APPLICATION OF WRITING SKILLS AND KNOWLEDGE TO CLASSROOM INSTRUCTION 198
Skill 8.1: Use prewriting to generate and organize ideas *(including freewriting and using outlines)* 198
Skill 8.2: Identify and use appropriate reference materials 200
Skill 8.3: Draft and revise *(including composing or refining a thesis statement, writing focused and organized paragraphs, and writing a conclusion)* 200
Skill 8.4: Edit written documents for clarity, grammar, sentence integrity *(run-ons and sentence fragments)*, **word usage, punctuation, and spelling** 210
Skill 8.5: Write for different purposes and audiences *(including using appropriate language and taking a position for or against something)* 214
Skill 8.6: Recognize and write in different modes and forms *(e.g., descriptive essays, persuasive essays, narratives, letters)* 215

SAMPLE TEST
WRITING 225
Answer Key 231
Rigor Table 231

PRAXIS
PARAPRO ASSESSMENT
0755

SECTION 1
ABOUT XAMONLINE

XAMonline—A Specialty Teacher Certification Company
Created in 1996, XAMonline was the first company to publish study guides for state-specific teacher certification examinations. Founder Sharon Wynne found it frustrating that materials were not available for teacher certification preparation and decided to create the first single, state-specific guide. XAMonline has grown into a company of over 1,800 contributors and writers and offers over 300 titles for the entire PRAXIS series and every state examination. No matter what state you plan on teaching in, XAMonline has a unique teacher certification study guide just for you.

XAMonline—Value and Innovation
We are committed to providing value and innovation. Our print-on-demand technology allows us to be the first in the market to reflect changes in test standards and user feedback as they occur. Our guides are written by experienced teachers who are experts in their fields. And our content reflects the highest standards of quality. Comprehensive practice tests with varied levels of rigor means that your study experience will closely match the actual in-test experience.

To date, XAMonline has helped nearly 600,000 teachers pass their certification or licensing exams. Our commitment to preparation exceeds simply providing the proper material for study—it extends to helping teachers **gain mastery** of the subject matter, giving them the **tools** to become the most effective classroom leaders possible, and ushering today's students toward a **successful future**.

SECTION 2
ABOUT THIS STUDY GUIDE

Purpose of This Guide
Is there a little voice inside of you saying, "Am I ready?" Our goal is to replace that little voice and remove all doubt with a new voice that says, "I AM READY. **Bring it on!**" by offering the highest quality of teacher certification study guides.

Organization of Content

You will see that while every test may start with overlapping general topics, each is very unique in the skills they wish to test. Only XAMonline presents custom content that analyzes deeper than a title, a subarea, or an objective. Only XAMonline presents content and sample test assessments along with **focus statements**, the deepest-level rationale and interpretation of the skills that are unique to the exam.

Title and field number of test
→Each exam has its own name and number. XAMonline's guides are written to give you the content you need to know for the specific exam you are taking. You can be confident when you buy our guide that it contains the information you need to study for the specific test you are taking.

Subareas
→These are the major content categories found on the exam. XAMonline's guides are written to cover all of the subareas found in the test frameworks developed for the exam.

Objectives
→These are standards that are unique to the exam and represent the main subcategories of the subareas/content categories. XAMonline's guides are written to address every specific objective required to pass the exam.

Focus statements
→These are examples and interpretations of the objectives. You find them in parenthesis directly following the objective. They provide detailed examples of the range, type, and level of content that appear on the test questions. **Only XAMonline's guides drill down to this level.**

How Do We Compare with Our Competitors?

XAMonline—drills down to the focus statement level.
CliffsNotes and REA—organized at the objective level
Kaplan—provides only links to content
MoMedia—content not specific to the state test

Each subarea is divided into manageable sections that cover the specific skill areas. Explanations are easy to understand and thorough. You'll find that every test answer contains a rejoinder so if you need a refresher or further review after taking the test, you'll know exactly to which section you must return.

How to Use This Book

Our informal polls show that most people begin studying up to eight weeks prior to the test date, so start early. Then ask yourself some questions: How much do you really know? Are you coming to the test straight from your teacher-education program or are you having to review subjects you haven't considered in ten years? Either way, take a **diagnostic or assessment test** first. Also, spend time on sample tests so that you become accustomed to the way the actual test will appear.

This guide comes with an online diagnostic test of 30 questions found online at *www.XAMonline.com*. It is a little boot camp to get you up for the task and reveal things about your compendium of knowledge in general. Although this guide is structured to follow the order of the test, you are not required to study in that order. By finding a time-management and study plan that fits your life you will be more effective. The results of your diagnostic or self-assessment test can be a guide for how to manage your time and point you toward an area that needs more attention.

After taking the diagnostic exam, fill out the **Personalized Study Plan** page at the beginning of each chapter. Review the competencies and skills covered in that chapter and check the boxes that apply to your study needs. If there are sections you already know you can skip, check the "skip it" box. Taking this step will give you a study plan for each chapter.

Week	Activity
8 weeks prior to test	Take a diagnostic test found at www.XAMonline.com
7 weeks prior to test	Build your Personalized Study Plan for each chapter. Check the "skip it" box for sections you feel you are already strong in. ✘ SKIP IT ☐
6-3 weeks prior to test	For each of these four weeks, choose a content area to study. You don't have to go in the order of the book. It may be that you start with the content that needs the most review. Alternately, you may want to ease yourself into plan by starting with the most familiar material.
2 weeks prior to test	Take the sample test, score it, and create a review plan for the final week before the test.
1 week prior to test	Following your plan (which will likely be aligned with the areas that need the most review) go back and study the sections that align with the questions you may have gotten wrong. Then go back and study the sections related to the questions you answered correctly. If need be, create flashcards and drill yourself on any area that makes you anxious.

SECTION 3
ABOUT THE PRAXIS EXAMS

What Is PRAXIS?

PRAXIS II tests measure the knowledge of specific content areas in K-12 education. The test is a way of insuring that educators are prepared to not only teach in a particular subject area, but also have the necessary teaching skills to be effective. The Educational Testing Service administers the test in most states and has worked with the states to develop the material so that it is appropriate for state standards.

PRAXIS Points

1. The PRAXIS Series comprises more than 140 different tests in over seventy different subject areas.

2. Over 90% of the PRAXIS tests measure subject area knowledge.

3. The purpose of the test is to measure whether the teacher candidate possesses a sufficient level of knowledge and skills to perform job duties effectively and responsibly.

4. Your state sets the acceptable passing score.

5. Any candidate, whether from a traditional teaching-preparation path or an alternative route, can seek to enter the teaching profession by taking a PRAXIS test.

6. PRAXIS tests are updated regularly to ensure current content.

Often **your own state's requirements** determine whether or not you should take any particular test. The most reliable source of information regarding this is either your state's Department of Education or the Educational Testing Service. Either resource should also have a complete list of testing centers and dates. Test dates vary by subject area and not all test dates necessarily include your particular test, so be sure to check carefully.

If you are in a teacher-education program, check with the Education Department or the Certification Officer for specific information for testing and testing timelines. The Certification Office should have most of the information you need.

If you choose an alternative route to certification you can either rely on our Web site at *www.XAMonline.com* or on the resources provided by an alternative certification program. Many states now have specific agencies devoted to alternative certification and there are some national organizations as well:

National Center for Education Information
http://www.ncei.com/Alt-Teacher-Cert.htm

National Associate for Alternative Certification
http://www.alt-teachercert.org/index.asp

Interpreting Test Results

Contrary to what you may have heard, the results of a PRAXIS test are not based on time. More accurately, you will be scored on the raw number of points you earn in relation to the raw number of points available. Each question is worth one raw point. It is likely to your benefit to complete as many questions in the time allotted, but it will not necessarily work to your advantage if you hurry through the test.

Follow the guidelines provided by ETS for interpreting your score. The web site offers a sample test score sheet and clearly explains how the scores are scaled and what to expect if you have an essay portion on your test.

Scores are usually available by phone within a month of the test date and scores will be sent to your chosen institution(s) within six weeks. Additionally, ETS now makes online, downloadable reports available for 45 days from the reporting date.

It is **critical** that you be aware of your own state's passing score. Your raw score may qualify you to teach in some states, but not all. ETS administers the test and assigns a score, but the states make their own interpretations and, in some cases, consider combined scores if you are testing in more than one area.

What's on the Test?

PRAXIS tests vary from subject to subject and sometimes even within subject area. For PRAXIS ParaPro Assessment (0755), the test lasts for 2.5 hours and consists of approximately 90 multiple-choice questions. The use of calculators is not permitted for this test. The breakdown of the questions is as follows:

Category	Approximate Number of Questions	Approximate Percentage of the test
I: Reading Skills and Knowledge	18	20%
II: Application of Reading Skills and Knowledge to Classroom Instruction	12	13%

Table continued on next page

Category	Approximate Number of Questions	Approximate Percentage of the test
III: Mathematics Skills and Knowledge	18	20%
IV: Application of Mathematics Skills and Knowledge to Classroom Instruction	12	13%
V: Writing Skills and Knowledge	18	20%
VI: Application of Writing Skills and Knowledge to Classroom Instruction	12	13%

This chart can be used to build a study plan. Twenty percent may seem like a lot of time to spend on Reading, Mathematics, and Writing each, but when you consider that amounts to about one out of five multiple choice questions in each part of the test, it might change your perspective.

Question Types

You're probably thinking, enough already, I want to study! Indulge us a little longer while we explain that there is actually more than one type of multiple-choice question. You can thank us later after you realize how well prepared you are for your exam.

1. Complete the Statement. The name says it all. In this question type you'll be asked to choose the correct completion of a given statement. For example:

   > The Dolch Basic Sight Words consist of a relatively short list of words that children should be able to?
   >
   > A. Sound out
   >
   > B. Know the meaning of
   >
   > C. Recognize on sight
   >
   > D. Use in a sentence

   The correct answer is A. In order to check your answer, test out the statement by adding the choices to the end of it.

2. **Which of the Following.** One way to test your answer choice for this type of question is to replace the phrase "which of the following" with your selection. Use this example:

> **Which of the following words is one of the twelve most frequently used in children's reading texts:**
> A. There
> B. This
> C. The
> D. An

Don't look! Test your answer. ____ is one of the twelve most frequently used in children's reading texts. Did you guess C? Then you guessed correctly.

3. **Roman Numeral Choices.** This question type is used when there is more than one possible correct answer. For example:

> **Which of the following two arguments accurately supports the use of cooperative learning as an effective method of instruction?**
> I. Cooperative learning groups facilitate healthy competition between individuals in the group.
> II. Cooperative learning groups allow academic achievers to carry or cover for academic underachievers.
> III. Cooperative learning groups make each student in the group accountable for the success of the group.
> IV. Cooperative learning groups make it possible for students to reward other group members for achieving.
>
> A. I and II
> B. II and III
> C. I and III
> D. III and IV

Notice that the question states there are **two** possible answers. It's best to read all the possibilities first before looking at the answer choices. In this case, the correct answer is D.

4. **Negative Questions.** This type of question contains words such as "not," "least," and "except." Each correct answer will be the statement that does **not** fit the situation described in the question. Such as:

> **Multicultural education is not:**
> A. An idea or concept
> B. A "tack-on" to the school curriculum
> C. An educational reform movement
> D. A process

Think to yourself that the statement could be anything but the correct answer. This question form is more open to interpretation than other types, so read carefully and don't forget that you're answering a negative statement.

5. **Questions that Include Graphs, Tables, or Reading Passages.** As always, read the question carefully. It likely asks for a very specific answer and not a broad interpretation of the visual. Here is a simple (though not statistically accurate) example of a graph question:

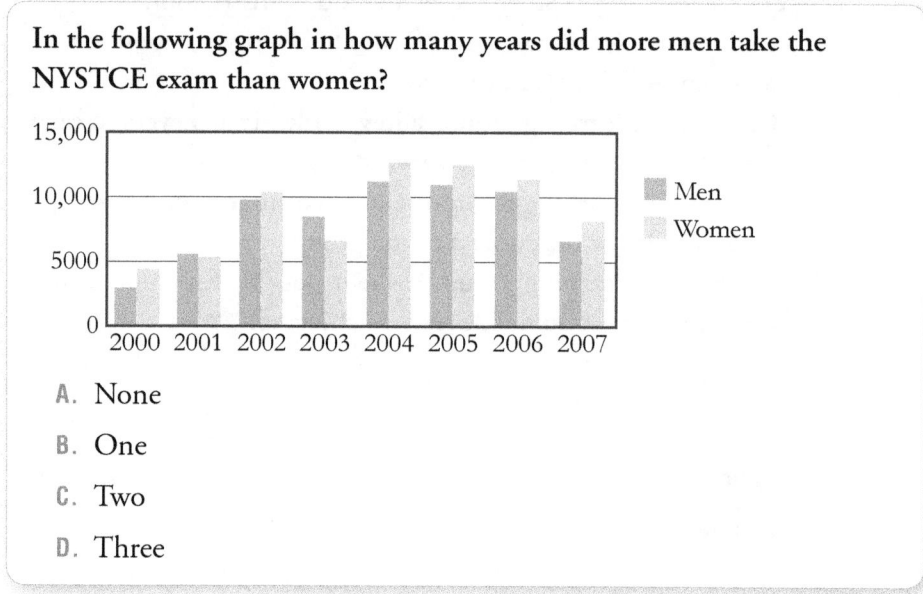

> **In the following graph in how many years did more men take the NYSTCE exam than women?**
>
> A. None
> B. One
> C. Two
> D. Three

It may help you to simply circle the two years that answer the question. Make sure you've read the question thoroughly and once you've made your determination, double check your work. The correct answer is C.

SECTION 4
HELPFUL HINTS

Study Tips

1. **You are what you eat.** Certain foods aid the learning process by releasing natural memory enhancers called CCKs (cholecystokinin) composed of tryptophan, choline, and phenylalanine. All of these chemicals enhance the neurotransmitters associated with memory and certain foods release memory enhancing chemicals. A light meal or snacks of one of the following foods fall into this category:

   - Milk
   - Rice
   - Eggs
   - Fish
   - Nuts and seeds
   - Oats
   - Turkey

   The better the connections, the more you comprehend!

2. **See the forest for the trees.** In other words, get the concept before you look at the details. One way to do this is to take notes as you read, paraphrasing or summarizing in your own words. Putting the concept in terms that are comfortable and familiar may increase retention.

3. **Question authority.** Ask why, why, why? Pull apart written material paragraph by paragraph and don't forget the captions under the illustrations. For example, if a heading reads *Stream Erosion* put it in the form of a question (Why do streams erode? What is stream erosion?) then find the answer within the material. If you train your mind to think in this manner you will learn more and prepare yourself for answering test questions.

4. **Play mind games.** Using your brain for reading or puzzles keeps it flexible. Even with a limited amount of time your brain can take in data (much like a computer) and store it for later use. In ten minutes you can: read two paragraphs (at least), quiz yourself with flash cards, or review notes. Even if you don't fully understand something on the first pass, your mind stores it for recall, which is why frequent reading or review increases chances of retention and comprehension.

5. **The pen is mightier than the sword.** Learn to take great notes. A by-product of our modern culture is that we have grown accustomed to getting our information in short doses. We've subconsciously trained ourselves to assimilate information into neat little packages. Messy notes fragment the flow of information. Your notes can be much clearer with proper formatting. *The Cornell Method* is one such format. This method was popularized in *How to Study in College*, Ninth Edition, by Walter Pauk. You can benefit from the method without purchasing an additional book by simply looking up the method online. Below is a sample of how *The Cornell Method* can be adapted for use with this guide.

← 2" → **Cue Column**	← 6" → **Note Taking Column**
	1. Record: During your reading, use the note-taking column to record important points.
	2. Questions: As soon as you finish a section, formulate questions based on the notes in the right-hand column. Writing questions helps to clarify meanings, reveal relationships, establish community, and strengthen memory. Also, the writing of questions sets the state for exam study later.
	3. Recite: Cover the note-taking column with a sheet of paper. Then, looking at the questions or cue-words in the question and cue column only, say aloud, in your own words, the answers to the questions, facts, or ideas indicated by the cue words.
	4. Reflect: Reflect on the material by asking yourself questions.
	5. Review: Spend at least ten minutes every week reviewing all your previous notes. Doing so helps you retain ideas and topics for the exam.
↑ 2" ↓	**Summary** After reading, use this space to summarize the notes from each page.

*Adapted from How to Study in College, Ninth Edition, by Walter Pauk, ©2008 Wadsworth

6. Place yourself in exile and set the mood. Set aside a particular place and time to study that best suits your personal needs and biorhythms. If you're a night person, burn the midnight oil. If you're a morning person set yourself up with some coffee and get to it. Make your study time and place as free from distraction as possible and surround yourself with what you need, be it silence or music. Studies have shown that music can aid in concentration, absorption, and retrieval of information. Not all music, though. Classical music is said to work best

7. Get pointed in the right direction. Use arrows to point to important passages or pieces of information. It's easier to read than a page full of yellow highlights. Highlighting can be used sparingly, but add an arrow to the margin to call attention to it.

8. Check your budget. You should at least review all the content material before your test, but allocate the most amount of time to the areas that need the most refreshing. It sounds obvious, but it's easy to forget. You can use the study rubric above to balance your study budget.

The proctor will write the start time where it can be seen and then, later, provide the time remaining, typically fifteen minutes before the end of the test.

Testing Tips

1. Get smart, play dumb. Sometimes a question is just a question. No one is out to trick you, so don't assume that the test writer is looking for something other than what was asked. Stick to the question as written and don't overanalyze.

2. Do a double take. Read test questions and answer choices at least twice because it's easy to miss something, to transpose a word or some letters. If you have no idea what the correct answer is, skip it and come back later if there's time. If you're still clueless, it's okay to guess. Remember, you're scored on the number of questions you answer correctly and you're not penalized for wrong answers. The worst case scenario is that you miss a point from a good guess.

3. Turn it on its ear. The syntax of a question can often provide a clue, so make things interesting and turn the question into a statement to see if it changes the meaning or relates better (or worse) to the answer choices.

4. Get out your magnifying glass. Look for hidden clues in the questions because it's difficult to write a multiple-choice question without giving away part of the answer in the options presented. In most questions you can readily eliminate one or two potential answers, increasing your chances of answering correctly to 50/50, which will help out if you've skipped a question and gone back to it (see tip #2).

5. Call it intuition. Often your first instinct is correct. If you've been studying the content you've likely absorbed something and have subconsciously retained the knowledge. On questions you're not sure about trust your instincts because a first impression is usually correct.

6. Graffiti. Sometimes it's a good idea to mark your answers directly on the test booklet and go back to fill in the optical scan sheet later. You don't get extra points for perfectly blackened ovals. If you choose to manage your test this way, be sure not to mismark your answers when you transcribe to the scan sheet.

7. Become a clock-watcher. You have a set amount of time to answer the questions. Don't get bogged down laboring over a question you're not sure about when there are ten others you could answer more readily. If you choose to follow the advice of tip #6, be sure you leave time near the end to go back and fill in the scan sheet.

Do the Drill

No matter how prepared you feel it's sometimes a good idea to apply Murphy's Law. So the following tips might seem silly, mundane, or obvious, but we're including them anyway.

1. Remember, you are what you eat, so bring a snack. Choose from the list of energizing foods that appear earlier in the introduction.

2. You're not too sexy for your test. Wear comfortable clothes. You'll be distracted if your belt is too tight or if you're too cold or too hot.

3. Lie to yourself. Even if you think you're a prompt person, pretend you're not and leave plenty of time to get to the testing center. Map it out ahead of time and do a dry run if you have to. There's no need to add road rage to your list of anxieties.

4. Bring sharp number 2 pencils. It may seem impossible to forget this need from your school days, but you might. And make sure the erasers are intact, too.

5. No ticket, no test. Bring your admission ticket as well as **two** forms of identification, including one with a picture and signature. You will not be admitted to the test without these things.

6. You can't take it with you. Leave any study aids, dictionaries, notebooks, computers, and the like at home. Certain tests **do** allow a scientific or four-function calculator, so check ahead of time to see if your test does.

7. **Prepare for the desert.** Any time spent on a bathroom break **cannot** be made up later, so use your judgment on the amount you eat or drink.

8. **Quiet, Please!** Keeping your own time is a good idea, but not with a timepiece that has a loud ticker. If you use a watch, take it off and place it nearby but not so that it distracts you. And **silence your cell phone**.

To the best of our ability, we have compiled the content you need to know in this book and in the accompanying online resources. The rest is up to you. You can use the study and testing tips or you can follow your own methods. Either way, you can be confident that there aren't any missing pieces of information and there shouldn't be any surprises in the content on the test.

If you have questions about test fees, registration, electronic testing, or other content verification issues please visit *www.ets.org*.

Good luck!

Sharon Wynne
Founder, XAMonline

DOMAIN I
READING

READING

PERSONALIZED STUDY PLAN

PAGE	COMPETENCY AND SKILL	KNOWN MATERIAL/ SKIP IT
3	**1: Reading Skills and Knowledge**	☐
	1.1: Identify the main idea or primary purpose	☐
	1.2: Identify supporting ideas	☐
	1.3: Identify how a reading selection is organized	☐
	1.4: Determine the meanings of words or phrases in context	☐
	1.5: Draw inferences or implications from directly stated content	☐
	1.6: Determine whether information is presented as fact or opinion	☐
	1.7: Interpret information from tables, diagrams, charts, and graphs	☐
16	**2: Application of Reading Skills and Knowledge**	☐
	2.1: Sounding out words	☐
	2.2: Breaking down words into parts	☐
	2.3: Decoding words or phrases using context clues	☐
	2.4: Distinguishing among synonyms, antonyms, and homonyms	☐
	2.5: Alphabetizing words	☐
	2.6: Prereading strategies, such as skimming or making predictions	☐
	2.7: Asking questions about a reading selection to understand the selection	☐
	2.8: Making observations about ability to understand and interpret text	☐
	2.9: How to use a dictionary	☐
	2.10: Understand how to help students interpret written directionsr	☐

COMPETENCY 1
READING SKILLS AND KNOWLEDGE

SKILL 1.1 Identify the main idea or primary purpose

The MAIN IDEA of a passage or paragraph is the basic message, idea, point concept, or meaning that the author wants to convey to you, the reader. Understanding the main idea of a passage or paragraph is the key to understanding the more subtle components of the author's message. The main idea is what is being said about a topic or subject. Once you have identified the basic message, you will have an easier time answering other questions that test critical skills.

Main ideas are either stated or implied. A stated main idea is explicit: It is directly expressed in a sentence or two in the paragraph or passage. An implied main idea is suggested by the overall reading selection. In the first case, you need not pull information from various points in the paragraph or passage in order to form the main idea because it is already stated by the author. If a main idea is implied, however, you must formulate, in your own words, a main idea statement by condensing the overall message contained in the material itself.

> **MAIN IDEA:** basic message, idea, point concept, or meaning that the author wants to convey to you, the reader

READING

Practice Question

Read the following passage and select an answer.

Sometimes too much of a good thing can become a very bad thing indeed. In an earnest attempt to consume a healthy diet, dietary supplement enthusiasts have been known to overdose. Vitamin C, for example, long thought to help people ward off cold viruses, is currently being studied for its possible role in warding off cancer and other diseases that cause tissue degeneration. Unfortunately, an overdose of vitamin C—more than 10,000 mg—on a daily basis can cause nausea and diarrhea. Calcium supplements commonly taken by women are helpful in warding off osteoporosis. More than just a few grams a day, however, can lead to stomach upset and even kidney and bladder stones. Niacin, proven useful in reducing cholesterol levels, can be dangerous in large doses to those who suffer from heart problems, asthma, or ulcers.

1. **The main idea expressed in this paragraph is:**

    A. Supplements taken in excess can be a bad thing

    B. Dietary supplement enthusiasts have been known to overdose

    C. Vitamins can cause nausea, diarrhea, and kidney or bladder stones

    D. People who take supplements are preoccupied with their health

Answer Key

1. Answer A is a paraphrase of the first sentence and provides a general framework for the rest of the paragraph: Excess supplement intake is bad. The rest of the paragraph discusses the consequences of taking too many vitamins. Options B and C refer to major details and Option D introduces the idea of preoccupation, which is not included in this paragraph.

Sample Test Questions and Rationale

For sample test questions and rationales requiring a reading passage, see page 72.

READING SKILLS AND KNOWLEDGE

SKILL 1.2 Identify supporting ideas

SUPPORTING DETAILS are examples, facts, ideas, illustrations, cases, and anecdotes used by a writer to explain, expand on, and develop the more general main idea. A writer's choice of supporting materials is determined by the nature of the topic being covered. Supporting details are specifics that relate directly to the main idea. Writers select and shape material according to their purposes. An advertisement writer seeking to persuade the reader to buy a particular running shoe, for instance, will emphasize only the positive characteristics of the shoe for advertisement copy. A columnist for a running magazine, on the other hand, might list the good and bad points about the same shoe in an article recommending appropriate shoes for different kind of runners. Both major details (those that directly support the main idea) and minor details (those that provide interesting, but not always essential, information) help create a well-written and fluid passage.

> **SUPPORTING DETAILS:** examples, facts, ideas, illustrations, cases, and anecdotes used by a writer to explain, expand on, and develop the more general main idea

In the following paragraph, the sentences in **bold print** provide a skeleton of a paragraph on the benefits of recycling. The sentences in bold are generalizations that by themselves do not explain the need to recycle. The sentences in *italics* add details to EXPLAIN the general points in bold. Notice how the supporting details help you understand the necessity for recycling.

> **While one day recycling may become mandatory in all states, right now it is voluntary in many communities.** *Those of us who participate in recycling are amazed by how much material is recycled.* **For many communities, the blue-box recycling program has had an immediate effect.** *By just recycling glass, aluminum cans, and plastic bottles, we have reduced the volume of disposable trash by one third, thus extending the useful life of local landfills by more than a decade. Imagine the difference if those dramatic results were achieved nationwide.* **The amount of reusable items we thoughtlessly dispose of is staggering.** *For example, Americans dispose of enough steel every day to supply Detroit car manufacturers for three months. Additionally, we dispose of enough aluminum annually to rebuild the nation's air fleet. These statistics, available from the Environmental Protection Agency (EPA), should encourage all of us to watch what we throw away.* **Clearly, recycling in our homes and in our communities directly improves the environment.**

Notice how the author's supporting examples enhance the message of the paragraph and relate to the author's thesis noted above. If you only read the boldface sentences, you get a glimpse at the topic. This paragraph of illustration, however, is developed through numerous details creating specific images: *reduced the volume of disposable trash by one-third, extended the useful life of local landfills by more than*

READING

a decade, enough steel every day to supply Detroit car manufacturers for three months, enough aluminum to rebuild the nation's air fleet. If the writer had merely written a few general sentences, such as those shown in boldface, you would not fully understand the vast amount of trash involved in recycling or the positive results of current recycling efforts.

SKILL 1.3 Identify how a reading selection is organized

> **ORGANIZATION:** the order in which the writer has chosen to present the different parts of the discussion or argument, and the relationships he or she constructs among these parts

The ORGANIZATION of a written work includes two factors: the order in which the writer has chosen to present the different parts of the discussion or argument, and the relationships he or she constructs among these parts.

Written ideas need to be presented in a logical order so that a reader can follow the information easily and quickly. There are many different ways in which to order a series of ideas but they all share one thing in common: the goal is to lead the reader along a desired path while avoiding backtracking and skipping around in order to give a clear, strong presentation of the writer's main idea. Some of the ways in which a paragraph may be organized are:

Sequence of Events	In this type of organization, the details are presented in the order in which they have occurred. Paragraphs that describe a process or procedure, give directions, or outline a given period of time (such as a day or a month) are often arranged chronologically.
Statement Support	In this type of organization, the main idea is stated and the rest of the paragraph explains or proves it. This is also referred to as relative or order of importance organization. There are four ways in which this type of order is organized: most to least, least to most, most-least-most, and least-most-least.
Comparison and Contrast	In this type of organization, the compare-contrast pattern is used when a paragraph describes the differences or similarities of two or more ideas, actions, events, or things. Usually the topic sentence describes the basic relationship between the ideas or items and the rest of the paragraph explains this relationship.
Classification	In this type of organization, the paragraph presents grouped information about a topic. The topic sentence usually states the general category and the rest of the sentences show how various elements of the category have a common base—and also how they differ from the common base.

Table continued on next page

READING SKILLS AND KNOWLEDGE

Cause and Effect	This pattern describes how two or more events are connected. The main sentence usually states the primary cause(s) and the primary effect(s) and how they are basically connected. The rest of the sentences explain the connection—how one event caused the next.
Spatial/Place	In this type of organization, certain descriptions are organized according to the location of items in relation to each other and to a larger context. The orderly arrangement guides the reader's eye as he or she mentally envisions the scene or place being described.
Example, Clarification, and Definition	These types of organizations show, explain, or elaborate on the main idea. This can be done by showing specific cases, examining meaning multiple times, or extensive description of one term.

SKILL 1.4 Determine the meanings of words or phrases in context

Context Clues

CONTEXT CLUES help readers determine the meaning of words they are not familiar with. The context of a word is the sentence or sentences that surround the word.

Read the following sentences and attempt to determine the meanings of the words in bold print.

> The **luminosity** of the room was so incredible that there was no need for lights.

If there was no need for lights then one must assume that the word luminosity has something to do with giving off light. The definition of luminosity is: the emission of light.

> Jamie could not understand Joe's feelings. His mood swings made him somewhat of an **enigma**.

The fact that he could not be understood made him somewhat of a puzzle. The definition of enigma is: a mystery or puzzle.

Familiarity with word ROOTS (the basic elements of words) and with PREFIXES can also help one determine the meanings of unknown words. Following is a partial list of roots and prefixes. It might be useful to review these.

CONTEXT CLUES: help readers determine the meaning of words they are not familiar with

ROOTS: the basic elements of words

PREFIXES: a letter or group of letters attached to the beginning of a word to help indicate meaning

READING

Root	Meaning	Example
aqua	water	aqualung
astro	stars	astrology
bio	life	biology
carn	meat	carnivorous
circum	around	circumnavigate
geo	earth	geology
herb	plant	herbivorous
mal	bad	malicious
neo	new	neonatal
tele	distant	telescope

Prefix	Meaning	Example
un-	not	unnamed
re-	again	reenter
il-	not	illegible
pre-	before	preset
mis-	incorrectly	misstate
in-	not	informal
anti-	against	antiwar
de-	opposite	derail
post-	after	postwar
ir-	not	irresponsible

Word Forms

Sometimes a very familiar word can appear as a different part of speech.

You may have heard that *fraud* involves a criminal misrepresentation, so when it appears as the adjective form *fraudulent* ("He was suspected of fraudulent activities"), you can make an educated guess.

You probably know that something out of date is *obsolete*; therefore, when you read about "built-in *obsolescence*," you can detect the meaning of the unfamiliar word.

Practice Questions

Read the following sentences and attempt to determine the meanings of the underlined words.

1. Farmer John got a two-horse plow and went to work. Straight <u>furrows</u> stretched out behind him.

    The word <u>furrows</u> means:
    A. Long cuts made by plow
    B. Vast, open fields
    C. Rows of corn
    D. Pairs of hitched horses

2. The survivors struggled ahead, <u>shambling</u> through the terrible cold, doing their best not to fall.

    The word <u>shambling</u> means:
    A. Frozen in place
    B. Running
    C. Shivering uncontrollably
    D. Walking awkwardly

Answer Key

1. A.

    The words "straight" and the expression "stretched out behind him" are your clues.

2. D.

    The words "ahead" and "through" are your clues.

Sentence Clues

Often, a writer will actually define a difficult or particularly important word for you the first time it appears in a passage. Phrases like *that is, such as, which is,* or *is called* might announce the writer's intention to give just the definition you need. Occasionally, a writer will simply use a synonym (a word that means the same thing) or near-synonym joined by the word *or*. Look at the following examples:

> Nothing would <u>assuage</u> or lessen the child's grief.
>
> The <u>credibility</u>, that is to say the believability, of the witness was called into question by evidence of previous perjury.

Punctuation at the sentence level is often a clue to the meaning of a word. Commas, parentheses, quotation marks, and dashes tell the reader that a definition is being offered by the writer.

> A tendency toward <u>hyperbole</u>, extravagant exaggeration, is a common flaw among persuasive writers.
>
> Political <u>apathy</u>—lack of interest—can lead to the death of the state

A writer might simply give an explanation in other words that you can understand, in the same sentence:

> The <u>xenophobic</u> townspeople were suspicious of every foreigner.

Writers also explain a word in terms of its opposite at the sentence level:

> His <u>incarceration</u> was ended, and he was elated to be out of jail.

Adjacent Sentence Clues

The context for a word goes beyond the sentence in which it appears. At times, the writer uses adjacent (adjoining) sentences to present an explanation or definition:

> The $200 for the car repair would have to come out of the <u>contingency</u> fund. Fortunately, Angela's father had taught her to keep some money set aside for just such emergencies.

The second sentence offers a clue to the definition of *contingency* as used in this sentence: "emergencies." Therefore, a fund for contingencies would be money tucked away for unforeseen and/or urgent events.

READING SKILLS AND KNOWLEDGE

Entire Passage Clues

On occasion, you must look at an entire paragraph or passage to figure out the definition of a word or term. In the following paragraph, notice how the word *nostalgia* undergoes a form of extended definition throughout the selection rather than in just one sentence.

> The word nostalgia links Greek words for "away from home" and "pain." If you're feeling nostalgic, then, you are probably in some physical distress or discomfort, suffering from a feeling of alienation and separation from loved ones or loved places. Nostalgia is that awful feeling you remember you felt the first time you went away to camp or spent the weekend with a friend's family—homesickness, or some condition even more painful than that. But in common use, nostalgia has come to have more sentimental associations. A few years back, for example, a nostalgia craze had to do with the 1950s. We resurrected poodle skirts and saddle shoes, built new restaurants to look like old ones, and tried to make chicken a la king just as mother probably never made it. In TV situation comedies, we recreated a pleasant world that probably never existed and relished our nostalgia, longing for a homey, comfortable lost time.

SKILL 1.5 Draw inferences or implications from directly stated content

An INFERENCE is sometimes called an "educated guess" because it requires that you go beyond the strictly obvious to create additional meaning by taking the text one logical step further. Inferences and conclusions are based on the content of the passage—that is, on what the passage says or how the writer says it—and are derived by reasoning.

> **INFERENCE:** using the text to make an educated guess

Inference is an essential and automatic component of most reading. For example, it is important in making educated guesses about the meaning of unknown words, the author's main idea, and whether he or she is writing with a bias. Such is the essence of inference: You use your own ability to reason in order to figure out what the writer implies. As a reader, then, you must often logically extend meaning that is only implied.

> *Inference is an essential and automatic component of most reading.*

Consider the following example. Assume you are an employer, and you are reading over the letters of reference submitted by a prospective employee for the position of clerk/typist in your real estate office. The position requires the applicant to be neat, careful, trustworthy, and punctual. You come across this letter of reference submitted by an applicant:

READING

> To whom it may concern,
>
> Todd Finley has asked me to write a letter of reference for him. I am well qualified to do so because he worked for me for three months last year. His duties included answering the phone, greeting the public, and producing some simple memos and notices on the computer. Although Todd initially had few computer skills and little knowledge of telephone etiquette, he did acquire some during his stay with us. Todd's manner of speaking, both on the telephone and with the clients who came to my establishment, could be described as casual. He was particularly effective when communicating with peers. Please contact me by telephone if you wish to have further information about my experience.

Here the writer implies, rather than openly states, the main idea. This letter calls attention to itself because there's a problem with its tone. A truly positive letter would say something like "I have the distinct honor of recommending Todd Finley." Here, however, the letter simply verifies that Todd worked in the office. Second, the praise is obviously lukewarm. For example, the writer says that Todd "was particularly effective when communicating with peers." An educated guess translates that statement into a nice way of saying Todd was not serious about his communication with clients.

In order to draw inferences and make conclusions, a reader must use prior knowledge and apply it to the current situation. A conclusion or inference is never stated. You must rely on your common sense.

Practice Questions

Read the following passages and select an answer.

1. The Smith family waited patiently around carousel number seven for their luggage to arrive. They were exhausted after their five-hour trip and were anxious to get to their hotel. After about an hour, they realized that they no longer recognized any of the other passengers' faces. Mrs. Smith asked the person who appeared to be in charge if they were at the right carousel. The man replied, "Yes, this is it, but we finished unloading that baggage almost half an hour ago."

   From the man's response we can infer that:

   A. The Smiths were ready to go to their hotel
   B. The Smiths' luggage was lost
   C. The man had their luggage
   D. They were at the wrong carousel

2. Tim Sullivan had just turned 15. As a birthday present, his parents had given him a guitar and a certificate for ten guitar lessons. He had always shown a love for music and a desire to learn an instrument. Tim began his lessons and before long, he was making up his own songs. At the music studio, Tim met Josh, who played the piano, and Roger, whose instrument was the saxophone. They all shared the same dream—to start a band—and each was praised by his teacher as having real talent.

   From this passage one can infer that:

   A. Tim, Roger, and Josh are going to start their own band
   B. Tim is going to give up his guitar lessons
   C. Tim, Josh, and Roger will no longer be friends
   D. Josh and Roger are going to start their own band

READING

> **Answer Key**
>
> 1. **B.**
>
>   Since the Smiths were still waiting for their luggage, we know that they were not yet ready to go to their hotel. From the man's response, we know that they were not at the wrong carousel and that he did not have their luggage. Therefore, though not directly stated, it appears that their luggage was lost.
>
> 2. **A.**
>
>   Given the facts that Tim wanted to be a musician and start his own band, after meeting others who shared the same dreams, we can infer that they joined together in an attempt to make their dreams become a reality.

SKILL 1.6 Determine whether information is presented as fact or opinion

FACTS: statements that are verifiable

OPINIONS: statements that must be supported in order to be accepted

FACTS are statements that are verifiable. OPINIONS are statements that must be supported in order to be accepted such as beliefs, values, judgments, or feelings. Facts are objective statements used to support subjective opinions. For example, "Jane is a bad girl" is an opinion. However, "Jane hit her sister with a baseball bat" is a *fact* upon which the opinion is based.

Judgments are opinions—decisions or declarations based on observation or reasoning that express approval or disapproval. Facts report what has happened or exists and come from observation, measurement, or calculation. Facts can be tested and verified, whereas opinions and judgments cannot. They can only be supported with facts.

Most statements cannot be so clearly distinguished. "I believe that Jane is a bad girl" is a fact. The speaker knows what he/she believes. However, it obviously includes a judgment that could be disputed by another person who might believe otherwise. Judgments are not usually so firm. They are, rather, plausible opinions that provoke thought or lead to factual development.

Joe DiMaggio, a Yankees center fielder, was replaced by Mickey Mantle in 1952.

READING SKILLS AND KNOWLEDGE

This is a fact. If necessary, evidence can be produced to support this.

First year players are more ambitious than seasoned players.

This is an opinion. There is no proof to support that this is true in every case.

Practice Questions

Decide if the statement is fact or opinion.

1. The Inca were a group of Indians who ruled an empire in South America.
   A. Fact
   B. Opinion

2. The Inca were clever.
   A. Fact
   B. Opinion

3. The Inca built very complex systems of bridges.
   A. Fact
   B. Opinion

Answer Key

1. **A.**
   Research can prove this to be true.

2. **B.**
   It is doubtful that all people who have studied the Inca agree with this statement. Therefore, no proof is available.

3. **A.**
   As with question number one, research can prove this to be true.

SKILL 1.7 Interpret information from tables, diagrams, charts, and graphs

See Skill 5.1

COMPETENCY 2
APPLICATION OF READING SKILLS AND KNOWLEDGE TO CLASSROOM INSTRUCTION

SKILL 2.1 Understand how to help students sound out words (e.g., recognize long and short vowels, consonant sounds, rhymes)

Decoding

In the late 1960s and the 1970s, many reading specialists, most prominently Fries (1962), believed that successful decoding resulted in reading comprehension. This meant that if children could sound out the words, they would then automatically be able to comprehend the words. Many teachers of reading and many reading texts still subscribe to this theory after more than thirty years.

Phonological Awareness

PHONOLOGICAL AWARENESS is the ability of the reader to recognize the sound of spoken language. This recognition includes how these sounds can be blended together, segmented (divided up), and manipulated (switched around). This awareness then leads to phonics, a method for teaching children to read. It helps them sound out words.

Development of phonological skills may begin during pre-K years. Indeed by the age of five, a child who has been exposed to rhyme can recognize a rhyme. That child can demonstrate phonological awareness by filling in the missing rhyming word in a familiar rhyme or rhymed picture book.

Phonological Awareness Skills include:

- Rhyming and syllabification
- Blending sounds into words—such as pic-tur-boo-k
- Identifying the beginning or starting sounds of words and the ending or closing sounds of words
- Breaking words down into sounds—also called "segmenting" words
- Recognizing other smaller words in the big word, by removing starting sounds—such as hear to ear

> **PHONOLOGICAL AWARENESS:** the ability of the reader to recognize the sounds of spoken language

You teach children phonological awareness when you teach them the sounds made by the letters and the sounds made by various combinations of letters, and when you teach them to recognize individual sounds in words.

APPLICATION OF READING SKILLS AND KNOWLEDGE TO CLASSROOM INSTRUCTION

The Role of Phonological Awareness in Reading Development

Instructional methods to teach phonological awareness may include any or all of the following:

- Play auditory games and drills during which children recognize and manipulate the sounds of words, separate or segment the sounds of words, take out sounds, blend sounds, add in new sounds, or take apart sounds to recombine them in new formations.

- Play the snap game. The teacher says two words. The children snap their fingers if the two words share a sound, which might be at the beginning, middle or end of the word. Silence occurs if the words share no sounds. Children love this simple game and it also helps with classroom management.

- Language games model for children identification of rhyming words. These games help inspire children to create their own rhymes.

- Word strip activities and experiences help children concretely experience that words are made up of syllables, and that words can be broken down into separate sounds. Word strips help kinesthetic and spatial learners work to enhance this auditory skill.

- Read books that rhyme such as *Sheep in Jeep* by Nancy Shaw or *The Fox on a Box* by Barbara Gregorich.

- Share books with children that use alliteration (words that all begin with the same sound) such as *Avalanche, A to Z*.

Assessment of Phonological Awareness

These skills can be assessed by having the child listen to the teacher say two words. Then ask the child to decide if these two words are the same word repeated twice or two different words.

When you make this assessment, if you do use two different words, make certain that they only differ by one phoneme, such as /d/ and /g/.

Children can be assessed on words that are not real words or words that are not familiar to them. Words used can be make-believe words.

READING

Phonemic Awareness

> *The two best predictors of early reading success are alphabetic recognition and phonemic awareness.* — **Marilyn Jager Adams**
>
> *In order to benefit from formal reading instruction, children must have a certain level of phonemic awareness... phonemic awareness is both a prerequisite for and a consequence of learning to read.* — **Hallie Kay Yopp**

Phonemic awareness is understanding that words are comprised of sounds. To be phonemically aware means that the reader and listener can recognize and manipulate specific sounds in spoken words.

PHONEMIC AWARENESS deals with sounds in words that are spoken. The majority of phonemic awareness tasks, activities, and exercises are **oral**.

Theorist Marilyn Jager Adams, who researches early reading, has outlined five basic types of phonemic awareness tasks.

> **PHONEMIC AWARENESS:** understanding that words are composed of sounds

Task 1: Ability to hear rhymes and alliteration. Children could listen to a poem, rhyming picture book, or song and identify the rhyming words heard which the teacher might then record or list on an experiential chart.

Task 2: Ability to do oddity tasks (recognize the member of a set that is different [odd] among the group). Children could look at the pictures of grass, a garden, and a rose and tell which starts with a different sound.

Task 3: Ability to orally blend words and split syllables. Children can say the first sound of a word and then the rest of the word and put it together as a single word.

Task 4: Ability to orally segment words. Children can count sounds. They could be asked as a group to count the sounds in "hamburger."

Task 5: Ability to do phonics manipulation tasks. Children can replace the "r" sound in rose with a "p" sound.

The Role of Phonemic Awareness in Reading Development

Children who have problems with phonics generally have not acquired or been exposed to phonemic awareness activities usually fostered at home and in preschool through second grade. This includes extensive songs, rhymes, and read-alouds.

APPLICATION OF READING SKILLS AND KNOWLEDGE TO CLASSROOM INSTRUCTION

Instructional Methods

Since the ability to distinguish between individual sounds, or phonemes, within words is a prerequisite to association of sounds with letters and manipulating sounds to blend words—a fancy way of saying "reading"—the teaching of phonemic awareness is crucial to emergent literacy (early childhood K-2 reading instruction). Children need a strong background in phonemic awareness in order for phonics instruction (sound–spelling relationship–printed materials) to be effective.

Instructional methods that may be effective for teaching phonemic awareness can include:

- Clapping syllables in words
- Distinguishing between a word and a sound
- Using visual cues and movements to help children understand when the speaker goes from one sound to another
- Incorporating oral segmentation activities which focus on easily distinguished syllables rather than sounds
- Singing familiar songs (e.g., "Happy Birthday," "Knick Knack Paddy Wack") and, replacing key words in them with words with a different ending or middle sound (oral segmentation)
- Dealing children a deck of picture cards and having them sound out the words for the pictures on their cards or calling for a picture by asking for its first and second sound

The Difference Between Phonological Awareness and Phonemic Awareness

Phonological awareness involves the recognition that spoken words are composed of a set of smaller units including syllables and sounds.

Phonemic awareness is a specific type of phonological awareness that focuses on the ability to distinguish, manipulate, and blend specific sounds or phonemes within a given word.

Think of phonological awareness as an umbrella and phonemic awareness as a specific spoke under this umbrella.

Phonics deals with printed words and the learning of sound-spelling correlations, while phonemic awareness activities are for the most part oral.

> *Phonological awareness involves the recognition that spoken words are composed of a set of smaller units including syllables and sounds.*

READING

Sample Test Questions and Rationale

(Rigorous)

1. The major difference between phonemic and phonological awareness is:

   A. One deals with a series of discrete sounds and sound spelling relationships

   B. One is involved with teaching and learning alliteration and rhymes

   C. Phonemic awareness is a specific type phonological awareness that deals with separate phonemes within a given word

   D. Phonological awareness is associated with printed words

   Answer is C.

   This is a sheer "memorize the definition and get it right" question. By definition, phonemic awareness falls under the phonological awareness umbrella. All of the other choices do not deal with the DIFFERENCE between the two types of awareness.

(Rigorous)

2. All of the following are true about phonological awareness except:

   A. It may involve print

   B. It is a prerequisite for spelling and phonics

   C. Activities can be done by the children with their eyes closed

   D. Starts before letter recognition is taught

   Answer is A.

   The key word here is except which will be highlighted in uppercase on the test as well. All of the options are correct aspects of phonological awareness except the first one, A, because phonological awareness DOES NOT involve print.

SKILL 2.2 Understand how to help students break down words into parts *(e.g., recognize syllables, root words, prefixes, and suffixes)*

This aspect of vocabulary development helps children look for structural elements within words that they can use independently to help them determine meaning.

Some teachers choose to directly teach structural analysis. In particular, those who teach by following the phonics-centered approach for reading do this. Other teachers, who follow the balanced literacy approach, introduce the structural components as part of mini lessons that are focused on the students' reading and writing.

Structural analysis of words as defined by J. David Cooper (2004) involves the study of significant word parts. This analysis can help the child with pronunciation and constructing meaning.

Key structural analysis components are found in the list below.

- Root word: A word from which another word is developed. The second word can be said to have its "root" in the first. The meaning of this structural component can be shown to children in an illustration of a tree with roots. Children may also want to literally construct root words using cardboard trees and/or actual roots from plants to create word family models. ELL learners can construct these models for their native language root word families, as well for the English language words they are learning. ELL learners in the fifth and sixth grades may even appreciate analyzing the different root structures for contrasts and similarities between their native language and English. Special needs learners can focus in small groups or individually with a para-professional on building root word models.

- Base word: A stand-alone linguistic unit that cannot be deconstructed or broken down into smaller words. For example, in the word "retell," the base word is "tell."

- Contraction: A shortened form of two words in which a letter or letters have been deleted. These deleted letters have been replaced by an apostrophe.

- Prefix: Beginning units of meaning which can be added (the vocabulary word for this type of structural adding is "affixed") to a base word or root word. They cannot stand alone. They are also sometimes known as "bound morphemes," meaning that they cannot stand alone as a base word.

- Suffix: Ending units of meaning which can be "affixed" or added onto the ends of root or base words. Suffixes transform the original meanings of base and root words. Like prefixes, they are also known as "bound morphemes," because they cannot stand alone as words.

- Compound word: Occurs when two or more base words are connected to form a new word. The meaning of the new word is in some way connected with that of the base word.

- Inflectional ending: Type of suffix that imparts a new meaning to the base or root word. These endings in particular change the gender, number, tense, or form of the base or root words. Just like other suffixes, these are termed "bound morphemes."

Comments

Definitions are included because the structural analysis components are explicitly taught in schools that advocate the phonics-centered approach and are also incorporated into the word work component of the schools that advocate the balanced literacy approach for instruction.

Definition questions are included because these multiple choice questions that have only a single right answer test whether the teacher candidate has memorized the appropriate content usage of the terms. They constitute no less than 15 percent of the multiple choice questions on the test. Taking the time to memorize these easy definitions will likely improve your score.

What about the use of these concepts to engage children in successful reading? One activity was detailed above related to root families, and a few more will be provided further on. Some of you may want to know why some of the activities are presented in such detail. This is deliberate and these activities have been bolded for easy identification.

Often constructed response questions form the foundations of reading tests and certification tests, asking the teacher to explain how a certain concept would be taught in a given grade for a certain student population. This type of constructed response question is simple for a teacher who is already teaching that concept to precisely that group of students in precisely that grade. There are a certain number of working teacher educators who take these tests to get additional certification or to be become certified, so for them, these detailed "How would you teach ____?" questions are a breath of tension-free air.

However, as both a trainer of working teachers in elementary schools and a graduate education teacher, I know first-hand the tension level caused by these constructed response questions for the graduate education student who has not set foot in an elementary school since the day he or she left there as a child.

I also know how unnerving it is for many educators who are career changers, who find the challenge of describing how they would teach something they can easily "do" themselves to children on the elementary level. Indeed these constructed response questions upset even experienced, currently teaching educators who may work full time as kindergarten or special needs instructors and are suddenly being asked how they would differentiate (memorize that key in-vogue education term) instruction to support children from an ELL background or to align with the U.S. history theme mandated for fifth graders. If the question doesn't focus on grades the teacher candidate has taught, even the most experienced teacher can come up high and dry as far as explaining how to teach an unfamiliar concept to an unfamiliar student population (in education circles, we use the shorthand "student pop"). Therefore, the detailed activities which have been deliberately strewn throughout the guide are constructed response models, which teacher candidates are invited, enjoined, and *urged* to review at least twice before the examination. I hope that if a "How would you teach _____ to _____?" question calls for a constructed response, but you haven't taught that subject or you haven't taught that to the designated population, you can easily use my experiences with my best wishes and hopes that they will work for you as they have for me.

So back to giving gifts the teacher may not particularly relish at this point in his or test preparation, but may need to keep in reserve for the exam or for that new student population assignment you get when the teacher who was on maternity leave decides to return.

Structural Analysis Sing-Along: Memorizing the Definitions of These Structural Word Components

Learning how to distinguish among and to correctly define these structural word components is seemingly daunting for young children. Actually they can quite easily accomplish memorizing these set definitions, which is the first necessary step for correctly using them as they construct the meaning. Pleasure in structural analysis is just a melodic song away.

Use a familiar song, which is actually a definition, for a sing-along, using "Do-Re-Mi" from *The Sound of Music* or any children's song that is regularly used in the classroom.

Model for the children how the familiar song "Do-Re-Mi" can be "changed" to be the "sung" definitions of these structural components:

> "Re," a prefix, at the beginning of a word
> "Ful," a suffix, when someone is fearful
> "Ed," an inflectional at the end of walk, it means he walked in the past
> "Don't," a contraction made up of do and not.
> That will bring us back to…

Once the teacher models the opening stanza, the children can then be challenged to come up with the next stanza's lines. The teachers will set the structural component for the line, let's say, "compound words." Then the children as either a whole class, in small groups, or as a guided writing activity will author a line to share a compound word and explain what it is. Once this is successfully done the child or group of children who wrote the correct lyric can select another structural component. They can challenge other class members to complete the next line and the structural song writing can continue for the time allotted to vocabulary development or writing workshop.

READING

This activity can develop into a structural song writing lyric wall, center, and/ or sound recording. The teacher or one of the children (if the children are on grade three level or above), can write down each lyric line contributed and then routinely sing it with small groups or the whole class as practice for reviewing structural components or just for fun! The songs can be shared with other classes. They can also be used as student-centered (written by and for students) exercises for a Structural Analysis Center where peers do activities in word study using work actually done by their classmates.

Using singing to help support children in necessary structural analysis definitions also differentiates instruction and helps the teacher to draw children whose learning styles and strengths are auditory and musical into the circle of engaged readers and writers.

Knowledge of Greek and Latin Roots that Form English Words

Knowledge of Greek and Latin roots that form English words can measurably enhance children's reading skills and can also enrich their writing.

Strategy One: word webs

Sharon Taberski (2000) does not advocate teaching Greek and Latin derivatives in the abstract to young children. However, when she comes across (as is common and natural) specific Greek and Latin roots in her readings with and to children, she uses that opportunity to introduce children to these rich resources.

Knowledge of Greek and Latin roots that form English words can measurably enhance children's reading skills and can also enrich their writing.

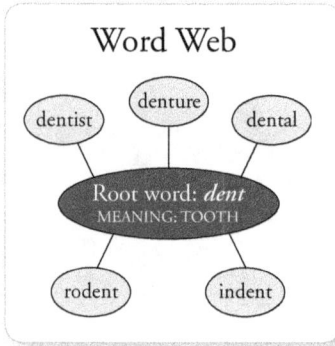

For example, during readings on rodents (a favorite of first and second graders), Taberski draws her class's attention to the fact that beavers gnaw at things with their teeth. She then connects the "dent" root or derivative to the children's lives, other words they are familiar with, or other experiences. The children then volunteer "dentist," "dental," "denture," etc. Taberski begins to place these in a graphic organizer, or word web.

When she has tapped the extent of the children's prior knowledge of "dent" words, she shares with them the fact that "dent/dentis" is the Latin word for teeth. Then she introduces the word "indent," which she has already previewed with them as part of their conventions of print study. She helps them to see that the "indenting" of the first line of a paragraph can even be related to the Latin root "teeth" in that it looks like a "print" bite was taken out of the paragraph.

Taberski displays the word web in the Word Wall Chart section of her room. The class is encouraged throughout the week to look for other words to add to the web. Taberski stresses that for her, as an elementary teacher of reading and writing, the key element of the Greek and Latin word root web activity is the children's coming to understand that if they know what a Greek or Latin word root means, they can use that knowledge to figure out what other words mean.

She feels the key concept is to model and demonstrate for children how fun and fascinating Greek and Latin root study can be.

Strategy Two: Greek and Latin roots word webs with an assist from the Internet

Older children in grades three through six can build on this initial print activity by searching online for additional words for a particular Greek or Latin root that has been introduced in class.

They can easily do this in a way that authentically ties in with their own interests and experiences by reading online reviews for a book that has been a read-aloud or by just reading online summaries of the day's news and printing out those words in the stories that share the root discussed.

Children can be encouraged to print and then circle or cut these online identified instances of their Latin or Greek root and also to document the exact date and URL for the citation. These can be posted as part of their own online web in the word wall section study area. If the school or class has a website or webpage, the children can post this data there as a special Greek and Latin root word page.

Expanding the concept of the Greek and Latin word web from the printed page to the World Wide Web nicely inculcates the child in the habits of lifelong reading and researching online. This beginning expository research will serve them well in upper elementary subject content area work and beyond.

Use of Syllabification as a Word Identification Strategy

Strategy: Clap hands and count those syllables as they come (Taberski, 2000). The objective of this activity is for children to understand that every syllable in a polysyllabic word can be studied for its spelling patterns in the same way that monosyllabic words are studied for their spelling patterns.

The easiest way for the K–3 teacher to introduce this activity to the children is to share a familiar poem from the poetry chart (or to write out a familiar poem on a large experiential chart).

First the teacher reads the poem with the children. As they are reading it aloud, the children clap the beats of the poem and the teacher uses a colored marker to place a tic (/) above each syllable.

Next, the teacher takes letter cards and selects one of the polysyllabic words from the poem that the children have already "clapped" out.

The children use letter cards to spell that word on the sentence strip holder or it can be placed on a felt board or up against a window on display. Together the children and teacher divide the letters into syllables and place blank letter cards between the syllables. The children identify spelling patterns they know.

Finally and as part of continued small group syllabification study, the children identify other polysyllabic words they clapped out from the poem. They make up the letter combinations of these words. Then they separate them into syllables with blank letter cards between the syllables.

Children who require special support in syllabification can be encouraged to use lots of letter cards to create a large butcher paper syllabic representation (in letter cards with spaces) of the poem or at least a few lines of the poem. They can be told that this will be used as a teaching tool for others. In this way, they authenticate their study of syllabification with a real product that can actually be referenced by peers.

Use of Context Cues (e.g., semantic, syntactic) to Help Identify Words and to Verify the Pronunciation and Meaning of Words

Semantic feature analysis

This technique for enhancing vocabulary skills by using semantic cues is based on the research of Johnson and Pearson (1984) and Anders and Bos (1986). Young children set up a feature analysis grid of various subject content words that is an outgrowth of their discussion about these words.

For instance, Cooper (2004) includes a sample of a Semantic Features Analysis Grid for Vegetables.

Vegetables	Green	Have Peels	Eat Raw	Seeds
Carrots	−	+	+	−
Cabbage	+	−	+	−

Note: The use of the + for yes, − for no, and possible use for both + and − if a vegetable like squash could be both green and yellow. Make this grid very accessible for young readers and very easy to do on their own as part of their independent word analysis.

Teachers of children in grade one and beyond can design their own semantic analysis grids to meet their students' needs and to align with the topics the kids are learning.

Select a category or class of words (could be planets, rodent family members, winter words, weather words).

APPLICATION OF READING SKILLS AND KNOWLEDGE TO CLASSROOM INSTRUCTION

Use the left side of the grid to list at least three items that fit this category. The number of actual items listed will depend on the age and grade level of the children, with three or four items for K–1 and up to ten or fifteen for grades five and six.

The teacher may brainstorm with the children, or if better suited to the class list on his or her own, features that the items have in common. As can be noted from the example excerpted from Cooper's *Literacy: Helping Children Construct Meaning* (2004), these common features such as vegetables' color, peels, and seeds are usually pretty easy to identify.

Show the children how to insert the notations +, −, or ? (If they are not certain) on the grid. Explore with the children the possibility that an item could get both a + and a −. For example, a vegetable like broccoli might be eaten cooked or raw, and squash can be green or yellow.

Whatever the length of the grid when first presented to the children (perhaps as a semantic cue lesson in and of itself tied in to a text being read in class), make certain that the grid as presented and filled out is not the end of the activity.

Children can use it as a model for developing their own semantic features grid and share them during the share time with the whole class. Child developed grids can become part of a Word Work center in the classroom or even be published in a Word Study Games book by the class as a whole. Such a publication can be shared with parents during open school week and evening visits and with peer classes.

Contextual redefinition

This strategy helps children use context more effectively by presenting them with sufficient context *before* they begin reading. It models for the children the use of contextual clues to make informed guesses about word meanings.

To apply this strategy, the teacher should first select unfamiliar words to teach. No more than two or three words should be selected for direct teaching. The teacher should then write a sentence in which there are sufficient clues supplied for the child to successfully figure out the meaning. Among the types of context clues the teacher can use are: compare/contrast, synonyms, and direct definition.

Then the teacher should present the words only on the experiential chart or as letter cards. Have the children pronounce the words. As they pronounce them, challenge them to come up with a definition for each word. After more than one definition is offered, encourage the children to decide as a whole group what the definition is. Write down their agreed upon definition with no comment as to its true meaning.

Then share with the children the contexts (sentences the teacher wrote with the words and explicit context clues). Ask that the children read the sentences aloud. Then have them come up with a definition for each word. Make certain that as they present their definitions, the teacher does not comment. Ask that they justify their definitions by making specific references to the context clues in the sentences.

As the discussion continues, direct the children's attention to their previously agreed upon definition of the word. Facilitate them in discussing the differences between their guesses about the word when they saw only the word itself and their guesses about the word when they read it in context. Finally have the children check their use of context skills to correctly define the word by using a dictionary.

This type of direct teaching of word definitions is useful when the children have dictionary skills and the teacher is aware of the fact that there are not sufficient clues about the words in the context to help the students define it. In addition, struggling readers and students from ELL backgrounds may benefit tremendously from being walked through this process that highly proficient and successful readers apply automatically.

By using this strategy, the teacher can also "kid watch" and note the students' prior knowledge as they guess the word in isolation. The teacher can also actually witness and hear how various students use context skills.

Through their involvement in this strategy, struggling readers gain a feeling of community as they experience the ways in which their struggles and guesses resonate in other peers' responses to the text. They are also getting a chance to be "walked through" this maze of meaning and learning how to use context clues in order to navigate it themselves.

APPLICATION OF READING SKILLS AND KNOWLEDGE TO CLASSROOM INSTRUCTION

Sample Test Questions and Rationale

(Easy)

1. The word "bat" is a ___ word for "batter-up":

   A. suffix
   B. prefix
   C. root word
   D. inflectional ending

   Answer is C.

   The key word in this question is "best" and the answer is C because this type of a book is best for teaching and display.

(Rigorous)

2. As part of study about the agricultural products of their state, children have identified twenty two different types of apples produced in the state. They can use a _____ to compare and contrast these different types of apples.

   A. word web
   B. semantic map
   C. semantic features analysis grid
   D. all of the above

   Answer is D.

   The answer here is Choice D and all of these graphic organizers would work with the apples.

SKILL 2.3 Understand how to help students decode words or phrases using context clues

WORD ANALYSIS (also called phonics or decoding) is the process readers use to figure out unfamiliar words based on written patterns. WORD RECOGNITION is the process of automatically determining the pronunciation and some degree of the meaning of an unknown word. In other words, fluent readers recognize most written words easily and correctly, without consciously decoding or breaking them down. The elements of literacy below are skills readers need for word recognition.

WORD ANALYSIS: the process readers use to figure out unfamiliar words based on written patterns

WORD RECOGNITION: the process of automatically determining the pronunciation and some degree of the meaning of an unknown word

Alphabetic Principle

The Alphabetic Principle is sometimes called graphophonemic awareness. This multisyllabic technical reading foundation term means the understanding that written words are composed of patterns of letters that represent the sounds of spoken words.

READING

> **MORPHOLOGY:** the study of word structure

> **SYNTAX:** refers to the rules or patterned relationships that correctly create phrases and sentences from words

> **SEMANTICS:** refers to the meaning expressed when words are arranged in a specific way

> **DECODE:** to change communication signals into messages

> **ENCODING:** involves changing a message into symbols

Morphology, Syntax, and Semantics

MORPHOLOGY is the study of word structure. When readers develop morphemic skills, they are developing an understanding of patterns they see in words. For example, English speakers realize that cat, cats, and caterpillar share some similarities in structure. This understanding helps readers to recognize words at a faster and easier rate, since each word doesn't need individual decoding.

SYNTAX refers to the rules or patterned relationships that correctly create phrases and sentences from words. When readers develop an understanding of syntax, they begin to understand the structure of how sentences are built, and eventually the beginning of grammar.

> *Example: "I am going to the movies."*

This statement is syntactically and grammatically correct

> *Example: "They am going to the movies."*

This statement is syntactically correct since all the words are in their correct place, but it is grammatically incorrect with the use of the word "They" rather than "I."

SEMANTICS refers to the meaning expressed when words are arranged in a specific way. Semantics includes connotation and denotation of words, which eventually plays a role for readers.

All of these skill sets are important to eventually develop effective word recognition skills, which helps emerging readers develop fluency.

To DECODE means to change communication signals into messages. (*See Skill 2.1.*) Reading comprehension requires that the reader learn the code in which a message is written and be able to decode it to get the message.

ENCODING involves changing a message into symbols. Examples of encoding include changing oral language into writing (spelling), changing an idea into words, and changing a mathematical or physical idea into appropriate symbols.

Although effective reading comprehension requires identifying words automatically (Adams, 1990, Perfetti, 1985), children do not have to be able to identify every single word or know the exact meaning of every word in a text to understand it. Indeed, Nagy (1988) says that children can read a work with a high level of comprehension even if they do not fully know as many as 15 percent of the words within it.

Children develop the ability to decode and recognize words automatically. They then can extend their ability to decode to multisyllabic words.

Explicit and Implicit Strategies for Teaching Phonics

Uta Frith has done work on the sequence of children's phonic learning. Frith has identified three phases that describe the progression of children's phonic learning from ages four through eight.

PHASES OF PHONIC LEARNING	
Logographic Phase	Children recognize whole words that have significance for them such as their own names or the names of stores they frequent or products that their parents buy. Strategies that nurture development in this phase can include explicit labeling in the classroom using the children's names and those of classroom objects, components, furniture, and materials. In addition, during snack time and lunch time, explicit attention and talk can be focused on new brands of foods and drink. Toward the end of this phase children start to notice initial letters in words and the sounds that they represent.
Analytic Phase	During this phase children make associations between the spelling patterns in the words that they know and the new words that they encounter.
Orthographic Phase	In this phase children recognize words almost automatically. They can rapidly identify an increasing number of words because they know a good deal about the structure of words and how they're spelled. To best support these phases and the development of emergent and early readers, teachers should focus on elements of phonics learning, which help children analyze words by looking at their letters, spelling patterns, and structural components. Children need to be involved in activities in which they can use what they know about words to learn new ones. The teacher needs to build on what the children know to introduce new spelling patterns, vowel combinations, and short and long vowel investigations. The teacher must do this and be aware that these will be reintroduced again and again as needed.

Activities

Suggested activities to support phonics instruction to address the needs of these three phases of phonics learning are detailed below.

These activities have specifically been provided in detail so that the educator can study them and use them in the sample constructed response questions that have been provided at the end of the guide. Since the role of phonics in promoting reading development is so crucial, it is highly likely that a constructed response question on the certification test will focus on the use of such strategies. Therefore it is a good idea for the certification candidate to study the examples closely. As a bonus, the detail with which these strategies are set

> *Keep in mind that children's learning of phonics and other key components of reading is not linear, but rather falls back to review and then flows forward to build new understandings.*

READING

forth also makes them easy to use in classes the teacher is currently teaching or anticipates teaching after successfully passing the certification exam.

Sorting words

Start with monosyllabic words. Have the children group them by their length, common letters, sound, and/or spelling pattern.

Prepare for the activity by writing ten to fifteen words on oaktag strips and place them randomly on the sentence strip holder. These words should come from a book previously shared in the classroom or a language experience chart.

Next begin to sort out the word with the children, perhaps by where a particular letter appears in a word. While the children sort the place of a particular letter in a given word, they should also be coached (or facilitated) by the teacher to recognize that sometimes a letter in the middle of the word can still be the last sound that we hear and that some letters at the end of a word are silent (such as "e").

Children should be encouraged to make their own categories for word sorts and to share their own discoveries as they do the word sorts. The children's discoveries should be recorded and posted in the rooms with their names so they have ownership of their phonics learning.

> *This activity allows children to focus closely on the specific features of words and to begin to understand the basic elements of letter sound relationships.*

Spelling pattern word wall

Create a spelling pattern word wall in your classroom. Wylie and Durrell have identified spelling patterns that are in their classic thirty-seven "dependable" rhymes. The spelling word wall can be created by stapling a piece of 3" x 5" butcher block paper to the bulletin board. Then attach spelling pattern cards around the border with thumbtacks, so that the cards can be easily removed to use at the meeting area.

Once you decide on a spelling pattern for instruction, remove the corresponding card from the word wall. Then take a 1" x 3" piece of a contrasting color of butcher block paper and tape the card to the top end of a sheet the children will use for their investigation. Next read one of Wylie and Durrell's short rimes with the children and have them identify the pattern.

After the pattern is identified the children can try to come up with other words that have the same spelling pattern. The teacher can write these on the spelling pattern sheet, using a different color marker to highlight the spelling pattern within the word. The children have to add to the list until the sheet is full, which might take two days or more.

After the sheet is full, the completed spelling pattern is attached to the wall.

> *One of the understandings emergent readers come to about a word is that if they know how to read, write, and spell one word, they can write, read, and spell many other words as well.*

Letter holder making words

Use a 2" x 3" piece of foam board to make a letter holder. On the front of the board, attach sixteen library pockets—one for each letter from A to P. Use the back of the board to attach another ten pockets for the rest of the alphabet.

Write the letter name on each pocket and use clear bookbinding tape to secure each row of cards. Make twelve cards for each letter. On the front of each 2" x 6" strip make a capital letter, and on its back write that letter in lower case. Write consonants in black marker and vowels in red marker.

Through use of this letter holder, children can experience how letters can be rearranged, added, or removed to make new words. They can use these cards also to focus as needed on letter sequences and to support them in recognizing spelling patterns in words.

You can choose the words for this activity from Patricia Cunningham and Dorothy P. Hall's *Making Words* (1994).

Select a word that is called the "secret word." Build up toward the creation of that word through a focus on the smaller words within it. Words should be chosen that reflect the spelling patterns being studied by the class.

You can create letter holders for the children by folding up the bottom third of a used manila file folder and taping the ends to form a shallow pocket. Give them letter cards that are made of 2" x 6" oaktag. So, for example, if the secret word is bicycle, the children would be given the separate letter cards that would make up that word. The children keep the letters on the floor in front of them and only place them in the holder when they are actually making a word. Making words should begin with making two letter words and then progress to making larger words depending on the individual child's progress. The teacher tells the child which two letters to use to make a word. After the instruction is given, the children select the correct letters and make the word in their folder. The teacher then writes the word down and the children check their letter holder word against it. The teacher goes around checking through and reviewing the letter holders to see which children are getting it and then continues to build up words with more letters if the children are ready.

Through use of letter holders, children can experience how letters can be rearranged, added, or removed to make new words.

Word splits

Word splits involve splitting compound words. Through working with compound words, children can experience that big words are often made up of smaller words. By working with five to ten compound words on oaktag cards, children can analyze letter–sound relationships and meaning.

By splitting compound words, children can experience that big words are often made up of smaller words.

Before children meet in a group, write five to ten words on oaktag cards and arrange them on the sentence strip holder. After the words have been read, cut each of the words into its two smaller words and randomly arrange them on the sentence strip holder. Allow the children to randomly take turns arranging the smaller words into the original compound words. Also encourage them to form new compound words. For example, if one of two original compound words is "rainbow" and the other is "dropping," the children should be able to come with "raindrop." The new words the children come up with should be written on blank oaktag cards with the names of the children who came up with them attached. In this way the children can add to their growing bank of new words and have ownership in the words that they have added.

Role of Phonics in Developing Rapid, Automatic Word Recognition, Decoding, and Reading Comprehension

Decoding means changing communication signals into messages. Reading comprehension requires that the reader learn the code within which a message is written and be able to decode it to get the message.

Children develop the ability to decode and recognize words automatically. They then can extend their ability to decode to multisyllabic words.

Blending letter sounds and prompts for graphophonic cues

Here are some prompts.

- You said [the child's incorrect attempt]. Does that match the letters you see?
- If it were [the child's incorrect attempt], what would it have to start with?
- If it were [the child's incorrect attempt], what would it have to end with?

Look at the first letter/s . . . look at the middle letter/s . . . look at the last letter . . . What could it be?

If you were writing [the child's incorrect attempt], what letter would you write first? What letters would go in the middle? What letter would go last?

A good strategy to use in working with individual children is to have them explain how they finally correctly identified a word that was troubling them. If prompted and habituated through one-on-one teacher/tutoring conversations, they can be quite clear about what they did to get the word.

If the children are already writing their own stories, the teacher might say to them: "You know when you write your own stories, you would never write any story that did not make sense. You wouldn't and probably this writer didn't either. If you read something that does make sense, but doesn't match the letters, then it's probably not what the author wrote. Right now this is the author's story, not yours, so go back to the work and see if you can find out the author's story. Later on, you might write your own story."

Letter–sound correspondence and beginning decoding

- Focus on a particular letter that you want the child to investigate. It is good to choose one from a shared text that the children are familiar with. Make certain that the directions to the children are clear and either focuses them on looking for a specific letter or listening for sounds.

- Next, begin a list of words that meet the task given to the children. Use chart paper to list the words that the children identify. This list can be continued into the next week as long as the children's focus is maintained on the list. This can be easily done by challenging the children to identify a specific number of letters or sounds and urging them as a class team to go beyond those words or sounds.

- Continue to add to the list. Focus the children at the beginning of the day on the goal of their individually adding to the list. Give them an adhesive note (sticky pad sheet) on which they can individually write down the words they find. Then they can attach the newly found words with their names on them to the chart. This provides the children with a sense of ownership and pride in their letter-sounding abilities. During shared reading, discuss the children's proposed additions and have the group decide if these meet the directed category. If all the children agree that they do meet the category, include the words on the chart.

- Do a word sort from all the words generated and have the children put the words into categories that demonstrate similarities and differences. They can be prompted to see if the letter appeared at the beginning of the word or in the middle of the word. They might also be prompted to see that one sound could have two different letter representations. The children can then "box" the word differences and similarities by drawing colors established in a chart key.

- Finally, before the children go off to read, ask them to look for new words in the texts that they can now recognize because of the letter–sound relationships on their chart. During shared reading, make certain that they have time to share the words they were able to decode because of their explorations.

READING

Strategies for helping students decode single syllable words that follow common patterns and multisyllable words

This activity is presented in detail so it can actually be implemented with children in a classroom and also to provide detail for a potential constructed response question on a certification examination.

Use this procedure for letter–sound investigations that support beginning decoding.

The CVC Phonic Card game developed by Jackie Montierth, a computer teacher in South San Diego for use with grade five and six students, is a good one to adapt to the needs of any group with appropriate modification for age, grade level, and language needs.

The children use the vehicle of the card game to practice and enhance their use of consonants and vowels. This fluency will increase their ability to decode words.

Potential uses beyond whole classroom instruction include use as part of the small group word work component of the reading workshop and as part of cooperative team learning.

This strategy also is particularly helpful for grade four and beyond ELL who are in a regular English language classroom setting.

The card game works well because the practice of the content is implicit for transfer as the children continue to improve their reading skills. In addition, the card game format allows "instructional punctuation" using a student centered high interest exploration.

Teachers of ELL learners can play this game in their native language first and then transition into English, facilitating native language reading skills and second language acquisition. They can develop appropriate decks to meet the vocabulary needs of their children and to complement the curricula Using Phonics to Decode Words in Connected Text.

CARD DESIGN

The teacher can use the computer, 5" x 8" index cards, or actual card-sized oaktag cards to create a deck. For repeated use and durability, laminate the cards.

The deck should consist of the following:

44 consonant cards (including the blends)

15 vowel cards (including 3 of each vowel)

5 wild cards (which can be used as any vowel)

6 final e-cards

The design of this project can also focus on particular CVC words that are part of a particular book, topic, or theme (i.e. study of American history, grade four appropriate; US, Canada, and Latin America Geography, grade five and six; or genre format). Before playing the game, children can also be directed to review the words on the word wall or other words on a word map.

APPLICATION OF READING SKILLS AND KNOWLEDGE TO CLASSROOM INSTRUCTION

PROCEDURE

The game is best introduced first as part of a mini lesson with the teacher reading the rules, and a pair of children demonstrating step by step, as the game is played in front of the class for the first time.

Have the children divide into pairs or small groups of no more than four per group. Each group needs one deck of CVC cards.

Have each group choose a dealer. The dealer shuffles the deck of cards. The dealer deals five cards to each player. The remaining cards are placed face down for drawing during the play. One card is turned over to form the discard pile.

Players may not show their cards to other players.

The first player to the left of the dealer looks at his/her cards and if possible, puts down three cards that make a consonant-vowel-consonant word. For more points, four cards forming a consonant-vowel-consonant word can be laid down. The player must then say the word and draw the number of cards he or she laid down.

If he or she is unable to form a word, he/she draws a card from either the draw or discard pile. The player then discards one card. All players must have five cards at all times.

The next player to the left now takes his/her turn. That player puts down any cards forming a CVC word. That player must then say the word and draw the number of cards that he or she laid down. Should the player not be able to say the word he/she draws from the pile, he/she draws a card from the discard or the draw pile.

The game continues until one or more of the following happens:

- There are no more cards in the draw pile.
- All players run out of cards.
- No player is able to form a word.

The winner is the player who has laid down the most cards during the game. Players may only lay down words at the beginning of their turn. Proper names may not be counted as words.

VARIATIONS

The game can be played with teams of individuals in a small group of four or less competing against one another (excellent for special needs or resource room students). It can also be done as a whole class activity in which all the students are divided into cooperative teams or small groups who compete against one another. This second approach will work well with a heterogeneous classroom that includes special needs and/or ELL children.

READING

Identifying new words

Some strategies to share with children during conferences or as part of shared reading include the following prompts:

- Look at the beginning letter/s. What sound do you hear?

- Stop to think about the text or story. What word with this beginning letter would make sense here?

- Look at the book's illustrations. Do they provide you with help in figuring out the new word?

- Think of what word would make sense, sound right, and match the letters that you see. Start the sentence over, making your mouth ready to say that word.

- Skip the word, read to the end of the sentence, and then come back to the word. How does what you've read help you with the word?

- Listen to whether what you are reading makes sense and matches the letters (this is asking the child to self-monitor). If it doesn't make sense, see if you can correct it on your own.

- Look for spelling patterns you know from the spelling pattern wall.

- Look for smaller words you might know within the larger word.

- Think of any place you may have seen this word before, or any story read to you or by you where you met up with this word.

- Read a little bit more, and then return to the part that confused you.

APPLICATION OF READING SKILLS AND KNOWLEDGE TO CLASSROOM INSTRUCTION

Sample Test Questions and Rationale

(Average)

1. Rina has been hired to work in a school that serves a local public housing project. She is working with kindergarten children and has been asked to focus on shared reading. She selects:

    A. Chapter books
    B. Riddle books
    C. Alphabet books
    D. Wordless picture books

Answer is D.

Given the fact this is a kindergarten in a public housing project, she will be most successful with wordless picture books, since there is no guarantee the children have had prior exposure to the other types of books listed. Choice D will allow them to construct a story from the pictures.

(Easy)

2. The term graphophonemic awareness refers to:

    A. Handwriting skills
    B. Letter to sound recognition
    C. Alphabetic principle
    D. Phonemic awareness

Answer is C.

(Easy)

3. To decode is to:

    A. Construct meaning
    B. Sound out a printed sequence of letters
    C. Use a special code to decipher a message
    D. None of the above

Answer is B.

(Average)

4. Asking a child if what he or she has read makes sense to him or her is prompting the child to use:

    A. Phonics cues
    B. Syntactic cues
    C. Semantic cues
    D. Prior knowledge

Answer is C.

This is one a literate test taker can get; the answer is Choice C.

READING

> **SKILL 2.4** Understand how to help students distinguish among synonyms, antonyms, and homonyms

SYNONYMS: words with similar or identical meanings that are interchangeable

SYNONYMS are words with similar or identical meanings that are interchangeable. Synonyms can be adjectives, nouns, verbs, or adverbs. Both synonyms must be the same part of speech. Here are some examples of synonyms:

Talk (v.)	Speak (v.)
Bucket (n.)	Pail (n.)
Large (adj.)	Big (adj.)
Beautiful (adj.)	Attractive (adj.)
Wet (adj.)	Moist (adj.)
Close (v.)	Shut (v.)
Infant (n.)	Baby (n.)

> I was <u>delighted</u> to volunteer at the women's shelter.
> I was <u>happy</u> to volunteer at the women's shelter.

ANTONYMS: words with opposite meanings

ANTONYMS are words with opposite meanings. Antonyms can express complementary or absolute opposites: "mortal" and "immortal," as well as gradable opposites, such as "tall" and "short." Here are some examples of antonyms:

Big	Small
Happy	Sad
Sharp	Dull
Cold	Hot
Hard	Soft
Capable	Incapable

> I was <u>sure</u> that my answer was correct.
> I was <u>unsure</u> whether my answer was correct.

APPLICATION OF READING SKILLS AND KNOWLEDGE TO CLASSROOM INSTRUCTION

Students frequently encounter problems with HOMONYMS. Homonyms are words that are pronounced the same as others but usually have different spellings and meanings, such as due and do. A special type of homonym is a homograph: words that are pronounced and spelled the same way but have different meanings, such as mean, which can be a verb that means "to intend," an adjective that means "unkind," and a noun or adjective that means "average."

A similar phenomenon that causes trouble is HETERONYMS (also sometimes called heterophones), words that are spelled the same but have different pronunciations and meanings (in other words, they are homographs that differ in pronunciation or, technically, homographs that are not homophones).

> *Examples: the homographs desert (abandon) and desert (arid region) are heteronyms (pronounced differently); but mean (intend) and mean (average) are not. They are pronounced the same, or are homonyms.*

Another similar occurrence in English is the CAPITONYM, a word that is spelled the same but has different meanings when it is capitalized and may or may not have different pronunciations.

> *Example: polish (to make shiny) and Polish (from Poland).*

Some of the most troubling homonyms are those that are spelled differently but sound the same.

> *Examples: its (third person singular neuter pronoun) and it's ("it is"); there, their (third person plural pronoun) and they're ("they are"); to, too, two.*

Some homonyms/homographs are particularly complicated and troubling. Fluke, for instance is a fish, a flatworm, the end parts of an anchor, the fins on a whale's tail, and a stroke of luck.

HOMONYMS: words that are pronounced the same as others but usually have different spellings and meanings

HETERONYMS: words that are spelled the same but have different pronunciations and meanings

CAPITONYM: a word that is spelled the same but has different meanings when it is capitalized and may or may not have different pronunciations

SKILL 2.5 Understand how to help students alphabetize words

Development of the Understanding that Print Carries Meaning

Understanding that print carries meaning is demonstrated every day in the elementary classroom as the teacher holds up a selected book to read it aloud to the class. The teachers explicitly and deliberately think aloud about how to hold the book, how to focus the class on looking at its cover, where to start reading, and in what direction to begin.

Even in writing the morning message on the board, the teacher targets the children on the placement of the message and its proper place at the top of the board, to be followed by additional activities and a schedule for the rest of the day.

When the teacher challenges children to make letter posters of a single letter and the items in the classroom, their home, or their knowledge base that start with that letter, the children are making concrete that print carries meaning.

Strategies for Promoting Awareness of the Relationship Between Spoken and Written Language

- Write what the children are saying on a chart.

- Highlight and celebrate the meanings, uses, and print products found in the classroom. These products include: posters, labels, yellow sticky pad notes, labels on shelves and lockers, calendars, rule signs, and directions.

- The intentional reading of big-print and oversized books teaches print conventions such as directionality.

- Practice exercises in reading to others (for K–1 or 2) where young children practice how to handle a book, how to turn pages, how to find tops and bottoms of pages, and how to tell the difference between the front and back covers of a book.

- Search and discuss adventures in word awareness and close observation where children are challenged to identify and talk about the length, appearance, and boundaries of specific words and the letters that comprise them.

- Have children match spoken words to printed words by forming an echo chorus as the teacher reads the story aloud. They echo the reading. Often this works best with poetry or rhymes.

- Have the children combine, manipulate, switch, and move letters to change words and spelling patterns.

- Work with letter cards to create messages and respond to the messages that they create.

The Role of Environmental Print in Developing Print Awareness

An environmental print book can be created by the teacher for the children that contains collaged symbols of their favorite lunch or breakfast foods. The environmental print book can be a collaged effort composed of alphabetically arranged cut and clipped symbols from the packaging of these foods. Then the class can add to it by clipping and placing symbols and logos from their favorite lunch and snack foods in the book. Newspapers are also an excellent source of environmental print. They are accessible every day and food ads, clothing ads, and other child-centered products and personalities lend themselves wonderfully to developing print awareness. Supermarket circulars and coupons distributed in chain drug stores are also excellent for engaging children in using environmental print as a reading device.

Environmental print is particularly effective in immediately helping a child from an ELL background develop print awareness through the familiarity of commercial logos and packaging symbols used.

Strategies for Promoting Letter Knowledge and Letter Formation

Engage the children in a Tale Trail game. Use a story they have already heard or read. Ask the children to circle certain letters and then reread the story, sharing the letters they have circled.

Give the children lots of opportunities to do letter sorts. Pass out word cards that have the targeted letter on them. Ask the children to come up and display their answers to questions like these about the letter R, for example.

> *R as the first letter—rose, rise, ran*
> *R as the last letter—car, star, far*
> *R with a t after it—start, heart, part, smart*
> *R, two r's in the middle of a word—carry, sorry, starry*

Play "what's in a name?" Select a student's name. Copy it on a sentence strip. Have the children count the number of letters in the name and how many of them appear twice. Allow them to talk about which letter is uppercase and which letters are lowercase. Have the students chant the name. Then rewrite the name on another sentence strip. Cut the strip into separate letters and see if someone from the class can put the name back correctly.

As you read a book with or to children, ask that they show you specific letters or lowercase or uppercase letters. Read the text first and encourage as many children to come up and identify the letters as possible. Use a big book and have felt letters available for display as well. If grade, age, and developmentally appropriate, have children then write the letter they identified themselves or, even more fun, construct it using pipe cleaners, craft sticks, or coded colored markers (different colors for uppercase and lowercase letters).

Play "letter leap" with the children and have them look carefully at the room to identify labeled items that begin with a specific letter by "leaping" over to them and placing a large lettered placard next to them. Children who have advanced in letter formation can then be challenged to "leap" through the classroom when called upon to literally "letter" unlabeled objects.

Use of Reading and Writing Strategies for Teaching Letter-Sound Correspondence

Provide children with a sample of a single letter book (or create one from environmental sources, newspapers, coupons, circulars, magazines, or your own text ideas). Make sure that your already published or created sample includes a printed version of the letter in both upper and lower case forms. Make certain that each page contains a picture of something that starts with that specific letter and also has the word for the picture. The book you select or create should be a predictable one in that when the picture is identified, the word can be read.

Once the children have been provided with your sample and have listened to it being read, challenge them to each make a one letter book. Often it is best to focus on familiar consonants for the single letter book or the first letter of the child's first name. Use of the first letter of the child's first name invites the child to develop a book that tells about him or her and the words that he or she finds. This is an excellent way to have the reading workshop aspect of the teacher's teaching of alphabetic principle complement and enhance the writing workshop. Encourage children to be active writers and readers by finding words for their book on the classroom word wall, in alphabet books in the special alphabet book bin, and in grade and age appropriate pictionaries (dictionaries for younger children that are filled with pictures).

Of course, the richest resource within the reading and writing workshop classroom for teaching and fostering the alphabetic principle lies in the use of alphabet books as anchor books for inspiring students writing. While young children in grades K–1 will do better with the one letter book authoring activity, children in grades 2 and beyond can truly be inspired and motivated by alphabet books to enhance their own reading, writing, and alphabetic skills. Furthermore, use of these books that have ben and are being produced in a variety of formats to enhance social studies, science, and mathematical themes provide an opportunity for even young children to create a meaningful product that authenticates their content study as it enhances alphabetic skills and, of course, print awareness.

An annotated bibliography of some of the newest alphabet books has been provided in the bibliography section of this guide. It was limited by space considerations, but the educator can, with no expanse and with much pleasure, catch ue on the latest titles and identify those most appropriate for the grade taught by visiting a bookstore. Hold the print book in hand and then consider selecting an alphabet book that has a particularly inviting concept, art style, or adaptable format within the children's capacity to use as a model.

For instance, Tana Hoban uses actual color photographs of letters in her *26 Letters and 99 Cents*. Children may want to make clay letters or create letter sculptures that develop their own "in style of" alphabet book similar to Hoban's. If nutrition is the science topic, children might want to examine Lois Ehlert's very accessible *Eating the Alphabet: Fruits and Vegetables from A to Z*. This, combined with an examination of the fruits and vegetables in a local store (perhaps a pleasant walk from the school and a quick break from the routine local outing), can yield a wonderful alphabet book on fruits and vegetables that can also include those fruits and vegetables eaten in various cultures (i.e., mangos, plantains, pomegranates, etc).

The alphabet book can also offer the class a chance to work collaboratively within a template created by the teacher. Completion of this collaborative work can be shared with peers in another class and parents and be kept as a model for the following year's class with their recognition and acceptance of the authors!

Assessment Throughout the Year of Graphophonemic Awareness

The teacher will want to maintain individual records of children's reading behaviors demonstrating alphabetic principle/graphophonemic awareness.

The following performance standards should be part of a record template form for each child in grades K–1 and beyond as needed (depending on ELL or special needs):

- Match all consonant and short vowel sounds.
- Read one's own name.
- Read one syllable words and high frequency words.
- Demonstrate ability to read and understand that as letters in words change, so do the sounds.
- Generate the sounds from all letters including consonant blends and long vowel patterns. Blend those different sounds into recognizable words.
- Read common sight words.
- Read common word families.
- Recognize and use knowledge of spelling patterns when reading—run/running, hop/hopping.

READING

- Decode (sound out) regular words with more than one syllable (vacation, graduation).

- Recognize regular abbreviations (Feb., Mr., PS).

Any record kept of an individual child's progress should include each date of observation and some legend or rubric detailing the level of performance, standard acquisition, or mastery.

Some teachers use Y for "exhibits the reading behavior consistently," M for "making progress toward the standard," and N for "has not yet exhibited the behavior." Beyond this objective legend for the assessment, the teacher may want to and should include any other comments that detail the child's progress in this awareness.

Sample Test Questions and Rationale

(Average)

1. **Environmental print is available at all of the following except:**

   A. Within a newspaper
   B. On the page of a library book
   C. On a supermarket circular
   D. In a commercial flyer

   Answer is B.

   The key word here is "except" and environmental print is not defined as print in a library book, so Choice B is the right one here because it is incorrect.

(Average)

2. **The best way for a primary grade teacher to model directionality and one to one word matching would be:**

   A. Using a regular library or classroom text book
   B. Using her own person reading book
   C. Using a big book
   D. Using a book dummy

   Answer is C.

SKILL 2.6 Understand how to help students use prereading strategies, such as skimming or making predictions

The point of comprehension instruction is not necessarily to focus just on the text(s) students are using at the very moment of instruction, but rather to help them learn the strategies that they can use independently with any other text.

COMMON METHODS OF TEACHING INSTRUCTION	
Summarization	Students go over the main point of the text, along with strategically chosen details that highlight the main point. This is not the same as paraphrasing, which is saying the same thing in different words. Teaching students how to summarize is very important because it will help them look for the most critical areas in a text and in nonfiction. For example, it will help them distinguish between main arguments and examples. In fiction, it helps students to learn how to focus on the main characters and events and distinguish those from the lesser characters and events.
Question Answering	While this tends to be overused in many classrooms, it is still a valid method of teaching students to comprehend. Students answer questions regarding a text, either out loud, in small groups, or individually on paper. The best questions are those that cause students to think about the text (rather than just find an answer within the text).
Question Generating	This is the opposite of question answering, although students can then be asked to answer their own questions or the questions of peers. In general, we want students to constantly question texts as they read. This is important because it causes students to become more critical readers. To teach students to generate questions helps them to learn the types of questions they can ask, and it gets them thinking about how best to be critical of texts.
Graphic Organizers	Graphic organizers are graphical representations of content within a text. For example, Venn diagrams can be used to highlight the difference between two characters in a novel or two similar political concepts in a social studies textbook. Or, a teacher can use flow-charts with students to talk about the steps in a process, such as the steps of setting up a science experiment or the chronological events of a story. Semantic organizers are similar in that they graphically display information. The difference, usually, is that semantic organizers focus on words or concepts. For example, a word web can help students make sense of a word by mapping out from the central word all the similar and related concepts to that word.
Text Structure	Often in nonfiction—particularly in textbooks—and sometimes in fiction, text structures will give important clues to readers about what to look for. Students may not know how to make sense of all the types of headings in a textbook and do not realize that, for example, the side-bar story about a character in history is not the main text on a particular page in the history textbook. Teaching students how to interpret text structures gives them tools with which to tackle similar texts.

Table continued on next page

READING

Monitoring Comprehension	Students need to be aware of their comprehension, or lack of it, in particular texts. So, it is important to teach students what to do when suddenly text stops making sense. For example, students can go back and reread the description of a character. Or, they can go back to the table of contents or the first paragraph of a chapter to see where they are headed.
Textual Marking	This is where students interact with the text as they read. For example, armed with Post-it Notes, students can insert questions or comments regarding specific sentences or paragraphs within the text. This helps students focus on the importance of the small things, particularly when they are reading larger works (such as novels in high school). It also gives students a reference point on which to go back into the text when they need to review something.
Discussion	Small group or whole-class discussion stimulates thoughts about texts and gives students a larger picture of the impact of those texts. For example, teachers can strategically encourage students to discuss related concepts to the text. This helps students learn to consider texts within larger societal and social concepts. Or teachers can encourage students to provide personal opinions in discussion. By listening to various students' opinions, this will help all students in a class to see the wide range of possible interpretations and thoughts regarding one text.

Many people mistakenly believe that the terms "research-based," "research-validated," or "evidence-based" relate mainly to specific programs, such as early reading textbook programs. While research does validate that some of these programs are effective, much research has been conducted regarding the effectiveness of particular instructional strategies. In reading, many of these strategies have been documented in the report from the National Reading Panel (2000).

Just because a strategy has not been validated as effective by research, however, does not necessarily mean that it is not effective with certain students in certain situations. The number of strategies out there far outweighs researchers' ability to test their effectiveness. Some of the strategies listed above have been validated by rigorous research, while others have been shown consistently to help improve students' reading abilities in localized situations. There simply is not enough space to list all the strategies out there that have been proven effective; just know that the above strategies are very commonly cited as working in a variety of situations.

SKILL 2.7 Understand how to ask questions about a reading selection to help students understand the selection

The Relationship Between Oral and Written Vocabulary Development and Reading Comprehension

Biemiller's (2003) research documents that those children entering fourth grade with significant vocabulary deficits demonstrate increasing reading comprehension problems. Evidence shows that these children do not catch up, but rather continue to fall behind.

Strategy One: word map strategy

This strategy is a good one for children grades three through six and beyond. The target group of children for this strategy includes those who need to improve their independent vocabulary acquisition abilities. The strategy is essentially teacher-directed learning where children are "walked through" the process. They are helped by the teacher to identify the type of information that makes a definition. They are also assisted in using context clues and background understanding to construct meaning.

The word map strategy helps children to visually represent the elements of a given concept.

The word map graphic organizer is the tool teachers use to complete this strategy with children. Word map templates are available online from the Houghton Mifflin Web site and from READWRITETHINK, the Web site of the NCTE.

The children's literal articulation of the concept can be prompted by three key questions: What is it? What is it like? What are some examples?

For instance, the word "oatmeal" might yield a word map with "What?", and in a rectangular box a hot cereal you eat in the morning; "What is it like?": hot, mushy, salty; "What are some examples?": instant oatmeal you make in a minute, apple-flavor oatmeal, Irish Oatmeal.

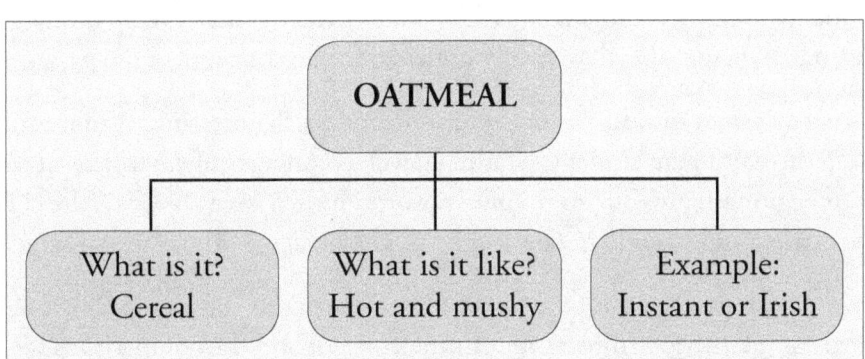

The procedure to be used in sharing this strategy with children is to select three concepts the children are familiar with. Then show them the template of a word map. Tell them that the three questions asked on the map and the boxes to fill in beneath them helps readers to see what they need to know about a word. The teacher of balanced literacy will also mention that these same three things are necessary for writers to know when they write about a word.

Next, help the children to complete at least two word maps for two of the three concepts that were pre-selected. Then have the children select a concept of their own to map either independently or in a small group. As the final task for this first part of the strategy, have the children, in teams or individually, write a definition for at least one of the concepts using the key things about it listed on the map. Have the children share these definitions aloud and talk about how they used the word maps to help them with the definitions.

For the next part of this strategy, the teacher should pick up an expository text or a textbook the children are already using to study: mathematics, science, or social studies. The teacher should either locate a short excerpt where a particular concept is defined or use the content to write model passages of definition on his or her own.

After the passages are selected or authored, the teacher should duplicate them. Then they should be distributed to the children along with blank word map templates. The children should be asked to read each passage and then to complete the word map for the concept in each passage.

Finally, have the children share the word maps they have developed for each passage. Give them a chance to explain how they used the word in the passage to help them fill out their word map. End by telling them that the three components of the concept—class, properties, concept—are just three of the many components for any given concept.

This strategy has assessment potential for the teacher because the teacher can literally see how the students understand specific concepts by looking at their maps and hearing their explanations. The maps the students develop on their own demonstrate whether they have really understood the concepts in the passages.

This strategy serves to ready students for independently inferring word meanings. By using the word map strategy, children develop concepts of what they need to know to begin to figure out an unknown word on their own. It assists the children in grades three and beyond to connect prior knowledge with new knowledge.

This word map strategy can be adapted by the teacher to suit the specific needs and goals of instruction. Illustrations of the concept and the comparisons to other concepts can be included in the word mapping for children grades five and beyond. This particular strategy is one that can be used with a research theme in the social studies content areas.

Strategy Two: preview in context

Before beginning the strategy, the teacher selects only two or three key concept words. Then the teacher reads the text carefully to identify passages within the text that evidence strong context clues for the word.

> Preview in context is a direct teaching strategy that allows the teacher to guide the students as they examine words in their context prior to reading a passage.

Then the teacher presents the word and the context to the children. As the teacher reads aloud, the children follow along. Once the teacher has finished the read aloud, the children reread the material silently.

After the silent rereading, the children will be facilitated or coached by the teacher to a definition of one of the key words selected for study. This is done through a child-centered discussion. As part of the discussion, the teacher asks questions that get the children to activate their prior knowledge and to use the contextual clues to figure out the correct meaning of the selected key concept words. Make certain that the definition of the key concept word is finally made by the children.

Next, help the children to begin to expand the word's meaning. Do this by having them consider the following for the given key concept word: synonyms, antonyms, and other contexts or other kinds of stories or texts where the word might appear. This is the time to have the children check their responses to the challenge of identifying word synonyms and antonyms by having them go to the thesaurus or the dictionary to confirm their responses. In addition, have the children place the synonyms or antonyms they find in their word boxes or word journals. The recording of their findings will guarantee them ownership of the words and deepen their capacity to use contextual clues.

The main point to remember in using this strategy is that it should only be used when the context is strong. It will not work with struggling readers who have no prior knowledge. Through listening to the children's responses as the teacher helps them to define the word and its potential synonyms and antonyms, the teacher can assess their ability to successfully use context clues.

The key to this simple strategy is that it allows the teacher to draw the child out and to grasp through the child's responses the individual child's contextual clue process. The more talk from the child the better.

The Role of Systematic, Noncontextual Vocabulary Strategies

Strategy One: hierarchical and linear arrays

The very complexity of the vocabulary used in this strategy description may be unnerving for the teacher. Yet this strategy included in the Cooper (2004) literacy instruction is really very simple once it is outlined very directly for children.

By using the term "hierarchical and linear" arrays, Cooper really is talking about how some words are grouped based on associative meanings. The words may have a "hierarchical" relationship to one another. For instance, an undergraduate or a first grader is lower in the school hierarchy than the graduate student and second grader. Within an elementary school, the fifth grader is at the top of the hierarchy and the pre–K child or kindergartener is at the bottom of the hierarchy. By the way, the term for this strategy obviously need not be explained in this detail to K–3 children, but might be shared with some grade and age appropriate modifications with children in grades three and beyond. It will enrich their vocabulary development and ownership of arrays they create.

Words can have a linear relationship to one another in that they run a spectrum from bad to good—for example, from K–3 experiences—such as bad, better, good, best/perfect.

Once you get past the seemingly daunting vocabulary words, the arrays turn out to be another neat graphic organizer tool that can help children see how words relate to one another.

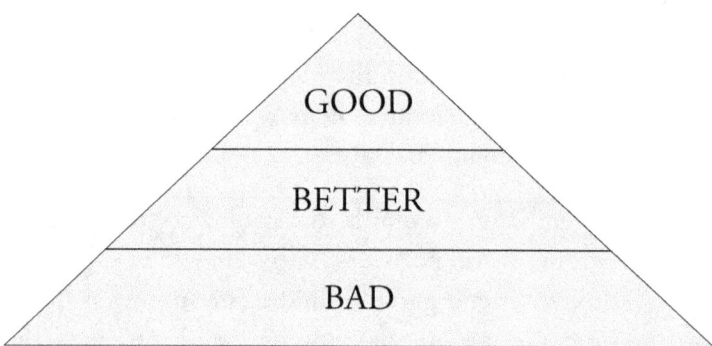

To use this graphic organizer tool, the teacher should pre-select a group of words from a read aloud or from the children's writing. Show the children how the array will look using arrows for the linear array and just straight lines for the hierarchy. Invite some children up to draw the straight hierarchy lines as it is presented, so they have a role in developing even the first hierarchical model.

Do one hierarchy array and one linear array with the preselected word with the children. Talk them through filling out (or helping the teacher to fill out) the array. After the children have had their own successful experience with arrays, they can select the words from their independent texts or familiar, previously read favorites to study. They will also need to decide which type of array—hierarchical or linear—is appropriate. For fifth and sixth graders, this choice can and should be voiced using the now "owned" vocabulary words: "hierarchical array" and "linear array."

This strategy is best used after reading, since it will help the children to expand their word banks.

APPLICATION OF READING SKILLS AND KNOWLEDGE TO CLASSROOM INSTRUCTION

Strategy Two: contextual vocabulary skills through vocabulary self-collection

This strategy is one that can be introduced by the teacher early in the year, perhaps even the first day or week. The format for self-collection can then be started by the children. It may take the form of a journal with photocopied template pages. It can be continued throughout the year.

To start, ask the children to read a required text or story. Invite them to select one word for the class to study from this text or story. The children can work individually, in teams, or in small groups. The teacher can also do the self-collecting so that this becomes the joint effort of the class community of literate readers. Tell the children that they should select words that particularly interest them or that are unique in some way.

After the children have had time to make their selections and to reflect on them, make certain that they have time to share them with their peers as a whole class. When each child shares the word that he or she has selected, have them provide a definition for the word. Each word that is given should be listed on a large experiential chart or even in a BIG BOOK format, if that is age and grade appropriate. The teacher should also share the word he or she selected and provide a definition. The teacher's definition and sharing should be somewhere in the middle of the children's recitations.

The dictionary should be used to verify the definitions. When all the definitions have been checked, a final list of child-selected (and single teacher-selected) words should be made.

Once this final list has been compiled, the children can record it in their word journals or they may opt to record only those words they find interesting in their individual journals. It is up to the teacher at the onset of the vocabulary self-collection activity to decide whether the children have to record all the words on the final list or if they can eliminate some. The decision made at the beginning by the teacher must be adhered to throughout the year.

To further enhance this strategy, children—particularly those in grades three and beyond—can be encouraged to use their collected words as part of their writings or to record and clip the appearance of these words in newspaper stories or online. This type of additional recording demonstrates that the child has truly incorporated the word into his or her reading and writing. It also habituates children to be lifelong readers, writers, and researchers.

Assessment is built into the strategy. As the children select the word for the list, they share how they used contextual clues and, through the children's response to the definitions offered by their peers, their prior knowledge can be assessed.

> *This strategy is one in which children, even on the emergent level from grade two and up, take responsibility for their learning. It is also, by definition, a student-centered strategy that demonstrates student ownership of their chosen vocabulary.*

> *This simple but versatile strategy works equally well with expository and narrative texts. It also provides children with an opportunity to use the dictionary.*

What is most useful about this strategy is that it documents that children can learn to read and write by reading and writing. The children take ownership of the words in the self-collection journals, and that can also be the beginning of writer observation journals as they include their own writings. They also use the word lists as a start for writer's commonplace books. These books are filled with newspaper, magazine, and functional document clippings using the journal words. This activity is a good one for demonstrating the balanced literacy belief that vocabulary study works best when the words studied are child-centered.

The Relationship between Oral Vocabulary and the Process of Identifying and Understanding Written Words

One way to explore the relationship between oral vocabulary and the comprehension of written words is through the use of oral records (which are discussed at length in the appendix).

In *On Solid Ground Strategies for Teaching Reading K–3*, Sharon Taberski (2000), discusses how oral reading records can be used by the K–3 teacher to assess how well children are using cueing systems. She notes that the running record format can also show visual depictions for the teacher of how the child thinks as the child reads. The notation of miscues in particular shows how a child "walks through" the reading process. They indicate if and in what ways the child may require guided support in understanding the words he or she reads aloud (oral language).

Taberski notes that when children read they need to think about several things at once:

- They must consider whether what they are reading makes sense (semantic or meaning cues).

- They must know whether their reading "sounds right" in terms of Standard English (syntactic and structural cues).

- They have to weigh whether their oral language actually and accurately matches the letters the words represent (visual or graphophonic cues).

In taking the running record and having the opportunity first-hand to listen to the children talk about the text, the teacher can analyze the relationship between the child's oral language and word comprehension. Information from the running record and the teacher–child talk as it is taken provide the teacher with a road map for differentiated cueing system instruction.

For example, when a running record is taken, a child often makes a mistake but then self-corrects. The child may select from various cueing systems when he or she self-corrects. These include: "M" for meaning, "S" for syntax, and "V" for visual. The use of a visual cue means that the child is drawing on his or her knowledge of spelling patterns. Of course, Taberski cautions that any relationship between oral language and comprehension that the teacher draws from an examination of the oral-reading records must be drawn using a series of several of the child's oral reading records taken over time, not just one instance.

A teacher can review children's running records over time to note their pattern of miscues and which cues they have the greatest tendency to use in their self-corrections. Whichever cue system the children use to the greatest extent, it is necessary for the teacher to offer their individual support in also using the other cueing systems to construct correct meaning. Taberski suggests that while assessing running records to determine the relationship between oral language and meaning, the children read from "just right" books.

Knowledge of Levels of Reading Comprehension and Strategies for Promoting Comprehension of Imaginative Literary Texts at All Levels

Sharon Taberski (2000) recommends that initially strategies for promoting comprehension of imaginative literary texts at all levels be done with the whole class. Here are Taberski's four main strategies for promoting comprehension of imaginative literary texts. She feels that if repeated sufficiently during the K–3 years and even if introduced as late as grade four, these strategies will even serve the adult lifelong reader in good stead.

Strategy One: stopping to think

As part of this strategy of reflecting on the text as a whole, the reader is challenged to come up with the answer to three questions:

- What do I think is going to happen? (Inferential)

- Why do I think this is going to happen? (Evaluative and inferential)

- How can I prove that I am right by going back to the story? (Inferential)

Taberski recommends that teachers introduce these key strategies with books that can be read in one sitting and recommends the use of picture books for these instructive strategies. Taberski also suggests that books that are read aloud and used for this strategy also contain a strong storyline, some degree of predictability, and a narrative with obvious stopping points. The text should also invite discussion.

Strategy Two: story mapping

Taberski recommends this strategy for promoting comprehension of imaginative/literary texts that are familiar to most elementary teachers.

For stories that suit this strategy, Taberski selects those that have distinct episodes, few characters, and obvious problems. In particular, she tries to use a story where a single, central problem or issue is introduced at the beginning of the story and then resolved or at least followed through by the close of the story. To make a story map of a particular story, Taberski divides the class into groups and asks one group of children to illustrate the "Characters" in the book. Another group of children is asked to draw the "Setting," while a third and fourth group of children tackles "Problem" and "Resolution."

The story may also help children hold together their ideas for writing in the writing workshop as they take their reading of an author's story to a new level. Best suited to the story mapping techniques are those books that have a story with a conflict resolution format, such as a main problem introduced at the beginning of the story that is at least somewhat resolved at the end of the story.

Strategy Three: character mapping

The character mapping strategy also used by Taberski focuses the children as readers on the ways in which the main character's personal traits can determine what will happen in the story. Character mapping works best when the character is not your daily run of the mill individual, has been featured perhaps in other books by the same author, has a personality that is somewhat predictable, and is capable of changing behavior as a consequence of what happens.

Using writing to share, deepen, and expand understanding of literary texts is a cornerstone of the balanced literacy approach.

Strategy Four: modeled writing

In line with the modeled writing component of balanced literacy, where the teacher first reads something that inspires the teacher's writing and then shares that individual "modeled" (teacher written) writing with the children, Taberski advocates having the teacher read sections of stories aloud, pause to reflect on what's happened in the story, and write down a response to it.

Within the confines of the elementary classroom, the teacher can use a chart to record his or her response to the events or personalities of a particular story being read, and the children can also contribute their comments for the chart. Later on, the children can start reflective reader's notebooks or journals where they will record their reactions to their readings independently. These independent reactions may or may not be shared with the teacher or with their families.

The best types of texts for this type of response are those that relate to age appropriate issues for young children (i.e. homework, testing, bullies, and friendship), a plot that can be interpreted in different ways, a text that is filled with questions, and a text full of suspense or wonder.

APPLICATION OF READING SKILLS AND KNOWLEDGE TO CLASSROOM INSTRUCTION

Development of Literary Response Skills

Literary response skills are dependent on prior knowledge, schemata, and background. SCHEMATA (the plural of schema) are those structures that represent generic concepts stored in our memory.

Without schemata and experiences to call upon as they read, children have little ability to comprehend. Of course, the reader's schemata and prior knowledge have more influence on the comprehension of plot or character information that is not directly stated than on plot or character information that is directly stated. Effective comprehenders of text, whether they are adults or children, use both their schemata and prior knowledge PLUS the ideas from the printed text for reading comprehension.

PRIOR KNOWLEDGE can be defined as all of an individual's prior experiences, learning, and development that precede his or her entering a specific learning situation or attempting to comprehend a specific text. Sometimes prior knowledge can be erroneous or incomplete. Obviously, if there are misconceptions in a child's prior knowledge, these must be corrected so that the child's overall comprehension skills can progress.

Even the prior knowledge of kindergarteners includes their accumulated positive and negative experiences both in and out of school. These might range from wonderful family travels, watching television, or visiting museums and libraries to visiting hospitals or prisons and surviving poverty. Whatever prior knowledge the child brings to the school setting, the independent reading and writing the child does in school immeasurably expands his prior knowledge and hence broadens that child's reading comprehension capabilities.

As he or she prepares to begin any imaginative/literary text, the teacher must consider the following about the students' level of prior knowledge:

- What prior knowledge needs to be activated for the text or theme or for the writing to be done successfully?
- How independent are the children in using strategies to activate their prior knowledge?

Holes and Roser (1987) have suggested five techniques for activating prior knowledge before starting an imaginative/literary text:

1. **Free recall:** Tell us what you know about _____.
2. **Unstructured discussion:** Let's talk about _____.
3. **Structured question:** Who exactly was Jane Aviles in the life of the hero of the story?

> **SCHEMATA:** those structures that represent generic concepts stored in our memory

> **PRIOR KNOWLEDGE:** all of an individual's prior experiences, learning, and development that precede his or her entering a specific learning situation or attempting to comprehend a specific text

4. Word association: When you hear these words . . . hatch, elephant, who, think . . . What author do you think of?

5. Recognition: Mulberry Street—what author comes to mind?

Previewing and predicting and story mapping are excellent strategies for activating prior knowledge.

Development of Literary Analysis Skills

There are many exciting ways to sensitize and to teach children about the features and formats of different literary genres.

Strategy One: genre switch-reader and writer transformation

This strategy should be introduced as a read-aloud with young children or with children who are struggling readers. In a similar fashion, it would be introduced as a read-aloud for ELL learners new to English Language read-alouds. Older children in grades 3–6 might just be "started off" by a teacher prompt and do the required reading on their own.

To begin, the teacher selects a particular genre book. If it is close to Halloween, a goblin or suspense story will do well. The teacher begins to read the story with the open invitation to the students to determine, as the story is being read, what type of story it is and what makes it that type of story.

Older children take notes in their reading journals, while younger children and those more in need of explicit teacher support contribute their ideas and responses as part of the discussion in class. Their responses are recorded on the experiential chart.

As the reading continues, the story type components are listed on the chart (most of the responses are those that have been elicited from the children).

At some point in what is either an oral read-aloud, a guided reading or an independent reading, the teacher directs the children's attention to the components that have emerged on the chart. They then use these components, which are generally components of character—setting, plot, style, conflict, language, etc.—to identify the story genre.

The teacher provides the children with an opportunity to expound at length on why this story is an example of the genre that they have identified.

Once they have done so, the teacher challenges them to consider how this story—with its set of given characters, plot, and setting—would be changed if the genre were different. The teacher can challenge the class as a whole with the idea of changing the story to a radically different genre—e.g., from suspense to a fairy tale or a comedy—or allow the children to come up another genre.

Then, depending on the children's developed writing abilities, they might be given time to rewrite the story on their own or retell it in class prior to writing and illustrating it.

In the balanced literacy approach, this transformation of the story into another genre is done as part of the writing workshop component, which uses the same reading material as the source for writing. The strategy results in the children having had the experience of an in-depth analysis of a particular genre as well as hands-on writing (or telling, if they cannot yet write or cannot yet write in English) experience of restyling that basic plot and characters into another genre. This authenticates the children's participation as readers and writers.

Strategy Two: author's point of view

Today, many elementary classrooms have an "author's chair" and posters celebrating the author but, alas, no actual authors present.

It is crucial for reading comprehension, test sophistication, and lifelong successful reading that a reader correctly interpret the author's point of view. The explicit teaching of this interpretive skill is vital in today's classroom. However, the problem that many young readers encounter as they enjoy their stories is that the author himself or herself is not a character in the stories and therefore, they cannot readily read his or her perspective.

This strategy involves having a volunteer from the class take on the role of the story author. This child studies the book carefully and then either writes down the author's point of view or explains it in conversation with the teacher. The child has to demonstrate to the teacher that he or she has picked up on the appropriate syntactic, semantic and other clues in the writing that express the author's point of view. If the author is also the illustrator, then the illustrations may also have to be referenced by the child reader acting as "author."

Once the child has satisfied the teacher that he or she can clearly communicate and justify the author's point of view, the story can be read aloud with the child/author explaining it to everyone. The story can also be presented as part of a reader's theater, where various children enact the plot and the child playing, the author then comes out and presents his or her point of view.

Actually having the opportunity to vie for the role of explaining author nicely focuses young readers' attention on the importance of correctly interpreting the author's perspective.

Use of Comprehension Strategies Before, During, and After Reading

Cooper (2004), Taberski (2000), Cox (2005), and other researchers recommend a broad array of comprehension strategies before, during, and after reading.

Posters and prompts to infuse into daily child reader routines

Cooper (2004) suggests a broad range of posters and explicit instruction in class so that children have prompts to monitor their own reading—for example, My Strategic Reading Guide:

1. Do I infer/predict important information, use what I know, think about what may happen or what I want to learn?

2. Identify important information about the story elements.

3. Self-question—generate questions and search for the answers.

4. Monitor—Ask: Does this make sense to me? Does this help me meet my purpose in reading?

5. If lost, what should I do—? Try fix-ups—re-read, read further ahead, look at the illustrations, ask for help, and think about the words. . . evaluate what I have read.

6. Summarize—Think about how the parts of the stories that I was reading came together.

The story maps previously discussed in connection with Taberski represent her comprehension strategies for predicting and visualizing. Storyboard panels, which are used by comic strip artists and by those artists who do advertising campaigns as well as television and film directors, are perfect for engaging children K–6 in a variety of comprehension strategies before, during, and after reading. They can storyboard the beginning of a story, read aloud, and then storyboard its predicted middle or end. Of course, after they experience or read the actual middle or ending of the story, they can compare and contrast what they produced with its actual structure. They can play familiar literature identification games with a buddy or as part of a center by storyboarding one key scene or characters from a book and challenging a partner or peer to identify the book and characters correctly.

APPLICATION OF READING SKILLS AND KNOWLEDGE TO CLASSROOM INSTRUCTION

Sample Test Question and Rationale

(Average)

1. When you ask a child if what he or she has just read "sounds right" to him or her, you are trying to get that child to use:

   A. Phonics cues
   B. Syntactic cues
   C. Semantic cues
   D. Prior knowledge

Answer is B.

This is another one of those "scripted" answers currently in use in reading. The answer has to be Choice B, syntactic clues.

SKILL 2.8 Understand how to make accurate observations about students' ability to understand and interpret text

Retelling

RETELLING needs to be very clearly defined so that the child reader does not think that the teacher wants him or her to spill the WHOLE story back in the retelling. A child should be able to talk comfortably and fluently about the story he or she has just read. He or she should be able to tell the main things that have happened in the story.

> **RETELLING:** being able to tell the main things that have happened in the story

When a child retells a story to a teacher, the teacher needs ways to help him or her assess the child's understanding. Ironically, the teacher can use some of the same strategies he or she suggests to the child to assess the child's understanding of a book which is not familiar to the teacher. These strategies include back cover reading, scanning the table of contents, looking at the pictures, and reading the book jacket.

If the child can explain how the story turned out and provide examples to support these explanations, try not to interrupt him or her with too many questions.

Children can use the text of the book to reinforce what they are saying and they can even read from it if they wish. It is also important to note that some children need to reread the text twice and their rereading of it is out of enjoyment.

When the teacher plans to use the retelling as a way of assessing the child, the following ground rules have to be set and made clear to the child.

The teacher explains the purpose of the retelling to determine how well the child is reading at the outset of the conference.

The teacher maintains in the child's assessment notebook or in his or her assessment record for him or her what the child is saying in phrases, not sentences. Just enough is recorded to indicate whether the child actually understood the story. The teacher also tries to analyze from the retelling why the child cannot comprehend a given text. If the child's accuracy rate with the text is below 95 percent, then the problem is at the word level, but if the accuracy rate for the text is above 95 percent, the difficulty lies at the text level.

Inferencing

> **INFERENCING:** evaluative process that involves the reader making a reasonable judgment based on the information given

INFERENCING is an evaluative process that involves the reader making a reasonable judgment based on the information given and engages children in literally constructing meaning. In order to develop and enhance this key skill in children, they might have a mini lesson where the teacher demonstrates this key skill by reading an expository book aloud (e.g., one on skyscrapers for young children) and then demonstrates for them the following reading habits: looking for clues, reflecting on what the reader already knows about the topic ("activating prior knowledge" in a teacher's jargon), and using the clues in the expository text to figure out what the author means.

Main Idea

> **MAIN IDEA:** the key information in a passage

Identifying MAIN IDEAS in an expository text can be improved when the children have an explicit strategy for identifying important information. They can make this strategy part of their everyday reading style by being focused and "walked" through the following exercises as part of a series of guided reading sessions. The child should read the passage so that the topic is readily identifiable to him or her. It will be what most of the information is about.

Next, the child should be asked to be on the lookout for a sentence within the expository passage that summarizes the key information in the paragraph or in the lengthier excerpt. Then the child should read the rest of the passage or excerpt in light of this information and also note which information in the paragraph is not important. The important information the child has identified in the paragraph can be used by the child reader to formulate the author's main idea. The child reader may even want to use some of the author's own language in formulating that idea.

APPLICATION OF READING SKILLS AND KNOWLEDGE TO CLASSROOM INSTRUCTION

Monitoring

MONITORING means self-clarifying: As a reader reads, the reader often realizes that what he or she is reading is not making sense. The reader then has to have a plan for making sensible meaning out of the excerpt. Cooper and other balanced literacy advocates have a stop-and-think strategy that they use with children. The child reflects, "Does this make sense to me?" When the child concludes that it does not, the child then either: rereads, reads ahead in the text, looks up unknown words, or asks for help from the teacher.

MONITORING: self-clarifying to make sure the passage makes sense

What is important about monitoring is that some readers ask these questions and try these approaches without ever being explicitly taught them in school by a teacher. However, the key philosophy of the foundations of reading theorists mentioned here is that these strategies need to be explicitly modeled and practiced under the guidance of the teacher by most, if not all, child readers.

Summarizing

SUMMARIZING engages the reader in pulling together into a cohesive whole the essential bits of information within a longer passage or excerpt of text. Children can be taught to summarize informational or expository text by following these guidelines. First they should look at the topic sentence of the paragraph or the text and delete the trivia. Then they should search for information that has been mentioned more than once and make sure it is included only once in their summary. Then find related ideas or items and group them under a unifying heading. Search for and identify a main idea sentence. Put the summary together using all these guidelines.

SUMMARIZING: identifying the cohesive information from within a long passage

Teachers should have a toolkit of instructional strategies, materials, and technologies to encourage and teach students how to problem solve and think critically about subject content. With each curriculum chosen by a district for school implementation comes an expectation that students must master benchmarks and standards of learning skills. There is an established level of academic performance and proficiency in public schools that students are required to master in today's classrooms. Research of national and state standards indicate that there additional benchmarks and learning objectives in the subject areas of science, foreign language, English language arts, history, art, health, civics, economics, geography, physical education, mathematics, and social studies that students are required to master in state assessments (Marzano & Kendall, 1996).

A critical thinking skill is a skill target that teachers help students develop to sustain learning in specific subject areas that can be applied within other subject areas. For example, when learning to understand algebraic concepts in solving a math word problem on how much fencing material is needed to build a fence around a backyard area that is 8' x 12', a math student must understand the order of numerical expression in how to simplify algebraic expressions. Teachers can provide instructional strategies that show students how to group the fencing measurements into an algebraic word problem that with minor addition, subtraction, and multiplication can produce a simple number equal to the amount of fencing materials needed to build the fence.

Higher-Ordered Thinking Skills

Developing critical thinking skills in students is not as simple as developing other simpler skills. In fact, many teachers mistakenly believe that these skills can be taught out of context (i.e., they can be taught as skills in and of themselves). Good teachers, however, realize that critical thinking skills must be taught within the contexts of specific subject matter. For example, language arts teachers can teach critical thinking skills through novels; social studies teachers can teach critical thinking skills through primary source documents or current events; science teachers can teach critical thinking skills by having students develop hypotheses prior to conducting experiments.

First, let's start with definitions of the various types of critical thinking skills. ANALYSIS is the systematic exploration of a concept, event, term, piece of writing, element of media, or any other complex item. Usually, people think of analysis as the exploration of the parts that make up a whole. For example, when someone analyzes a piece of literature, that person might focus on small pieces of the literature; yet, as they focus on the small pieces, they also call attention to the big picture and show how the small pieces create significance for the whole novel.

To carry this example further, if one were to analyze a novel, that person might investigate a particular character to determine how that character adds significance to the whole novel. In something more concrete like biology, one could analyze the findings of an experiment to see if the results might indicate significance for something even larger than the experiment itself. It is very easy to analyze political events, for example. A social studies teacher could ask students to analyze the events leading up to World War II; doing so would require that students look at the small pieces (i.e., smaller world events prior to World War II) and determine how those small pieces, when added up together, caused the war.

Next, let's consider synthesis. SYNTHESIS is usually thought of to be the opposite of analysis. In analysis, we take a whole, break it up into pieces, and look at the pieces. With synthesis, we take different things and make them one whole thing. For example, a language arts teacher could ask students to synthesize two works of distinct literature. Let's say that we take *The Scarlet Letter* and *The Crucible*, two

> **ANALYSIS:** the systematic exploration of a concept, event, term, piece of writing, element of media, or any other complex item

> **SYNTHESIS:** taking different things and making them one whole thing

works both featuring life during Puritanical America, written about one century apart. A student could synthesize the two works and come to conclusions about Puritanical life. An art teacher could ask students to synthesize two paintings from the Impressionist era and come to conclusions about the features that distinguish that style of art.

Finally, EVALUATION involves making judgments. Whereas analysis and synthesis seek answers and hypotheses based on investigations, evaluation seeks opinions. For example, a social studies teacher could ask students to evaluate the quality of Richard Nixon's resignation speech. To do so, they would judge whether or not they felt it was good. In contrast, analysis would keep judgment out of the assignment: it would have students focus possibly on the structure of the speech (i.e., Does an argument move from emotional to logical?). When evaluating a speech, a piece of literature, a movie, or a work of art, we seek to determine whether one thinks it is good or not. But keep in mind that teaching good evaluation skills requires not just that students learn how to determine whether something is good or not—it requires that they learn how to support their evaluations. So, if a student claims that Nixon's speech was effective in what the President intended the speech to do, the student would need to explain how this is so. Notice that evaluation will probably utilize the skills of analysis and/or synthesis, but that the purpose is ultimately different.

> **EVALUATION:** making judgments about things

Encouraging Independent Critical Thinking

Since most teachers want their educational objectives to use higher-level thinking skills, teachers need to direct students to these higher levels on the taxonomy. Questioning is an effective tool to build up students to these higher levels.

Low order questions are useful to begin the process. They ensure that the student is focused on the required information and understands what needs to be included in the thinking process. For example, if the objective is for students to be able to read and understand the story "Goldilocks and the Three Bears," the teacher may wish to start with low order questions (i.e., "What are some things Goldilocks did while in the bears home?" [Knowledge] or "Why didn't Goldilocks like the Papa Bear's chair?" [Analysis]).

Through a series of questions, the teacher can move the students up the taxonomy. (For example, "If Goldilocks had come to your house, what are some things she may have used?" [Application], "How might the story differed if Goldilocks had visited the three fishes?" [Synthesis], or "Do you think Goldilocks was good or bad? Why?" [Evaluation]). The teacher, through questioning, can control the thinking process of the class. As students become more involved in the discussion, they are systematically being lead to higher level thinking.

To develop a critical-thinking approach to the world, children need to know enough about valid and invalid reasoning to ask questions. Bringing into the classroom speeches or essays that demonstrate both valid and invalid examples can be useful in helping students develop the ability to question the reasoning of others. These will be published writers or televised speakers, so they can see that they are able even to question ideas that are accepted by some adults and talk about what is wrong in the thinking of apparently successful communicators.

If the teacher stays right on the cutting edge of children's experience, they will become more and more curious about what is out there in the world that they don't know about. A lesson on a particular country or tribe that the children may not even know exists, using various kinds of media to reveal to them what life is like there for children their age, is a good way to introduce the world outside their experience. In such a presentation, positive aspects of the lives of those other children should be included. Perhaps a correspondence with a village could be developed. It's good for children, some of whom may not live very high on the social scale in this country, to know what the rest of the world is like, and in so doing, they may develop an independent curiosity to know more.

In general, critical thinking skills should be taught through assignments, activities, lessons, and discussions that cause students to think on their own. While teachers can and should provide students with the tools to think critically, they will ultimately become critical thinkers if they have to use those tools themselves. But this one last point cannot be taken lightly: Teachers must provide students the tools to evaluate, analyze, and synthesize.

Let's take political speeches as an example. Students will be better analyzers, synthesizers, and evaluators if they understand some of the basics of political speeches. Therefore, a teacher might introduce concepts such as rhetoric, style, persona, audience, diction, imagery, and tone. The best way to introduce these concepts would be to provide students with multiple good examples of each. Once they are familiar with these critical tools, students will be in a better place to apply them individually to political speeches—and then be able to analyze, synthesize, and evaluate political speeches on their own.

APPLICATION OF READING SKILLS AND KNOWLEDGE TO CLASSROOM INSTRUCTION

Sample Test Question and Rationale

(Rigorous)

1. **To help children with "main idea" questions, the teacher should:**

   A. Give out a strategy sheet on the main idea for children to place in their reader's notebooks

   B. Model responding to such a question as part of the guided reading

   C. Have children create "main idea questions" to go with their writings

   D. All of the above

Answer is D.

All of the options given are correct.

SKILL 2.9 Understand how to help students use a dictionary

DICTIONARIES are useful for spelling, writing, and reading. It is very important for students to be exposed to, and learn to enjoy using, the dictionary. Cooper (2004) suggests that the following be kept in mind as the teacher of grades K–6 introduces and then habituates children in what is to be hoped, will be a lifelong fascination with the dictionary and vocabulary acquisition.

Requesting or suggesting that children look up a word in the dictionary should be an invitation to a wonderful exploration, not a punishment or busy work that has no reference to their current reading assignment.

Model the correct way to use the dictionary for children even as late as the third through sixth grade. Many have never been taught proper dictionary skills. The teacher needs to demonstrate to the children that, as an adult reader and writer, he or she routinely and happily uses the dictionary and learns new information that makes him or her better at reading and writing.

Do not routinely require children to look up every new spelling word in the dictionary (this is Cooper's view and many other theorists would disagree with him here).

DICTIONARIES: books that are useful for spelling, writing, and reading

Cooper believes in beginning dictionary study as early as kindergarten, and this is now very possible because of the proliferation of lush picture dictionaries which can be introduced at that grade level. He also suggests that children not only look at these picture dictionaries, but also begin to make dictionaries of their own at this grade level filled with pictures and beginning words. As children join the circle of lexicographers, they will begin to see themselves as compilers and users of dictionaries. Of course, this will support their ongoing vocabulary development.

On early grade levels, use of the dictionary can nicely complement the children's mastery of the alphabet. They should be given whole class and small group practice in locating words.

As the children progress with their phonetic skills, the dictionary can be used to show them phonetic respelling using the pronunciation key.

Older children in grades three and beyond need explicit teacher demonstrations and practice in use of guide words. They also need to begin to learn about the hierarchies of various word meanings. In the upper grades, children should also explore using special content dictionaries and glossaries in the backs of their books.

Key Words

Cooper (2004) feels that it is up to the teacher to preview the content area text to identify the main ideas. Then the teacher should compile a list of terms related to the content thrust. These terms and words become part of the key concepts list.

Next, the teacher sees which of the key concept words and terms are already defined in the text. These will not require direct teaching. Words, for which children have sufficient skills to determine their meaning—through base, root, prefixes, or suffixes—also will not require direct teaching.

Instruction in the remaining key words, which should not be more than two or three key words, can be provided before, during, or after reading. If students have previewed the content area and identified those words they need support on, the instruction should be provided before reading. Instruction can also easily be provided as part of guided reading support. After-reading support is indicated when the text offers the children an opportunity to enrich their own vocabularies.

Having children work as a whole class or in small groups on a content-specific dictionary for a topic regularly covered in their grade; social studies, science, or mathematics curricula offer an excellent collaborative opportunity for children to design a dictionary/word resource that can celebrate their own vocabulary learning. Such a resource can then be used with the next year's classes as well.

APPLICATION OF READING SKILLS AND KNOWLEDGE TO CLASSROOM INSTRUCTION

SKILL 2.10 Understand how to help students interpret written directions

How does one get from here to there, from kindergarten to graduate school or to a trade school? The answer of course is by one step at a time, carefully organizing one's courses of action, each phase building on the previous step and leading to the next.

Similarly, when taking a test you are asked to follow written instructions. The examiner wants to see how you manage your answer to the exam question. How do you organize your answer logically? How do you support your conclusions? How well connected are your ideas and the support you bring to your argument?

Look at how the writer does these tasks in the following essay:

> **Parenting Classes**
>
> Someone once said that the two most difficult jobs in the world—voting and being a parent—are given to rank amateurs. The consequences of this inequity are voter apathy and inept parenting leading to, on the one hand, an apparent failure of the democratic process and, on the other hand, misbehaving and misguided children.
>
> The antidote for the first problem is in place in most school systems. Classes in history, civics, history, government, and student government provide a kind of "hands on" training in becoming an active member of society so that the step from studenthood to citizenship is clear and expected.
>
> On the other hand, most school systems in the past have avoided or given only lip service to the issue of parenting and parenting skills. The moral issue of illegitimate births aside, the reality of the world is that each year there are large numbers of children born to unwed parents who have had little, or no, training in child rearing.
>
> What was done on the farm in the past is irrelevant here: the farm is gone and/or has been replaced by the inner city, and the pressing issue is how to train uneducated new parents in the child rearing tasks before them. Other issues are secondary to the immediate needs of newborns and their futures. And it is in their futures that the quality of life for all of us is found.
>
> Thus, while we can debate this issue all we wish, we cannot responsibly ignore that uneducated parents need to be educated in the tasks before them, and it is clear that the best way to do this is in the school system, where these new parents are already learning how to be responsible citizens in the civics and other classes currently in place.

Notice how the writer moves sequentially from one idea to the next, maintaining throughout the parallel of citizenship and parenthood, from the opening quotation, paragraph by paragraph to the concluding sentence. Each idea is developed from the preceding idea, and each new idea refers to the preceding ideas, and at no point do related but irrelevant issues sidetrack the writer.

READING

Sample Test Questions and Rationales

Read the passages and answer the questions that follow.

This writer has often been asked to tutor hospitalized children with cystic fibrosis. While undergoing all the precautionary measures to see these children (i.e., scrubbing thoroughly and donning sterilized protective gear, for the child's protection), she has often wondered why their parents subject these children to the pressures of schooling and trying to catch up on what they have missed because of hospitalization, which is a normal part of cystic fibrosis patients' lives. These children undergo so many tortuous treatments a day that it seems cruel to expect them to learn as normal children do, especially with their life expectancies being as short as they are.

(Average) (Skill 1.1)

1. **What is the main idea of this passage?**
   A. There is a lot of preparation involved in visiting a patient with cystic fibrosis
   B. Children with cystic fibrosis are incapable of living normal lives
   C. Certain concessions should be made for children with cystic fibrosis
   D. Children with cystic fibrosis die young

Answer is C.

The author states that she wonders "why parents subject these children to the pressures of schooling" and that "it seems cruel to expect them to learn as normal children do." In making these statements she appears to be expressing the belief that these children should not have to do what "normal" children do. They have enough to deal with — their illness itself.

(Rigorous) (Skill 1.1)

2. **What is the author's purpose?**
   A. To inform
   B. To entertain
   C. To describe
   D. To narrate

Answer is C.

The author is simply describing her experience in working with children with cystic fibrosis.

(Easy) (Skill 1.2)

3. **Why is the author familiar with the procedures used when visiting a child with cystic fibrosis?**
   A. She has read about it
   B. She works in a hospital
   C. She is the parent of one
   D. She often tutors them

Answer is D.

The writer states this fact in the opening sentence.

(Rigorous) (Skill 1.3)

4. **What type of organizational pattern is the author using?**
   A. Classification
   B. Explanation
   C. Comparison and contrast
   D. Cause and effect

APPLICATION OF READING SKILLS AND KNOWLEDGE TO CLASSROOM INSTRUCTION

Sample Test Questions and Rationale (cont.)

Answer is B.

In mentioning that their life expectancies are short, she is explaining by giving one reason why it is cruel to expect them to learn as normal children do.

(Rigorous) (Skill 1.3)

5. What kind of relationship is found within the last sentence that starts with "These children undergo..." and ends with "...as short as they are"?
   A. Addition
   B. Explanation
   C. Generalization
   D. Classification

Answer is A.

The writer clearly feels sorry for these children and gears her writing in that direction.

(Average) (Skill 1.4)

6. What is meant by the word "precautionary" in the second sentence?
   A. Careful
   B. Protective
   C. Medical
   D. Sterilizing

Answer is B.

The writer uses expressions such as "protective gear" and "child's protection" to emphasize this.

(Average) (Skill 1.5)

7. What is the author's tone?
   A. Sympathetic
   B. Cruel
   C. Disbelieving
   D. Cheerful

Answer is A.

The author states that "it seems cruel to expect them to learn as normal children do," thereby indicating that she feels sorry for them.

(Average) (Skill 1.6)

8. The author states that it is "cruel" to expect children with cystic fibrosis to learn as "normal" children do. Is this a fact or an opinion?
   A. Fact
   B. Opinion

Answer is B.

The author mentions tutoring children with cystic fibrosis in her opening sentence and goes on to explain some of these issues that are involved with her job.

(Rigorous) (Skill 1.6)

9. Is there evidence of bias in this paragraph?
   A. Yes
   B. No

Answer is B.

The fact that she states that it "seems" cruel indicates there is no evidence to support this belief.

Sample Test Questions and Rationale (cont.)

(Rigorous) (Skill 1.6)

10. Does the author present an argument that is valid or invalid concerning the schooling of children with cystic fibrosis?

   A. Valid
   B. Invalid

Answer is B.

Even though to most readers the writer's argument might make sense, it is biased and lacks real evidence.

Disciplinary practices have been found to affect diverse areas of child development such as the acquisition of moral values, obedience to authority, and performance at school. Even though the dictionary has a specific definition of the word "discipline," it is still open to interpretation by people of different cultures.

There are four types of disciplinary styles: assertion of power, withdrawal of love, reasoning, and permissiveness. Assertion of power involves the use of force to discourage unwanted behavior. Withdrawal of love involves making the love of a parent conditional on a child's good behavior. Reasoning involves persuading the child to behave one way rather than another. Permissiveness involves allowing the child to do as he or she pleases and face the consequences of his or her actions.

(Rigorous) (Skill 1.1)

11. Name four types of disciplinary styles.

   A. Reasoning, power assertion, morality, and permissiveness
   B. Morality, reasoning, permissiveness, and withdrawal of love
   C. Withdrawal of love, permissiveness, assertion of power, and reasoning
   D. Withdrawal of love, morality, reasoning, and power assertion

Answer is C.

This is directly stated in the second paragraph.

(Average) (Skill 1.3)

12. What organizational structure is used in the first sentence of the second paragraph?

   A. Addition
   B. Explanation
   C. Definition
   D. Simple listing

Answer is D.

The author simply states the types of disciplinary styles.

Sample Test Questions and Rationale (cont.)

(Average) (Skill 1.1)

13. What is the main idea of this passage?

   A. Different people have different ideas of how to discipline children

   B. Permissiveness is the most widely used disciplinary style

   C. Most people agree on their definition of discipline

   D. There are four disciplinary styles

Answer is A.

Choice C is not true; the opposite is stated in the passage. Choice B could be true, but we have no evidence of this. Choice D is just one of the many facts listed in the passage.

(Easy) (Skill 1.1)

14. What is the author's purpose in writing this?

   A. To describe
   B. To narrate
   C. To entertain
   D. To inform

Answer is D.

The author is providing the reader with information about disciplinary practices.

(Rigorous) (Skill 1.3)

15. What is the overall organizational pattern of this passage?

   A. Generalization
   B. Cause and effect
   C. Addition
   D. Summary

Answer is C.

The author has taken a subject—in this case discipline—and developed it point by point.

(Easy) (Skill 1.4)

16. What is the meaning of the word "diverse" in the first sentence?

   A. Many
   B. Related to children
   C. Disciplinary
   D. Moral

Answer is A.

Any of the other choices would be redundant in this sentence.

(Average) (Skill 1.5)

17. What is the author's tone?

   A. Disbelieving
   B. Angry
   C. Informative
   D. Optimistic

Answer is C.

The author appears to simply be stating the facts.

(Rigorous) (Skill 1.7)

18. Is this passage biased?

   A. Yes
   B. No

Answer is B.

If the reader were so inclined, he or she could research discipline and find this information.

SAMPLE TEST

READING

Read the passages and answer the questions that follow.

This writer has often been asked to tutor hospitalized children with cystic fibrosis. While undergoing all the precautionary measures to see these children (i.e., scrubbing thoroughly and donning sterilized protective gear, for the child's protection), she has often wondered why their parents subject these children to the pressures of schooling and trying to catch up on what they have missed because of hospitalization, which is a normal part of cystic fibrosis patients' lives. These children undergo so many tortuous treatments a day that it seems cruel to expect them to learn as normal children do, especially with their life expectancies being as short as they are.

(Average) (Skill 1.1)
1. **What is the main idea of this passage?**
   A. There is a lot of preparation involved in visiting a patient with cystic fibrosis
   B. Children with cystic fibrosis are incapable of living normal lives
   C. Certain concessions should be made for children with cystic fibrosis
   D. Children with cystic fibrosis die young

(Rigorous) (Skill 1.1)
2. **What is the author's purpose?**
   A. To inform
   B. To entertain
   C. To describe
   D. To narrate

(Easy) (Skill 1.2)
3. **Why is the author familiar with the procedures used when visiting a child with cystic fibrosis?**
   A. She has read about it
   B. She works in a hospital
   C. She is the parent of one
   D. She often tutors them

(Rigorous) (Skill 1.3)
4. **What type of organizational pattern is the author using?**
   A. Classification
   B. Explanation
   C. Comparison and contrast
   D. Cause and effect

(Rigorous) (Skill 1.3)
5. **What kind of relationship is found within the last sentence that starts with "These children undergo..." and ends with "...as short as they are"?**
   A. Addition
   B. Explanation
   C. Generalization
   D. Classification

(Average) (Skill 1.4)
6. **What is meant by the word "precautionary" in the second sentence?**
   A. Careful
   B. Protective
   C. Medical
   D. Sterilizing

(Average) (Skill 1.5)
7. What is the author's tone?

   A. Sympathetic
   B. Cruel
   C. Disbelieving
   D. Cheerful

(Average) (Skill 1.6)
8. The author states that it is "cruel" to expect children with cystic fibrosis to learn as "normal" children do. Is this a fact or an opinion?

   A. Fact
   B. Opinion

(Rigorous) (Skill 1.6)
9. Is there evidence of bias in this paragraph?

   A. Yes
   B. No

(Rigorous) (Skill 1.6)
10. Does the author present an argument that is valid or invalid concerning the schooling of children with cystic fibrosis?

    A. Valid
    B. Invalid

Disciplinary practices have been found to affect diverse areas of child development such as the acquisition of moral values, obedience to authority, and performance at school. Even though the dictionary has a specific definition of the word "discipline," it is still open to interpretation by people of different cultures.

There are four types of disciplinary styles: assertion of power, withdrawal of love, reasoning, and permissiveness. Assertion of power involves the use of force to discourage unwanted behavior. Withdrawal of love involves making the love of a parent conditional on a child's good behavior. Reasoning involves persuading the child to behave one way rather than another. Permissiveness involves allowing the child to do as he or she pleases and face the consequences of his or her actions.

(Rigorous) (Skill 1.1)
11. Name four types of disciplinary styles.

    A. Reasoning, power assertion, morality, and permissiveness
    B. Morality, reasoning, permissiveness, and withdrawal of love
    C. Withdrawal of love, permissiveness, assertion of power, and reasoning
    D. Withdrawal of love, morality, reasoning, and power assertion

(Average) (Skill 1.1)
12. What is the main idea of this passage?

    A. Different people have different ideas of how to discipline children
    B. Permissiveness is the most widely used disciplinary style
    C. Most people agree on their definition of discipline
    D. There are four disciplinary styles

(Easy) (Skill 1.1)
13. **What is the author's purpose in writing this?**
    A. To describe
    B. To narrate
    C. To entertain
    D. To inform

(Average) (Skill 1.3)
14. **What organizational structure is used in the first sentence of the second paragraph?**
    A. Addition
    B. Explanation
    C. Definition
    D. Simple listing

(Rigorous) (Skill 1.3)
15. **What is the overall organizational pattern of this passage?**
    A. Generalization
    B. Cause and effect
    C. Addition
    D. Summary

(Easy) (Skill 1.4)
16. **What is the meaning of the word "diverse" in the first sentence?**
    A. Many
    B. Related to children
    C. Disciplinary
    D. Moral

(Average) (Skill 1.5)
17. **What is the author's tone?**
    A. Disbelieving
    B. Angry
    C. Informative
    D. Optimistic

(Rigorous) (Skill 1.7)
18. **Is this passage biased?**
    A. Yes
    B. No

(Rigorous) (Skill 2.1)
19. **The major difference between phonemic and phonological awareness is:**
    A. One deals with a series of discrete sounds and sound spelling relationships
    B. One is involved with teaching and learning alliteration and rhymes
    C. Phonemic awareness is a specific type phonological awareness that deals with separate phonemes within a given word
    D. Phonological awareness is associated with printed words

(Rigorous) (Skill 2.1)
20. **All of the following are true about phonological awareness except:**
    A. It may involve print
    B. It is a prerequisite for spelling and phonics
    C. Activities can be done by the children with their eyes closed
    D. Starts before letter recognition is taught

(Easy) (Skill 2.2)
21. The word "bat" is a ___ word for "batter-up":

   A. suffix
   B. prefix
   C. root word
   D. inflectional ending

(Rigorous) (Skill 2.2)
22. As part of study about the agricultural products of their state, children have identified twenty-two different types of apples produced in the state. They can use a _____ to compare and contrast these different types of apples:

   A. word web
   B. semantic map
   C. semantic features analysis grid
   D. all of the above

(Average) (Skill 2.3)
23. Rina has been hired to work in a school that serves a local public housing project. She is working with kindergarten children and has been asked to focus on shared reading. She selects:

   A. Chapter books
   B. Riddle books
   C. Alphabet books
   D. Wordless picture books

(Easy) (Skill 2.3)
24. The term graphophonemic awareness refers to:

   A. Handwriting skills
   B. Letter to sound recognition
   C. Alphabetic principle
   D. Phonemic awareness

(Easy) (Skill 2.3)
25. To decode is to:

   A. Construct meaning
   B. Sound out a printed sequence of letters
   C. Use a special code to decipher a message
   D. None of the above

(Average) (Skill 2.3)
26. Asking a child if what he or she has read makes sense to him or her is prompting the child to use:

   A. Phonics cues
   B. Syntactic cues
   C. Semantic cues
   D. Prior knowledge

(Average) (Skill 2.5)
27. Environmental print is available at all of the following except:

   A. Within a newspaper
   B. On the page of a library book
   C. On a supermarket circular
   D. In a commercial flyer

(Average) (Skill 2.5)

28. The best way for a primary grade teacher to model directionality and one to one word matching would be:

    A. Using a regular library or classroom text book

    B. Using her own person reading book

    C. Using a big book

    D. Using a book dummy

(Average) (Skill 2.7)

29. When you ask a child if what he or she has just read "sounds right" to him or her, you are trying to get that child to use:

    A. Phonics cues

    B. Syntactic cues

    C. Semantic cues

    D. Prior knowledge

(Rigorous) (Skill 2.8)

30. To help children with "main idea" questions, the teacher should:

    A. Give out a strategy sheet on the main idea for children to place in their reader's notebooks

    B. Model responding to such a question as part of the guided reading

    C. Have children create "main idea questions" to go with their writings

    D. All of the above

Answer Key

1. C	11. C	21. C
2. C	12. A	22. D
3. D	13. D	23. D
4. B	14. D	24. C
5. A	15. C	25. B
6. B	16. A	26. C
7. A	17. C	27. B
8. B	18. B	28. C
9. B	19. C	29. B
10. B	20. A	30. D

Rigor Table

	Easy %20	Average Rigor %40	Rigorous %40
Question	3, 13, 16, 21, 24, 25	1, 6, 7, 8, 12, 14, 17, 23, 26, 27, 28, 29	2, 4, 5, 9, 10, 11, 15, 18, 19, 20, 22, 30

DOMAIN II
MATHEMATICS

MATHEMATICS

PERSONALIZED STUDY PLAN

KNOWN MATERIAL/SKIP IT ✗

PAGE	COMPETENCY AND SKILL	☐
83	**3: Number Sense and Basic Algebra**	☐
	3.1: Perform basic addition, subtraction, multiplication, and division of whole numbers, fractions, and decimals	☐
	3.2: Recognize multiplication as repeated addition and division as repeated subtraction	☐
	3.3: Recognize and interpret mathematical symbols	☐
	3.4: Understand the definitions of basic terms	☐
	3.5: Recognize the position of numbers in relation to one another	☐
	3.6: Recognize equivalent forms of a number	☐
	3.7: Demonstrate knowledge of place value for whole numbers and decimal numbers	☐
	3.8: Compute percentages	☐
	3.9: Demonstrate knowledge of basic concepts of exponents	☐
	3.10: Demonstrate knowledge of order of operations	☐
	3.11: Use mental math to solve problems by estimation	☐
	3.12: Solve word problems	☐
	3.13: Solve one-step, single-variable linear equations	☐
	3.14: Identify what comes next in a sequence of numbers	☐
117	**4: Geometry and Measurement**	☐
	4.1: Represent time and money in more than one way	☐
	4.2: Convert between units of measure in the same system	☐
	4.3: Identify basic geometrical shapes	☐
	4.4: Perform computations related to area, volume, and perimeter for basic shapes	☐
	4.5: Graph data on an xy-coordinate plane	☐
	7.6: Formal elements of a poetic text	☐
136	**5: Data Analysis**	☐
	5.1: Interpret information from tables, charts, and graphs	☐
	5.2: Interpret trends over time given a table, chart, or graph with time-related data	☐
	5.3: Create basic tables, charts, and graphs	☐
	5.4: Compute means, medians, and modes	☐
143	**6: Application of Mathematics Skills and Knowledge to Classroom Instruction**	☐

COMPETENCY 3
NUMBER SENSE AND BASIC ALGEBRA

SKILL 3.1 Perform basic addition, subtraction, multiplication, and division of whole numbers, fractions, and decimals

WHOLE NUMBERS are natural numbers and zero.
0, 1, 2, 3, 4, 5 ,6 ...

A FRACTION is an expression of numbers in the form x/y, where x is the numerator, and y is the denominator, which cannot be zero.

Example: $\frac{3}{7}$
3 is the numerator; 7 is the denominator

If the numerator and denominator in the fraction have common factors, divide both by the common factor to reduce the fraction to its lowest form.

Example: $\frac{13}{39} = \frac{1 \times 13}{3 \times 13} = \frac{1}{3}$
Divide by the common factor 13.

DECIMALS = deci = part of ten. To find the decimal equivalent of a fraction, use the denominator to divide the numerator as shown in the following example.

Example: Find the decimal equivalent of $\frac{7}{10}$.
Since 10 cannot divide into 7 evenly,
$\frac{7}{10} = 0.7$

RATIONAL NUMBERS can be expressed as the ratio of two integers, $\frac{a}{b}$ where $b \neq 0$, for example, $\frac{2}{3}$, $-\frac{4}{5}$, $5 = \frac{5}{1}$.

The rational numbers include integers, fractions and mixed numbers, and terminating and repeating decimals. Every rational number can be expressed as a repeating or terminating decimal and can be shown on a number line.

WHOLE NUMBERS: natural numbers and zero

FRACTION: an expression of numbers in the form x/y, where x is the numerator, and y is the denominator, which cannot be zero

DECIMALS: part of ten

RATIONAL NUMBERS: numbers that can be expressed as the ratio of two integers

MATHEMATICS

INTEGERS: positive and negative whole numbers and zero

NATURAL NUMBERS: the counting numbers

IRRATIONAL NUMBERS: real numbers that cannot be written as the ratio of two integers

MIXED NUMBER: has an integer part and a fractional part

PERCENT: per 100

INTEGERS are positive and negative whole numbers and zero.
   ...-6, -5, -4, -3, -2, -1, 0, 1, 2, 3, 4, 5, 6 ...

NATURAL NUMBERS are the counting numbers.
   1, 2, 3, 4, 5, 6, ...

IRRATIONAL NUMBERS are real numbers that cannot be written as the ratio of two integers. These are infinite non-repeating decimals.

Examples:
   $\sqrt{5} = 2.2360..$, pi $= \Pi = 3.1415927...$

A **MIXED NUMBER** has an integer part and a fractional part.

Example:
   $2\frac{1}{4}, -5\frac{1}{6}, 7\frac{1}{3}$

PERCENT = per 100 (written with the symbol %). Thus $10\% = \frac{10}{100} = \frac{1}{10}$.

Addition of Whole Numbers

Example: At the end of a day of shopping, a shopper had $24 remaining in his wallet. He spent $45 on various goods. How much money did the shopper have at the beginning of the day?

The total amount of money the shopper started with is the sum of the amount spent and the amount remaining at the end of the day.

```
   24
 + 45
 ----
   69
```

The orginal total was $69.

Example: A race took the winner 1 hr. 58 min. 12 sec. on the first half of the race and 2 hr. 9 min. 57 sec. on the second half of the race. How much time did the entire race take?

1 hr. 58 min. 12 sec.	
+ 2 hr. 9 min. 57 sec.	Add these numbers.
3 hr. 67 min. 69 sec.	
+ 1 min. -60 sec.	Change 60 seconds to 1 min.
3 hr. 68 min. 9 sec.	
+ 1 hr. -60 min.	Change 60 minutes to 1 hr.
4 hr. 8 min. 9 sec.	Final answer.

NUMBER SENSE AND BASIC ALGEBRA

Subtraction of Whole Numbers

Example: At the end of his shift, a cashier has $96 in the cash register. At the beginning of his shift, he had $15. How much money did the cashier collect during his shift?

The total collected is the difference of the ending amount and the starting amount.

$$\begin{array}{r} 96 \\ -\ 15 \\ \hline 81 \end{array}$$

The total collected was $81.

Multiplication of Whole Numbers

Multiplication is one of the four basic number operations. In simple terms, MULTIPLICATION is the addition of a number to itself a certain number of times. For example, 4 multiplied by 3 is the equal to $4 + 4 + 4$ or $3 + 3 + 3 + 3$. Another way of conceptualizing multiplication is to think in terms of groups. For example, if we have 4 groups of 3 students, the total number of students is 4 multiplied by 3. We call the solution to a multiplication problem the PRODUCT.

> **MULTIPLICATION:** the addition of a number to itself a certain number of times
>
> **PRODUCT:** the solution to a multiplication problem

The basic algorithm for whole number multiplication begins with aligning the numbers by place value, with the number containing more places on top.

$$\begin{array}{r} 172 \\ \times\ 43 \end{array}$$

Note that we placed 172 on top because it has more places than 43 does.

Next, we multiply the ones' place of the second number by each place value of the top number sequentially.

$$\begin{array}{r} (2) \\ 172 \\ \times\ 43 \\ \hline 516 \end{array} \quad \{3 \times 2 = 6, 3 \times 7 = 21, 3 \times 1 = 3\}$$

Note that we had to carry a 2 to the hundreds' column because $3 \times 7 = 21$. Note also that we add, not multiply, carried numbers to the product.

Next, we multiply the number in the tens' place of the second number by each place value of the top number sequentially. Because we are multiplying by a number in the tens' place, we place a zero at the end of this product.

$$\begin{array}{r} (2) \\ 172 \\ \times\ 43 \\ \hline 516 \\ 6880 \end{array} \quad \{4 \times 2 = 8, 4 \times 7 = 28, 4 \times 1 = 4\}$$

Finally, to determine the final product we add the two partial products.

```
   172
 ×  43
  ────
   516
 +6880
  ────
  7396
```

The product of 172 and 43 is 7,396.

Example: A student buys 4 boxes of crayons. Each box contains 16 crayons. How many total crayons does the student have?

The total number of crayons is 16 × 4.

```
   16
 ×  4
  ──
   64
```

Total number of crayons equals 64.

Division of Whole Numbers

DIVISION, the inverse of multiplication, is another of the four basic number operations. When we divide one number by another, we determine how many times we can multiply the divisor (number divided by) before we exceed the number we are dividing (dividend). For example, 8 divided by 2 equals 4 because we can multiply 2 four times to reach 8 (2 × 4 = 8 or 2 + 2 + 2 + 2 = 8). Using the grouping conceptualization we used with multiplication, we can divide 8 into 4 groups of 2 or 2 groups of 4. We call the answer to a division problem the QUOTIENT.

> **DIVISION:** the inverse of multiplication

> **QUOTIENT:** the answer to a division problem

If the divisor does not divide evenly into the dividend, we express the leftover amount either as a remainder or as a fraction with the divisor as the denominator. For example, 9 divided by 2 equals 4 with a remainder of 1 or $4\frac{1}{2}$.

The basic algorithm for division is long division. We start by representing the quotient as follows.

$$14\overline{)293}$$

14 is the divisor and 293 is the dividend. This represents 293 ÷ 14.

Next, we divide the divisor into the dividend starting from the left.

$$14\overline{)293}^{\,2}$$

14 divides into 29 two times with a remainder.

Next, we multiply the partial quotient by the divisor, subtract this value from the first digits of the dividend, and bring down the remaining dividend digits to complete the number.

NUMBER SENSE AND BASIC ALGEBRA

$$\begin{array}{r}2\\14\overline{)293}\\-28\\\hline 13\end{array}$$ $2 \times 14 = 28$, $29 - 28 = 1$, and bringing down the 3 yields 13.

Finally, we divide again (the divisor into the remaining value) and repeat the preceding process. The number left after the subtraction represents the remainder.

$$\begin{array}{r}20\\14\overline{)293}\\-28\\\hline 13\\-0\\\hline 13\end{array}$$

The final quotient is 20 with a remainder of 13. We can also represent this quotient as $20\frac{13}{14}$.

Example: Each box of apples contains 24 apples. How many boxes must a grocer purchase to supply a group of 252 people with one apple each?

The grocer needs 252 apples. Because he must buy apples in groups of 24, we divide 252 by 24 to determine how many boxes he needs to buy.

$$\begin{array}{r}10\\24\overline{)252}\\-24\\\hline 12\\-0\\\hline 12\end{array}$$

The quotient is 10 with a remainder of 12. Thus, the grocer needs 10 boxes plus 12 more apples. Therefore, the minimum number of boxes the grocer can purchase is 11.

Example: At his job, John gets paid $20 for every hour he works. If John made $940 in a week, how many hours did he work?

This is a division problem. To determine the number of hours John worked, we divide the total amount made ($940) by the hourly rate of pay ($20). Thus, the number of hours worked equals 940 divided by 20.

$$\begin{array}{r}47\\20\overline{)940}\\-80\\\hline 140\\-140\\\hline 0\end{array}$$

20 divides into 940, 47 times with no remainder. John worked 47 hours.

Addition and Subtraction of Decimals

When adding and subtracting decimals, we align the numbers by place value as we do with whole numbers. After adding or subtracting each column, we bring the decimal down, placing it in the same location as in the numbers added or subtracted.

Example: Find the sum of 152.3 and 36.342.

```
   152.300
+   36.342
   188.642
```

Note that we placed two zeroes after the final place value in 152.3 to clarify the column addition.

Example: Find the difference of 152.3 and 36.342.

```
   2 9 10          (4)11(12)
  152.300         152.300
 −  36.342      −  36.342
       58         115.958
```

Note how we borrowed to subtract from the zeroes in the hundredths' and thousandths' place of 152.300.

Multiplication of Decimals

When multiplying decimal numbers, we multiply exactly as with whole numbers and place the decimal moving in from the left the total number of decimal places contained in the two numbers multiplied. For example, when multiplying 1.5 and 2.35, we place the decimal in the product 3 places in from the left (3.525).

Example: Find the product of 3.52 and 4.1.

Note that there are 3 total decimal places in the two numbers.

```
     3.52
  ×  4.1
     352
+  14080
   14432
```

We place the decimal 3 places in from the left.

Thus, the final product is 14.432.

NUMBER SENSE AND BASIC ALGEBRA

Example: A shopper has 5 one-dollar bills, 6 quarters, 3 nickels, and 4 pennies in his pocket. How much money does he have?

$$5 \times \$1.00 = \$5.00 \qquad \begin{array}{c} \$0.25 \\ \times\ \ 6 \\ \hline \$1.50 \end{array} \qquad \begin{array}{c} \overset{3}{\$0.05} \\ \times\ \ 3 \\ \hline \$0.15 \end{array} \qquad \begin{array}{c} \$0.01 \\ \times\ \ 4 \\ \hline \$0.04 \end{array}$$

Note the placement of the decimals in the multiplication products. Thus, the total amount of money in the shopper's pocket is:

$$\begin{array}{r} \$5.00 \\ 1.50 \\ 0.15 \\ +\ 0.04 \\ \hline \$6.69 \end{array}$$

Division of Decimals

When dividing decimal numbers, we first remove the decimal in the divisor by moving the decimal in the dividend the same number of spaces to the right. For example, when dividing 1.45 into 5.3, we convert the numbers to 145 and 530 and perform normal whole number division.

Example: Find the quotient of 5.3 divided by 1.45.

Convert to 145 and 530.

Divide.

$$\begin{array}{r} 3 \\ 145\overline{)530} \\ -435 \\ \hline 95 \end{array} \qquad \begin{array}{r} 3.65 \\ 145\overline{)530.00} \\ -435 \\ \hline 950 \\ -870 \\ \hline 800 \end{array} \qquad \text{Note that we insert the decimal to continue division.}$$

Because one of the numbers divided contained one decimal place, we round the quotient to one decimal place. Thus, the final quotient is 3.7.

Addition and Subtraction of Fractions

Key points

You need a common denominator in order to add and subtract reduced and improper fractions.

Example:

$$\frac{1}{3} + \frac{7}{3} = \frac{1+7}{3} = \frac{8}{3} = 2\frac{2}{3}$$

Example:
$$\frac{4}{12}+\frac{6}{12}-\frac{3}{12}=\frac{4+6-3}{12}=\frac{7}{12}$$

Adding an integer and a fraction of the same sign results directly in a mixed fraction.

Example:
$$2+\frac{2}{3}=2\frac{2}{3}$$

Example:
$$-2-\frac{3}{4}=-2\frac{3}{4}$$

Adding an integer and a fraction with different signs involves the following steps:

- Get a common denominator
- Add or subtract as needed
- Change to a mixed fraction if possible

Example:
$$2-\frac{1}{3}=\frac{2\times 3-1}{3}=\frac{6-1}{3}=\frac{5}{3}=1\frac{2}{3}$$

Example: Add $7\frac{3}{8}+5\frac{2}{7}$.

Add the whole numbers; add the fractions and combine the two results:

$$7\frac{3}{8}+5\frac{2}{7}=(7+5)+(\frac{3}{8}+\frac{2}{7})$$
$$=12+\frac{(7\times 3)+(8\times 2)}{56} \quad \text{(LCM of 8 and 7)}$$
$$=12+\frac{21+16}{56}=12+\frac{37}{56}=12\frac{37}{56}$$

Example: Perform the operation.
$$\frac{2}{3}-\frac{5}{6}$$

We first find the LCM of 3 and 6, which is 6.

$$\frac{2\times 2}{3\times 2}-\frac{5}{6}=\frac{4-5}{6}=\frac{-1}{6}$$

(Using method A)

Example:
$$-7\frac{1}{4}+2\frac{7}{8}$$
$$-7\frac{1}{4}+2\frac{7}{8}=(-7+2)+(\frac{-1}{4}+\frac{7}{8})$$

NUMBER SENSE AND BASIC ALGEBRA

$$= (-5) + \frac{(-2+7)}{8} = (-5) + (\frac{5}{8})$$

$$= (-5) + \frac{5}{8} = \frac{(-5 \times 8)}{1 \times 8} + \frac{5}{8} = \frac{-40+5}{8}$$

$$= \frac{-35}{8} = -4\frac{3}{8}$$

Divide 35 by 8 to get 4, remainder 3.

Caution: Common error would be

$$-7\frac{1}{4} + 2\frac{7}{8} = -7\frac{2}{8} + 2\frac{7}{8} = -5\frac{9}{8} \quad \text{Wrong.}$$

It is correct to add -7 and 2 to get -5, but adding $\frac{2}{8} + \frac{7}{8} = \frac{9}{8}$ is wrong.

It should have been $\frac{-2}{8} + \frac{7}{8} = \frac{5}{8}$. Then, $-5 + \frac{5}{8} = -4\frac{3}{8}$ as before.

Multiplication of Fractions

Using the following example:

$$3\frac{1}{4} \times \frac{5}{6}$$

1. Convert each number to an improper fraction.

   $$3\frac{1}{4} = \frac{(12+1)}{4} = \frac{13}{4}$$

   $\frac{5}{6}$ is already in reduced form.

2. Reduce (cancel) common factors of the numerator and denominator if they exist.

   $$\frac{13}{4} \times \frac{5}{6}$$

   No common factors exist.

3. Multiply the numerators by each other and the denominators by each other.

   $$\frac{13}{4} \times \frac{5}{6} = \frac{65}{24}$$

4. If possible, reduce the fraction back to its lowest term.

   $\frac{65}{24}$ Cannot be reduced further.

5. Convert the improper fraction back to a mixed fraction by using long division.

   $$\frac{65}{24} = 24\overline{)65} \quad = 2\frac{17}{24}$$
   $$\quad \quad \underline{48}$$
   $$\quad \quad 17$$

Summary of sign changes for multiplication:

$$(+) \times (+) = (+)$$

$$(-)\times(+)=(-)$$
$$(+)\times(-)=(-)$$
$$(-)\times(-)=(+)$$

Example: Reduce like terms (22 and 11).

$$7\tfrac{1}{3}\times\tfrac{5}{11}=\tfrac{22}{3}\times\tfrac{5}{11}$$
$$=\tfrac{2}{3}\times\tfrac{5}{1}=3\tfrac{1}{3}$$

Example:

$$-6\tfrac{1}{4}\times\tfrac{5}{9}=\tfrac{-25}{4}\times\tfrac{5}{9}$$
$$=\tfrac{-125}{36}=-3\tfrac{17}{36}$$

Example: Negative times a negative equals positive.

$$\tfrac{-1}{4}\times\tfrac{-3}{7}$$
$$=\tfrac{1}{4}\times\tfrac{3}{7}=\tfrac{3}{28}$$

Division of Fractions

1. Change mixed fractions to improper fractions
2. Change the division problem to a multiplication problem by using the reciprocal of the number after the division sign
3. Find the sign of the final product
4. Cancel if common factors exist between the numerator and the denominator
5. Multiply the numerators together and the denominators together
6. Change the improper fraction to a mixed number

Example:

$$3\tfrac{1}{5}\div 2\tfrac{1}{4}=\tfrac{16}{5}\div\tfrac{9}{4}$$
$$=\tfrac{16}{5}\times\tfrac{4}{9} \qquad \text{Reciprocal of }\tfrac{9}{4}\text{ is }\tfrac{4}{9}.$$
$$=\tfrac{64}{45}=1\tfrac{19}{45}$$

NUMBER SENSE AND BASIC ALGEBRA

Example:

$$7\tfrac{3}{4} \div 11\tfrac{5}{8} = \tfrac{31}{4} \div \tfrac{93}{8}$$

$$= \tfrac{31}{4} \times \tfrac{8}{93} \qquad \text{Reduce like terms.}$$

$$= \tfrac{1}{1} \times \tfrac{2}{3} = \tfrac{2}{3}$$

Example:

$$(-2\tfrac{1}{2}) \div 4\tfrac{1}{6} = \tfrac{-5}{2} \div \tfrac{25}{6}$$

$$= \tfrac{-5}{2} \times \tfrac{6}{25} \qquad \text{Reduce like terms.}$$

$$= \tfrac{-1}{1} \times \tfrac{3}{5} = \tfrac{-3}{5}$$

Example:

$$(-5\tfrac{3}{8}) \div (\tfrac{-7}{16}) = \tfrac{-43}{8} \div \tfrac{-7}{16}$$

$$= \tfrac{-43}{8} \times \tfrac{-16}{7} \qquad \text{Reduce like terms.}$$

$$= \tfrac{43}{1} \times \tfrac{2}{7} \qquad \text{Negative times a negative equals a positive.}$$

$$= \tfrac{86}{7} = 12\tfrac{2}{7}$$

MATHEMATICS

Sample Test Questions and Rationale

(Average)

1. $\frac{-4}{9} + \frac{-7}{10} =$

   A. $\frac{23}{90}$

   B. $\frac{-23}{90}$

   C. $\frac{103}{90}$

   D. $\frac{-103}{90}$

   Answer is D.

   Find the LCD of $\frac{-4}{9}$ and $\frac{-7}{10}$. The LCD is 90, so you get $\frac{-40}{90} + \frac{-63}{90} = \frac{-103}{90}$, which is answer D.

(Average)

2. $5.6 \times -0.11 =$

   A. -0.616

   B. 0.616

   C. 6.110

   D. -6.110

   Answer is A.

   Simple multiplication. The answer will be negative because a positive times a negative is a negative number $5.6 \times -0.11 = -0.616$, which is answer A.

(Average)

3. $4\frac{2}{9} \times \frac{7}{10} =$

   A. $4\frac{9}{10}$

   B. $\frac{266}{90}$

   C. $2\frac{43}{45}$

   D. $2\frac{6}{20}$

   Answer is C.

   Convert any mixed number to an improper fraction: $\frac{38}{9} \times \frac{7}{10}$. Since no common factors of numerators or denominators exist, multiply the numerators and the denominators by each other $= \frac{266}{90}$. Convert back to a mixed number and reduce $2\frac{86}{90} = 2\frac{43}{45}$. The answer is C.

(Rigorous)

4. The price of gas was $3.27 per gallon. Your tank holds 15 gallons of fuel. You are using two tanks a week. How much will you save weekly if the price of gas goes down to $2.30 per gallon?

   A. $26.00

   B. $29.00

   C. $15.00

   D. $17.00

   Answer is B.

   15 gallons $\times$ 2 tanks = 30 gallons a week
   = 30 gallons $\times$ $3.27 = $98.10
   30 gallons $\times$ $2.30 = $69.00
   $98.10 − $69.00 = $29.10 is approximately $29.00. The answer is B.

NUMBER SENSE AND BASIC ALGEBRA

SKILL 3.2 Recognize multiplication as repeated addition and division as repeated subtraction

See Skill 3.1

SKILL 3.3 Recognize and interpret mathematical symbols

Symbol for inequality: The symbol > (greater than) or < (less than), the big open side of the symbol always faces the larger of the two numbers, and the point of the symbol always faces the smaller number.

Example: Compare 15 and 20 on the number line.

```
←——+——————+—+—+——→
   0       15 20 25
```

Because 20 is farther away from the zero than 15 is, then 20 is greater than 15, or $20 > 15$.

Example: Compare $\frac{3}{7}$ and $\frac{5}{10}$.

To compare fractions, they should have the same least common denominator (LCD). The LCD in this example is 70.

$$\frac{3}{7} = \frac{3 \times 10}{7 \times 10} = \frac{30}{70} \qquad \frac{5}{10} = \frac{5 \times 7}{10 \times 7} = \frac{35}{70}$$

Since the denominators are equal, compare only the denominators. $30 < 35$, so:

$$\frac{3}{7} < \frac{5}{10}$$

Sample Test Question and Rationale

(Easy)

1. $-9\frac{1}{4} \square -8\frac{2}{3}$

   A. $=$
   B. $<$
   C. $>$
   D. $\leq$

Answer is B.

The larger the absolute value of a negative number, the smaller the negative number is. The absolute value of $-9\frac{1}{4}$ is $9\frac{1}{4}$, which is larger than the absolute value of $-8\frac{2}{3}$, which is $8\frac{2}{3}$. Therefore, the sign should be $<$, which is answer B.

MATHEMATICS

SKILL 3.4 Understand the definitions of basic terms such as sum, difference, product, quotient, numerator, and denominator

SUM: the result of adding two numbers

DIFFERENCE: the result of subtracting two numbers

PRODUCT: the result of subtracting two numbers

QUOTIENT: the result of dividing one number by another

NUMERATOR: the number above the bar in a fraction that tells how many equal parts of the whole are being considered

DENOMINATOR: the number below the bar in a fraction that tells how many equal parts are in the whole

SUM: The result of adding two numbers.
Example: $12 + 6 = 18$

DIFFERENCE: The result of subtracting two numbers.
Example: $57 - 29 = 28$

PRODUCT: The result of two numbers being multiplied together.
Example: $5 \times 5 = 25$

QUOTIENT: The result of dividing one number by another.
Example: $32 \div 8 = 4$

NUMERATOR: The number above the bar in a fraction that tells how many equal parts of the whole are being considered

DENOMINATOR: The number below the bar in a fraction that tells how many equal parts are in the whole

Example: $\frac{3}{4}$ Numerator / Denominator

SKILL 3.5 Recognize the position of numbers in relation to one another

See Skills 3.1 and 3.7.

Sample Test Question and Rationale

(Easy)

1. $0.74 =$
   A. $\frac{74}{100}$
   B. 7.4%
   C. $\frac{33}{50}$
   D. $\frac{74}{10}$

Answer is A.

$0.74 \rightarrow$ the 4 is in the hundredths place, so the answer is $\frac{74}{100}$, which is A.

NUMBER SENSE AND BASIC ALGEBRA

SKILL 3.6 Recognize equivalent forms of a number

If we compare numbers in various forms, we see that:
The integer $400 = \frac{800}{2}$ (fraction) $= 400.0$ (decimal) $= 400\%$ (percent).

From this, you should be able to determine that fractions, decimals, and percents can be used interchangeably within problems.

- To change a percent into a decimal, move the decimal point two places to the left and drop off the percent sign.

- To change a decimal into a percent, move the decimal two places to the right and add on a percent sign.

- To change a fraction into a decimal, divide the numerator by the denominator.

- To change a decimal number into an equivalent fraction, write the decimal part of the number as the fraction's numerator. As the fraction's denominator, use the place value of the last column of the decimal. Reduce the resulting fraction as far as possible.

Example: J.C. Nickels has Hunch jeans for sale at $\frac{1}{4}$ off the usual price of $36.00. Shears and Roadster have the same jeans for sale at 30% off their regular price of $40. Find the cheaper price.

$\frac{1}{4} = .25$, so $.25(36) = \$9.00$ off; $\$36 - 9 = \$27$ sale price

$30\% = .30$, so $.30(40) = \$12$ off; $\$40 - 12 = \$28$ sale price

The price at J.C Nickels is $1 lower.

To convert a fraction to a decimal, as we did in the example above, simply divide the numerator (top) by the denominator (bottom). Use long division if necessary.

If a decimal has a fixed number of digits, the decimal is said to be a **TERMINATING DECIMAL**. To write such a decimal as a fraction, first determine what place value the digit farthest to the right has (for example: tenths, hundredths, thousandths, ten-thousandths, hundred-thousandths, etc.). Then drop the decimal point and place the string of digits over the number given by the place value.

If a decimal continues forever by repeating a string of digits, the decimal is said to be a **REPEATING DECIMAL**. To write a repeating decimal as a fraction, follow these steps:

1. Let x = the repeating decimal. (Ex. $x = .716716716...$)

TERMINATING DECIMAL: a decimal that has a fixed number of digits

REPEATING DECIMAL: a decimal that continues forever by repeating a string of digits

2. Multiply x by the multiple of 10 that will move the decimal just to the right of the repeating block of digits. (Ex. $1000x = 716.716716...$)

3. Subtract the first equation from the second.
   (Ex. $1000x - x = 716.716716... - .716716...$)

4. Simplify and solve this equation. The repeating block of digits will subtract out. (Ex. $999x = 716$ so $x = \frac{716}{999}$)

5. The solution will be the fraction for the repeating decimal.

COMMON EQUIVALENTS				
$\frac{1}{2}$	=	0.5	=	50%
$\frac{1}{3}$	=	$0.33\frac{1}{3}$	=	$33\frac{1}{3}\%$
$\frac{1}{4}$	=	0.25	=	25%
$\frac{1}{5}$	=	0.2	=	20%
$\frac{1}{6}$	=	$0.16\frac{2}{3}$	=	$16\frac{2}{3}\%$
$\frac{1}{8}$	=	$0.12\frac{1}{2}$	=	$12\frac{1}{2}\%$
$\frac{1}{10}$	=	0.1	=	10%
$\frac{2}{3}$	=	$0.66\frac{2}{3}$	=	$66\frac{2}{3}\%$
$\frac{5}{6}$	=	$0.83\frac{1}{3}$	=	$83\frac{1}{3}\%$
$\frac{3}{8}$	=	$0.37\frac{1}{2}$	=	$37\frac{1}{2}\%$
$\frac{5}{8}$	=	$0.62\frac{1}{2}$	=	$62\frac{1}{2}\%$
$\frac{7}{8}$	=	$0.87\frac{1}{2}$	=	$87\frac{1}{2}\%$
1	=	1.0	=	100%

NUMBER SENSE AND BASIC ALGEBRA

Sample Test Questions and Rationale

(Average)

1. 303 is what percent of 600?

   A. 0.505%
   B. 5.05%
   C. 505%
   D. 50.5%

   Answer is D.

   Use x for the percent.
   $600x = 303$.
   $\frac{600x}{600} = \frac{303}{600} \rightarrow x = 0.505$
   $= 50.5\%$, which is answer D.

(Rigorous)

2. An item that sells for $375 is put on sale at $120. What is the percent of decrease?

   A. 25%
   B. 28%
   C. 68%
   D. 34%

   Answer is C.

   Use $(1 - x)$ as the discount.
   $375x = 120$.

   $375(1 - x) = 120 \rightarrow$
   $375 - 375x = 120$
   $\rightarrow 375x = 255 \rightarrow x = 06.8 = 68\%$,

   which is answer C.

(Average)

3. A restaurant employs 465 people. There are 280 waiters and 185 cooks. If 168 waiters and 85 cooks receive pay raises, what percent of the waiters will receive a pay raise?

   A. 36.13%
   B. 60%
   C. 60.22%
   D. 40%

   Answer is B.

   The total number of waiters is 280 and only 168 of them get a pay raise. Divide the number getting a raise by the total number of waiters to get the percent.
   $\frac{168}{280} = 0.6 = 60\%$, which is answer B.

MATHEMATICS

SKILL 3.7 Demonstrate knowledge of place value for whole numbers and decimal numbers

Whole Number Place Value

Consider the number 792. We can assign a place value to each digit.

Reading from left to right, the first digit (7) represents the hundreds' place. The hundreds' place tells us how many sets of one hundred the number contains. Thus, there are 7 sets of one hundred in the number 792.

The second digit (9) represents the tens' place. The tens' place tells us how many sets of ten the number contains. Thus, there are 9 sets of ten in the number 792.

The last digit (2) represents the ones' place. The ones' place tells us how many ones the number contains. Thus, there are 2 sets of one in the number 792.

Therefore, there are 7 sets of 100, plus 9 sets of 10, plus 2 ones in the number 792.

Decimal Place Value

More complex numbers have additional place values to both the left and the right of the decimal point. Consider the number 374.8.

Reading from left to right, the first digit (3) is in the hundreds' place and tells us the number contains 3 sets of one hundred.

The second digit (7) is in the tens' place and tells us the number contains 7 sets of ten.

The third digit, 4, is in the ones' place and tells us the number contains 4 ones.

Finally, the number after the decimal (8) is in the tenths' place and tells us the number contains 8 tenths.

Place Value for Older Students

Each digit to the left of the decimal point increases progressively in powers of ten. Each digit to the right of the decimal point decreases progressively in powers of ten.

Example: 12345.6789 occupies the following powers of ten positions:

10^4	10^3	10^2	10^1	10^0	0	10^{-1}	10^{-2}	10^{-3}	10^{-4}
1	2	3	4	5	.	6	7	8	9

NUMBER SENSE AND BASIC ALGEBRA

NAMES OF POWER-OF-TEN POSITIONS:			
10^0	ones	(note that any non-zero base raised to power zero is 1)	
10^1	tens	number 1 and 1 zero or 10	
10^2	hundred	number 1 and 2 zeros or 100	
10^3	thousand	number 1 and 3 zeros or 1000	
10^4	ten thousand	number 1 and 4 zeros or 10000	
10^{-1}	$\frac{1}{10^1}$	tenths	1st digit after decimal point or 0.1
10^{-2}	$\frac{1}{10^2}$	hundredth	2nd digit after decimal point or 0.01
10^{-3}	$\frac{1}{10^3}$	thousandth	3rd digit after decimal point or 0.001
10^{-4}	$\frac{1}{10^4}$	ten thousandth	4th digit after decimal point or 0.0001

Example: Write 73169.00537 in expanded form.
We start by listing all the powers of ten positions.

$10^4 \quad 10^3 \quad 10^2 \quad 10^1 \quad 10^0 \quad . \quad 10^{-1} \quad 10^{-2} \quad 10^{-3} \quad 10^{-4} \quad 10^{-5}$

Multiply each digit by its power of ten. Add all the results.

Thus $73169.00537 = (7 \times 10^4) + (3 \times 10^3) + (1 \times 10^2) + (6 \times 10^1)$
$+ (9 \times 10^0) + (0 \times 10^{-1}) + (0 \times 10^{-2}) + (5 \times 10^{-3})$
$+ (3 \times 10^{-4}) + (7 \times 10^{-5})$

Example: Determine the place value associated with the underlined digit in 3.16<u>9</u>5.

$10^0 \quad . \quad 10^{-1} \quad 10^{-2} \quad 10^{-3} \quad 10^{-4}$

$3 \quad . \quad 1 \quad 6 \quad 9 \quad 5$

The place value for the digit 9 is 10^{-3} or $\frac{1}{1000}$.

Example: Find the number that is represented by
$(7 \times 10^3) + (5 \times 10^0) + (3 \times 10^{-3})$
$= 7000 + 5 + 0.003$
$= 7005.003$

Example: Write 21×10^3 in standard form.
$= 21 \times 1000 = 21,000$

Example: Write 739×10^{-4} in standard form.
$= 739 \times \frac{1}{10000} = \frac{739}{10000} = 0.0739$

Sample Test Question and Rationale

(Average)

1. $(3 \times 9)^4 =$

   A. $(3 \times 9)(3 \times 9)(27 \times 27)$
   B. $(3 \times 9)(3 \times 9)$
   C. (12×36)
   D. $(3 \times 9) + (3 \times 9) + (3 \times 9) + (3 \times 9)$

Answer is A.

$(3 \times 9)^4 = (3 \times 9)(3 \times 9)(3 \times 9)(3 \times 9)$, which, when solving two of the parentheses, is $(3 \times 9)(3 \times 9)(27 \times 27)$, which is answer A.

SKILL 3.8 Compute percentages

Percent means per 100 (represented by the symbol %).

Example: $10 \text{ percent} = \frac{10}{100} = \frac{1}{10} = 0.1$

Example: $10 \text{ percent of } 150 \text{ means } \frac{10}{100} \times \frac{150}{1} = 15$

Example: Add 75% of 25 to 10% of 1000.
$75\% \text{ of } 25 = \frac{75}{100} \times \frac{25}{1} = \frac{75}{4} \times \frac{1}{1} = \frac{75}{4} = 18\frac{3}{4}$ and
$10\% \text{ of } 1000 = \frac{10}{100} \times \frac{1000}{1} = \frac{10}{1} \times \frac{10}{1} = 100$
Adding the two numbers gives: $18\frac{3}{4} + 100 = 118\frac{3}{4}$

Example: 5 is what percent of 20?
This is the same as converting $\frac{5}{20}$ to % form.
$\frac{5}{20} \times \frac{100}{1} = \frac{5}{1} \times \frac{5}{1} = 25\%$

Example: An item on sale at 75% discount is now sold for $12.50. What was the selling price before the sale?
$12.50 is 75% of the price. What was full price?
$\frac{12.50}{75} \times \frac{100}{1} = \frac{50}{3} = \$16.667 \approx \$16.67$

Example: There are 64 dogs in the kennel. 48 are collies. What percent are collies?
Restate the problem.
48 is what percent of 64?

Write an equation.
$48 = n \times 64$

Solve.
$\frac{48}{64} = n$
$n = \frac{3}{4} = 75\%$
75% of the dogs are collies.

Example: The auditorium was filled to 90% capacity. There were 558 seats occupied. What is the capacity of the auditorium?
Restate the problem.
90% of what number is 558?

Write an equation.
$0.9n = 558$

Solve.
$n = \frac{588}{0.9}$
$n = 620$
The capacity of the auditorium is 620 people.

Example: A pair of shoes costs $42.00. Sales tax is 6%. What is the total cost of the shoes?
Restate the problem.
What is 6% of 42?

Write an equation.
$n = 0.06 \times 42$

MATHEMATICS

Solve.

$n = 2.52$

Add the sales tax to the cost. $42.00 + $2.52 = $44.52

The total cost of the shoes, including sales tax, is $44.52.

Sample Test Questions and Rationale

(Easy)

1. Choose the expression that is not equivalent to $5x + 3y + 15z$:

   A. $5(x + 3z) + 3y$

   B. $3(x + y + 5z)$

   C. $3y + 5(x + 3z)$

   D. $5x + 3(y + 5z)$

   Answer is B.

   $5x + 3y + 15z = (5x + 15z) + 3y = 5(x + 3z) + 3y$
   A. is true
   $= 5x + (3y + 15z)$
   $= 5x + 3(y + 5z)$
   D. is true
   $= 37 + (5x + 15z)$
   $= 37 + 5(x + 3z)$
   C. is true

   These can all be solved using the associative property and then factoring. However, in B. $3(x + y + 5z)$ by distributive property $= 3x + 3y + 15z$ does not equal $5x + 37 + 15z$. The answer is B.

(Average)

2. $\frac{7}{9} + \frac{1}{3} \div \frac{2}{3} =$

   A. $\frac{5}{3}$

   B. $\frac{3}{2}$

   C. 2

   D. $\frac{23}{18}$

   Answer is D.

   First, do the division.

   $\frac{1}{3} \div \frac{2}{3} = \frac{1}{3} \times \frac{3}{2} = \frac{1}{2}$

   Then add.

   $\frac{7}{9} + \frac{1}{2} = \frac{14}{18} + \frac{9}{18} = \frac{23}{18}$,

   which is answer D.

(Rigorous)

3. Choose the statement that is true for all real numbers.

   A. $a = 0, b \neq 0$, then $\frac{b}{a} =$ undefined.

   B. $-(a + (-a)) = 2a$

   C. $2(ab) = -(2a)b$

   D. $-a(b = 1) = ab - a$

   Answer is A.

   Any number divided by 0 is undefined.

NUMBER SENSE AND BASIC ALGEBRA

SKILL 3.9 Demonstrate knowledge of basic concepts of exponents

The **EXPONENT FORM** is a shortcut method to write repeated multiplication. Basic form: b^n, where b is called the base and n is the exponent. b and n are both real numbers. b^n implies that the base b is multiplied by itself n times.

EXPONENT FORM: a shortcut method to write repeated multiplication

Examples:
$3^4 = 3 \times 3 \times 3 \times 3 = 81$
$2^3 = 2 \times 2 \times 2 = 8$
$(-2)^4 = (-2) \times (-2) \times (-2) \times (-2) = 16$
$-2^4 = -(2 \times 2 \times 2 \times 2) = -16$

Key Exponent Rules

For a nonzero, and m and n real numbers:

1. $a^m \times a^n = a^{(m+n)}$

   Product rule

2. $\dfrac{a^m}{a^n} = a^{(m-n)}$

   Quotient rule

3. $\dfrac{a^{-m}}{a^{-n}} = \dfrac{a^n}{a^m}$

When 10 is raised to any power, the exponent tells the numbers of zeroes in the product.

Example: $10^7 = 10,000,000$

Caution: Unless the negative sign is inside the parentheses and the exponent is outside the parentheses, the sign is not affected by the exponent.

$(-2)^4$ implies that -2 is multiplied by itself 4 times.
-2^4 implies that 2 is multiplied by itself 4 times, then the answer is negated.

SCIENTIFIC NOTATION is a more convenient method for writing very large and very small numbers. It employs two factors. The first factor is a number between 1 and 10. The second factor is a power of 10. This notation is a "shorthand" for expressing large numbers (like the weight of 100 elephants) or small numbers (like the weight of an atom in pounds).

SCIENTIFIC NOTATION: a more convenient method for writing very large and very small numbers, which employs two factors: the first factor is a number between 1 and 10, the second factor is a power of 10

MATHEMATICS

10^n	=	$(10)^n$	Ten multiplied by itself n times.
10^0	=	1	Any nonzero number raised to power of zero is 1.
10^1	=	10	
10^2	=	$10 \times 10 = 100$	
10^3	=	$10 \times 10 \times 10 = 1000$	(kilo)
10^{-1}	=	1/10	(deci)
10^{-2}	=	1/100	(centi)
10^{-3}	=	1/1000	(milli)
10^{-6}	=	1/1,000,000	(micro)

Example: Write 46,368,000 in scientific notation.

1. Introduce a decimal point and decimal places
   46,368,000 = 46,368,000.0000

2. Make a mark between the two digits that give a number between -9.9 and 9.9
   4 ∧ 6,368,000.0000

3. Count the number of digit places between the decimal point and the ∧ mark. This number is the n—the power of ten
   So, 46,368,000 = 4.6368×10^7

Example: Write 0.00397 in scientific notation.

1. Decimal place is already in place

2. Make a mark between 3 and 9 to get a one number between -9.9 and 9.9

3. Move decimal place to the mark (3 hops)
   0.003∧97
   Motion is to the right, so n of 10^n is negative
   Therefore, 0.00397 = 3.97×10^{-3}

NUMBER SENSE AND BASIC ALGEBRA

SKILL 3.10 Demonstrate knowledge of order of operations *(parentheses, exponents, multiplication, division, addition, and subtraction)*

THE ORDER OF OPERATIONS is to be followed when evaluating algebraic expressions. Follow these steps in order:

1. Simplify inside grouping characters such as parentheses, brackets, square roots, fraction bars, etc.
2. Multiply out expressions with exponents
3. Do multiplication or division, from left to right
4. Do addition or subtraction, from left to right

THE ORDER OF OPERATIONS: sequence to be followed when evaluating algebraic expressions

Example: $3^3 - 5(b + 2)$
$= 3^3 - 5b - 10$
$= 27 - 5b - 10 = 17 - 5b$

Example: $2 - 4 \times 2^3 - 2(4 - 2 \times 3)$
$= 2 - 4 \times 2^3 - 2(4 - 6) = 2 - 4 \times 2^3 - 2(-2)$
$= 2 - 4 \times 2^3 + 4 = 2 - 4 \times 8 + 4$
$= 2 - 32 + 4 = 6 - 32 = -26$

SKILL 3.11 Use mental math to solve problems by estimation

To estimate measurement of familiar objects, it is first necessary to determine the units to be used.

EXAMPLES OF UNITS	
Length	The coastline of Florida
	The width of a ribbon
	The thickness of a book
	The depth of water in a pool

MATHEMATICS

EXAMPLES OF UNITS	
Weight or mass	A bag of sugar A school bus A dime
Capacity or volume	Paint to paint a bedroom Glass of milk
Money	Cost of a cup of coffee Exchange rate
Perimeter	The edge of a backyard The edge of a football field
Area	The size of a carpet The size of a state

Example: Estimate the measurements of the following objects:

Length of a dollar bill	6 inches
Weight of a baseball	1 pound
Distance from New York to Florida	1100 km
Volume of water to fill a medicine dropper	1 milliliter
Length of a desk	2 meters
Temperature of water in a swimming pool	80° F

Depending on the degree of accuracy needed, an object may be measured to different units. For example, a pencil may be 6 inches to the nearest inch, or $6\frac{3}{8}$ inches to the nearest eighth of an inch. Similarly, it might be 15 cm to the nearest cm or 154 mm to the nearest mm.

Given a set of objects and their measurements, the use of rounding procedures is helpful when attempting to round to the nearest given unit. When rounding to a given place value, it is necessary to look at the number in the next smaller place. If this number is 5 or more, the number in the place we are rounding to is increased by one and all numbers to the right are changed to zero. If the number is less than 5, the number in the place we are rounding to stays the same and all numbers to the right are changed to zero.

One method of rounding measurements can require an additional step. First, the measurement must be converted to a decimal number. Then the rules for rounding applied.

Example: Round the measurements to the given units.

Measurement	Round to Nearest	Answer
1 foot 7 inches	foot	2 ft
5 pound 6 ounces	pound	5 pounds
$5\frac{9}{16}$ inches	inch	6 inches

Convert each measurement to a decimal number. Then apply the rules for rounding.

1 foot 7 inches = $1\frac{7}{12}$ ft = 1.58333 ft, round up to 2 ft

5 pounds 6 ounces = $5\frac{6}{16}$ pounds = 5.375 pound, round to 5 pounds

$5\frac{9}{16}$ inches = 5.5625 inches, round up to 6 inches

Example: Janet goes into a store to purchase a CD on sale for $13.95. While shopping, she sees two pairs of shoes, prices $19.95 and $14.50. She only has $50. Can she purchase everything?
Solve by rounding:

$19.95 → $20.00
$14.50 → $15.00
$13.95 → $14.00
$49.00

Yes, she can purchase the CD and the shoes.

MATHEMATICS

Sample Test Questions and Rationale

(Average)

1. Given the formula $d = rt$, (where d = distance, r = rate, and t = time), calculate the time required for a vehicle to travel 585 miles at a rate of 65 miles per hour.

   A. 8.5 hours
   B. 6.5 hours
   C. 9.5 hours
   D. 9 hours

   Answer is D.

   We are given $d = 585$ miles and $r = 65$ miles per hour and $d = rt$. Solve for t. $585 = 65t \rightarrow t = 9$ hours, which is answer D.

(Rigorous)

2. Given $f(x) = (x)^3 - 3(x)^2 + 5$, find $x = (-2)$.

   A. 15
   B. -15
   C. 25
   D. -25

   Answer is B.

   Substitute $x = -2$.
   $f(-2) = (-2)^3 - 3 \times (-2)^2 + 5$
   $f(-2) = -8 - 3(4) + 5$
   $f(-2) = -8 - 12 + 5$
   $f(-2) = -15$

   The answer is B.

(Rigorous)

3. For each of the statements below, determine whether $x = \frac{1}{6}$ is a solution.

   i. $6x \leq 4x^2 + 2$
   ii. $10x + 1 = 3(4x - 3)$
   iii. $|x - 1| = x$

   A. i, ii, and iii
   B. i and iii
   C. i only
   D. iii only

   Answer is C.

   Substitute $x = \frac{1}{6}$ into each equation and solve.

   i. $6(\frac{1}{6}) \leq 4(\frac{1}{6})^2 + 2 =$
   $1 \leq 4(\frac{1}{36}) + 2 \rightarrow$
   $1 \leq \frac{1}{9} + 2 \rightarrow$
   $1 \leq 2\frac{1}{9}$
   True.

   ii. $10(\frac{1}{6}) + 1 = 3(4(\frac{1}{6}) - 3) =$
   $2\frac{2}{3} = 3(\frac{2}{3} - 3) \rightarrow$
   $2\frac{2}{3} = \frac{6}{3} - 9 \rightarrow$
   $2\frac{2}{3} = -7$
   False.

   iii. $|\frac{1}{6} - 1| = \frac{1}{6} \rightarrow$
   $|\frac{1}{6} - \frac{6}{6}| = \frac{1}{6} \rightarrow$
   $|\frac{-5}{6}| = \frac{1}{6} \rightarrow$
   $\frac{5}{6} = \frac{1}{6}$
   False.

   So, only (i) is true, which is answer C.

NUMBER SENSE AND BASIC ALGEBRA

Sample Test Questions and Rationale (cont.)

(Easy)

4. Choose the equation that is equivalent to the following:
$\frac{3x}{5} - 5 = 5x$

   A. $3x - 25 = 25x$
   B. $x - \frac{25}{3} = 25x$
   C. $6x - 50 = 75x$
   D. $x + 25 = 25x$

   Answer is A.

   A is the original equation multiplied by 5. The other choices alter the answer to the original equation.

(Rigorous)

5. If, $4x - (3 - x) = 7(x - 3) + 10$, then

   A. $x = 8$
   B. $x = -8$
   C. $x = 4$
   D. $x = -4$

   Answer is C.

   Solve for x. The answer is C.

SKILL 3.12 Solve word problems

Example: Mark and Mike are twins. Three times Mark's age plus four equals four times Mike's age minus 14. How old are the boys?

Since the boys are twins, their ages are the same. "Translate" the English into Algebra. Let x = their age.

$3x + 4 = 4x - 14$
$18 = x$

The boys are each 18 years old.

Example: The YMCA wants to sell raffle tickets to raise $32,000. If they must pay $7,250 in expenses and prizes out of the money collected from the tickets, how many tickets worth $25 each must they sell?

Let x = number of tickets sold
Then $25x$ = total money collected for x tickets
Total money minus expenses is greater than $32,000.

$25x - 7250 = 32{,}000$
$25x = 39350$

$x = 1570$

If they sell 1,570 tickets, they will raise $32,000.

Example: The Simpsons went out for dinner. All 4 of them ordered the aardvark steak dinner. Bert paid for the 4 meals and included a tip of $12 for a total of $84.60. How much was an aardvark steak dinner?

Let $x =$ the price of one aardvark dinner.
So, $4x =$ the price of 4 aardvark dinners.

Some word problems can be solved using a system (group) of equations or inequalities. Watch for words like *greater than*, *less than*, *at least*, or *no more than*, which indicate the need for inequalities.

Example: Farmer Greenjeans bought 4 cows and 6 sheep for $1,700. Mr. Ziffel bought 3 cows and 12 sheep for $2,400. If all the cows were the same price and all the sheep were another price, find the price charged for a cow or for a sheep.

Let $x =$ price of a cow; let $y =$ price of a sheep
    Then Farmer Greenjeans' equation would be: $4x + 6y = 1700$
    Mr. Ziffel's equation would be: $3x + 12y = 2400$

To solve by **addition-subtraction**:
    Multiply the first equation by -2: $-2(4x + 6y = 1700)$
    Keep the other equation the same: $3x + 12y = 2400$
    By doing this, the equations can be added to each other to eliminate one variable and solve for the other variable.
    $-8x - 12y = -3400$
    $3x + 12y = 2400$ Add these equations.
    $-5x = -1000$
    $x = 200$ The price of a cow was $200.
    Solving for y, $y = 150$ The price of a sheep, $150.

To solve by **substitution**:
    Solve one of the equations for a variable. (Try to make an equation without fractions if possible.) Substitute this expression into the equation that you have not yet used. Solve the resulting equation for the value of the remaining variable.
        $4x + 6y = 1700$
        $3x + 12y = 2400$ Solve this equation for x.
    It becomes $x = 800 - 4y$. Now substitute $800 - 4y$ in place of x in the OTHER equation. $4x + 6y = 1700$ now becomes:
        $4(800 - 4y) + 6y = 1700$

$$3200 - 16y + 6y = 1700$$
$$3200 - 10y = 1700$$
$$-10y = -1500$$
$$y = 150, \text{ or } \$150 \text{ for a sheep.}$$

Substituting 150 back into an equation for y, find x.
$$4x + 6(150) = 1700$$
$$4x + 900 = 1700$$
$$4x = 800 \text{ so } x = 200 \text{ for a cow.}$$

Example: Sharon's Bike Shoppe can assemble a 3-speed bike in 30 minutes or a 10-speed bike in 60 minutes. The profit on each bike sold is $60 for a 3 speed or $75 for a 10 speed bike. How many of each type of bike should they assemble during an 8 hour day (480 minutes) to make the maximum profit? Total daily profit must be at least $300.

Let x = number of 3-speed bikes.
Let y = number of 10-speed bikes.

Since there are only 480 minutes to use each day, $30x + 60y \leq 480$ is the first inequality.

Since the total daily profit must be at least $300, $60x + 75y \geq 300$ is the second inequality.

$32x + 65y \leq 480$ solves to $y \leq 8 - 1/2x$
$60x + 75y \geq 300$ solves to $y \geq 4 - 4/5x$

Graph these 2 inequalities:
$y \leq 8 - 1/2x$
$y \geq 4 - 4/5x$

MATHEMATICS

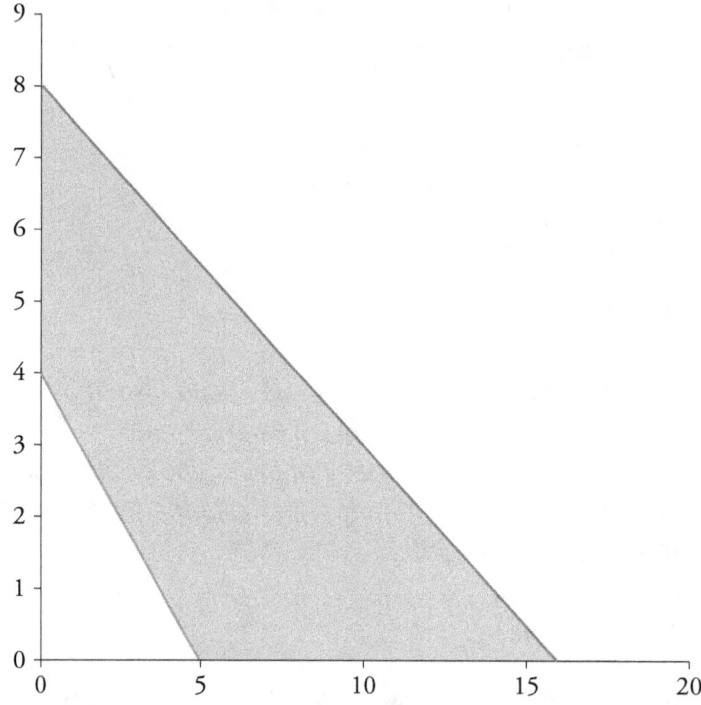

Realize that $x \geq 0$ and $y \geq 0$, since the number of bikes assembled cannot be a negative number. Graph these as additional constraints on the problem. The number of bikes assembled must always be an integer value, so points within the shaded area of the graph must have integer values. The maximum profit will occur at or near a corner of the shaded portion of this graph. Those points occur at (0,4), (0,8), (16,0), or (5,0).

Since profits are $60/3-speed or $75/10-speed, the profit would be:
    (0,4)   60(0)+75(4)=300
    (0,8)   60(0)+75(8)=600
    (16,0)   60(16)+75(0)=960 Maximum profit
    (5,0)   60(5)+75(0)=300

The maximum profit would occur if 16 of the 3-speed bikes are made daily.

NUMBER SENSE AND BASIC ALGEBRA

Sample Test Question and Rationale

(Easy)
1. Identify the missing term in the following harmonic sequence:
$\frac{1}{3}, \frac{1}{6}, \frac{1}{9}, \frac{1}{12}, \frac{1}{15}, ?$
   A. $\frac{1}{16}$
   B. $\frac{1}{17}$
   C. $\frac{1}{18}$
   D. 18

Answer is C.

The difference between the denominators is 3, so the next term in the progression is $\frac{1}{18}$, so the answer is C.

SKILL 3.13 Solve one-step, single-variable linear equations (find x if x + 4 = 2)

Procedure for solving algebraic equations

Example: Given the equation $3(x+3) = -2x+4$, solve for x.

1. Expand to eliminate all parentheses
   $3x + 9 = -2x + 4$

2. Multiply each term by the LCD to eliminate all denominators

3. Combine like terms on each side when possible

4. Use the properties to put all variables on one side and all constants on the other side

   $3x + 9 - 9 = -2x + 4 - 9$ Subtract nine from both sides.
   $3x = -2x - 5$
   $3x + 2x = -2x + 2x - 5$ Add 2x to both sides.
   $5x = -5$
   $\frac{5x}{5} = \frac{-5}{5}$ Divide both sides by 5.
   $x = -1$

MATHEMATICS

Example: Solve: 3(2x + 5) − 4x = 5(x + 9)

$6x + 15 − 4x = 5x + 45$

$2x + 15 = 5x + 45$

$−3x + 15 = 45$

$−3x = 30$

$x = −10$

SKILL 3.14 Identify what comes next in a sequence of numbers

Arithmetic Sequences

When given a set of numbers where the common difference between the terms is constant, use the following formula:

$$a_n = a_1 + (n − 1)d$$

where a_1 = the first term

n = the nth term (general term)

d = the common difference

Example: Find the 8th term of the arithmetic sequence 5, 8, 11, 14, ...

$a_n = a_1 + (n − 1)d$	
$a_1 = 5$	Identify the 1st term.
$d = 8 − 5 = 3$	Find d.
$a_n = 5 + (8 − 1)3$	Substitute.
$a_n = 26$	

Example: Given two terms of an arithmetic sequence, find a_1 and d.

$a_n = a_1 + (n − 1)d$	$a_4 = 21$
$21 = a_1 + (4 − 1)d$	$a_6 = 32$
$32 = a_1 + (6 − 1)d$	$a_4 = 21, n = 4$
	$a_6 = 32, n = 6$
$21 = a_1 + 3d$	Solve the system of equations.
$32 = a_1 + 5d$	
$21 = a_1 + 3d$	
$−32 = −a_1 − 5d$	Multiply by −1.
$\overline{−11 = −2d}$	Add the equations.
$5.5 = d$	
$21 = a_1 + 3(5.5)$	Substitute d = 5.5, into one of the equations.
$21 = a_1 + 16.5$	
$a_1 = 4.5$	

The sequence begins with 4.5 and has a common difference of 5.5 between numbers.

Geometric Sequences

When using geometric sequences, consecutive numbers are compared to find the common ratio.

$r = \frac{a_{n+1}}{a_n}$

where r = common ratio

a = the nth term

The ratio is then used in the geometric sequence formula:

$a_n = a_1 r^{n-1}$

Example: Find the 8th term of the geometric sequence 2, 8, 32, 128...

$r = \frac{a_{n+1}}{a_n}$	Use the common ratio formula to find the ratio.
$r = \frac{8}{2}$	Substitute $a_n = 2$, $a_{n+1} = 8$.
$r = 4$	
$a_n = a_1 \times r^{n-1}$	Use r = 4 to solve for the 8th term.
$a_n = 2 \times 4^{8-1}$	
$a_n = 32{,}768$	

COMPETENCY 4
GEOMETRY AND MEASUREMENT

> **SKILL 4.1** **Represent time and money in more than one way** *(e.g., 30 minutes = $\frac{1}{2}$ hour; 10:15 = quarter after 10; $0.50 = 50 cents = half dollar)*

Elapsed Time

Elapsed time problems are usually one of two types. One type of problem is the elapsed time between two times given in hours, minutes, and seconds. The other common type of problem is between two times given in months and years.

For any time of day past noon, change it into military time by adding 12 hours.

MATHEMATICS

For instance, 1:15 p.m. would be 13:15. Remember when you borrow a minute or an hour in a subtraction problem that you have borrowed 60 more seconds or minutes.

Example: Find the time from 11:34:22 a.m. until 3:28:40 p.m.
First change 3:28:40 p.m. to 15:28:40 p.m.
Now subtract   − 11:34:22 a.m.
                        :18
Borrow an hour and add 60 more minutes. Subtract.
    14:88:40 p.m.
  − 11:34:22 a.m.
    3:54:18   3 hours, 54 minutes, 18 seconds

Example: A race took the winner 1 hr. 58 min. 12 sec. on the first half of the race and 2 hr. 9 min. 57 sec. on the second half of the race. How much time did the entire race take?

    1 hr. 58 min. 12 sec.
  + 2 hr. 9 min. 57 sec.   Add these numbers.
    3 hr. 67 min. 69 sec.
  +   1 min. −60 sec.   Change 60 seconds to 1 min.
    3 hr. 68 min. 9 sec.
  + 1 hr. −60 min.   Change 60 minutes to 1 hr.
    4 hr. 8 min. 9 sec.   Final answer.

Example: It takes Cynthia 45 minutes to get ready each morning. How many hours does she spend getting ready each week?

45 minutes × 7 days = 315 minutes

$$\frac{315 \text{ minutes}}{60 \text{ minutes in an hour}} = 5.25 \text{ hours}$$

Money

Example: Janet goes into a store to purchase a CD on sale for $13.95. While shopping, she sees two pairs of shoes, prices $19.95 and $14.50. She only has $50. Can she purchase everything?

Solve by rounding:
  $19.95 → $20.00
  $14.50 → $15.00
  $13.95 → $14.00
           $49.00

Yes, she can purchase the CD and the shoes.

GEOMETRY AND MEASUREMENT

Weight

Example: The weight limit of a playground merry-go-round is 1,000 pounds. There are 11 children on the merry-go-round. 3 children weigh 100 pounds. 6 children weigh 75 pounds. 2 children weigh 60 pounds. George weighs 80 pounds. Can he get on the merry-go-round?

$3(100) + 6(75) + 2(60)$
$= 300 + 450 + 120$
$= 870$
$1000 - 870$
$= 130$

Since 80 is less than 130, George can get on the merry-go-round.

Sample Test Question and Rationale

(Rigorous)

1. It takes 5 equally skilled people 9 hours to shingle Mr. Joe's roof. Let t be the time required for only 3 of these men to do the same job. Select the correct statement of the given condition.

   A. $\frac{3}{5} = \frac{9}{t}$
   B. $\frac{9}{5} = \frac{3}{t}$
   C. $\frac{5}{9} = \frac{3}{t}$
   D. $\frac{14}{9} = \frac{t}{5}$

   Answer is A.

   $$\frac{3}{5} = \frac{9}{t}$$

   The answer is A.

SKILL 4.2 Convert between units of measure in the same system *(e.g., inches to feet, centimeters to meters)*

MEASUREMENTS OF LENGTH (ENGLISH SYSTEM)		
12 inches (in)	=	1 foot (ft)
3 ft	=	1 yard (yd)
1760 yd	=	1 mile (mi)

MATHEMATICS

MEASUREMENTS OF LENGTH (METRIC SYSTEM)		
kilometer (km)	=	1000 meters (m)
hectometer (hm)	=	100 meters (m)
decameter (dam)	=	1 mile (mi)
meter (m)	=	10 meters (m)
decimeter (dm)	=	1 meter (m)
centimeter (cm)	=	1/10 meter (m)
millimeter (mm)	=	1/100 meter (m)

CONVERSION OF LENGTH FROM ENGLISH TO METRIC		
1 inch	=	2.54 centimeters
1 foot	≈	30 centimeters
1 yard	≈	0.9 meters
1 mile	≈	1.6 kilometers

MEASUREMENTS OF WEIGHT (ENGLISH SYSTEM)		
28 grams (g)	=	1 ounce (oz)
16 ounces (oz)	=	1 pound (lb)
2000 pounds (lb)	=	1 ton (t) (short ton)
1.1 ton (t)	=	1 ton (t)

MEASUREMENTS OF WEIGHT (METRIC SYSTEM)		
kilogram (kg)	=	1000 grams (g)
gram (g)	=	1 gram (g)
milligram (mg)	=	1/1000 gram (g)

GEOMETRY AND MEASUREMENT

CONVERSION OF WEIGHT FROM ENGLISH TO METRIC		
1 ounce	≈	28 grams
1 pound	≈ ≈	0.45 kilogram 454 grams

MEASUREMENT OF VOLUME (ENGLISH SYSTEM)		
8 fluid ounces (oz)	=	1 cup (c)
2 cups (c)	=	1 pint (pt)
2 pints (pt)	=	1 quart (qt)
4 quarts (qt)	=	1 gallon (gal)

MEASUREMENT OF VOLUME (METRIC SYSTEM)		
kiloliter (kl)	=	1000 liters (l)
liter (l)	=	1 liter (l)
milliliter (ml)	=	1/1000 liters (ml)

CONVERSION OF VOLUME FROM ENGLISH TO METRIC		
1 teaspoon (tsp	≈	5 milliliters
1 fluid ounce	≈	15 milliliters
1 cup	≈	0.24 liters
1 pint	≈	0.47 liters
1 quart	≈	0.95 liters
1 gallon	≈	3.8 liters

MATHEMATICS

MEASUREMENT OF TIME		
1 second		
1 minute	=	60 seconds
1 hour	=	60 minutes
1 day	=	24 hours
1 week	=	7 days
1 year	=	365 days
1 century	=	100 years

Note: (') represents feet and (") represents inches.

Square Units

Square units can be derived with knowledge of basic units of length by squaring the equivalent measurements.

> 1 square foot (sq. ft.) = 144 sq. in.
> 1 sq. yd. = 9 sq. ft.
> 1 sq. yd. = 1296 sq. in.

Example:
14 sq. yd. = _____ sq. ft.
14 × 9 = 126 sq. ft.

Weight

Example: Kathy has a bag of potatoes that weighs 5 lbs., 10 oz. She uses one third of the bag to make mashed potatoes. How much does the bag weigh now?

1 lb. = 16 oz.
5(16 oz.) + 10 oz.
= 80 oz + 10 oz = 90 oz.

$90 - (\frac{1}{3})90$ oz.
= 90 oz. − 30 oz.
= 60 oz.
60 ÷ 16 = 3.75 lbs.
.75 = 75%
$75\% = \frac{75}{100} = \frac{3}{4}$

GEOMETRY AND MEASUREMENT

Sample Test Question and Rationale

(Average)

1. Round $1\frac{13}{16}$ of an inch to the nearest quarter of an inch.

   A. $1\frac{1}{4}$ inch
   B. $1\frac{5}{8}$ inch
   C. $1\frac{3}{4}$ inch
   D. 2 inches

Answer is C.

$1\frac{13}{16}$ inches is approximately $1\frac{12}{16}$, which is also $1\frac{3}{4}$, which is the nearest $\frac{1}{4}$ of an inch, so the answer is C.

SKILL 4.3 Identify basic geometrical shapes (e.g., isosceles triangle, right triangle, polygon)

POLYGONS—simple, closed two-dimensional figures composed of line segments—are named according to the number of sides they have.

A **QUADRILATERAL** is a polygon with four sides.

The sum of the measures of the angles of a quadrilateral is 360°.

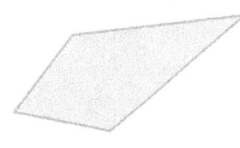 

A **TRAPEZOID** is a quadrilateral with exactly one pair of parallel sides.

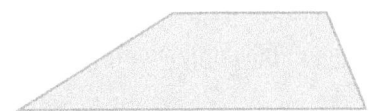 

In an **ISOSCELES TRAPEZOID**, the nonparallel sides are congruent.

POLYGONS: simple, closed two-dimensional figures composed of line segments, named according to the number of sides they have

QUADRILATERAL: a polygon with four sides

TRAPEZOID: a quadrilateral with exactly one pair of parallel sides

ISOSCELES TRAPEZOID: a quadrilateral where the nonparallel sides are congruent

MATHEMATICS

PARALLELOGRAM: a quadrilateral with two pairs of parallel sides

A **PARALLELOGRAM** is a quadrilateral with two pairs of parallel sides.

In a parallelogram:

- The diagonals bisect each other
- Each diagonal divides the parallelogram into two congruent triangles
- Both pairs of opposite sides are congruent
- Both pairs of opposite angles are congruent
- Two adjacent angles are supplementary

RECTANGLE: a parallelogram with a right angle

A **RECTANGLE** is a parallelogram with a right angle.

RHOMBUS: a parallelogram with all sides equal length

A **RHOMBUS** is a parallelogram with all sides equal length.

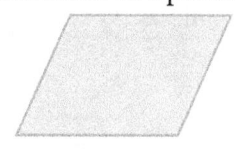

SQUARE: a rectangle with all sides of equal length

A **SQUARE** is a rectangle with all sides of equal length.

Example: True or false?

All squares are rhombuses.	True
All parallelograms are rectangles.	False—<u>some</u> parallelograms are rectangles
All rectangles are parallelograms.	True
Some rhombuses are squares.	True
Some rectangles are trapezoids.	False—trapezoids have only <u>one</u> pair of parallel sides

GEOMETRY AND MEASUREMENT

All quadrilaterals are parallelograms.	False—some quadrilaterals are parallelograms
Some squares are rectangles.	False—all squares are rectangles
Some parallelograms are rhombuses.	True

A **TRIANGLE** is a polygon with three sides. Triangles can be classified by the types of angles or the lengths of their sides.

An **ACUTE TRIANGLE** has exactly three acute angles.

A **RIGHT TRIANGLE** has one right angle.

An **OBTUSE TRIANGLE** has one obtuse angle.

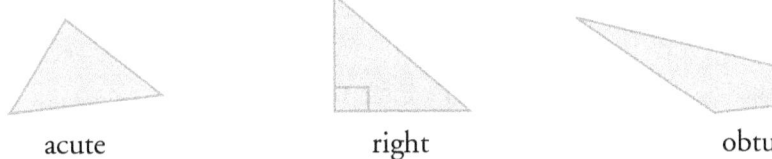

acute   right   obtuse

All three sides of an **EQUILATERAL TRIANGLE** are the same length.

Two sides of an **ISOSCELES TRIANGLE** are the same length.

None of the sides of a **SCALENE TRIANGLE** are the same length.

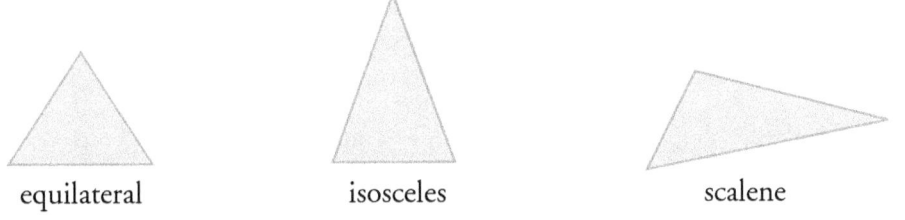

equilateral   isosceles   scalene

Example: Can a triangle have two right angles?
No. A right angle measures 90°; therefore the sum of two right angles would be 180° and there could not be a third angle.

Example: Can a triangle have two obtuse angles?
No. Because an obtuse angle measures more than 90°, the sum of two obtuse angles would be greater than 180°.

A **CYLINDER** has two congruent circular bases that are parallel.

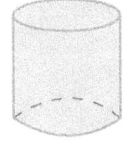

TRIANGLE: a polygon with three sides

ACUTE TRIANGLE: a triangle with exactly three acute angles

RIGHT TRIANGLE: a triangle with one right angle

OBTUSE TRIANGLE: a triangle with one obtuse angle

EQUILATERAL TRIANGLE: a triangle with all three sides the same length

ISOSCELES TRIANGLE: a triangle with two sides the same length

SCALENE TRIANGLE: a triangle with none of the sides the same length

CYLINDER: has two congruent circular bases that are parallel

MATHEMATICS

SPHERE: a space figure having all its points the same distance from the center

A **SPHERE** is a space figure having all its points the same distance from the center.

CONE: a space figure having a circular base and a single vertex

A **CONE** is a space figure having a circular base and a single vertex.

PYRAMID: a space figure with a square base and 4 triangle-shaped sides

A **PYRAMID** is a space figure with a square base and 4 triangle-shaped sides.

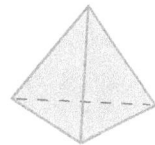

TETRAHEDRON: a 4-sided space triangle where each face is a triangle

A **TETRAHEDRON** is a 4-sided space triangle. Each face is a triangle.

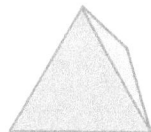

PRISM: a space figure with two congruent, parallel bases that are polygons

A **PRISM** is a space figure with two congruent, parallel bases that are polygons.

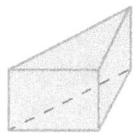

GEOMETRY AND MEASUREMENT

Sample Test Questions and Rationale

(Easy)

1. What type of triangle is △ABC?

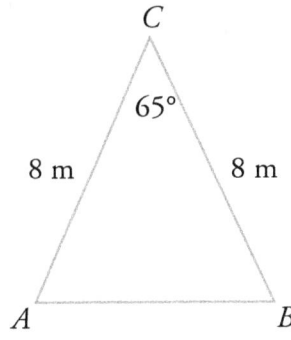

A. Right
B. Equilateral
C. Scalene
D. Isosceles

Answer is D.

Two of the sides are the same length, so we know the triangle is either equilateral or isosceles. ∡CAB and ∡CBA are equal, because their sides are. Therefore, $180° = 65° - 2x = \frac{115°}{2} = 57.5°$. Because all three angles are not equal, the triangle is isosceles, so the answer is D.

(Rigorous)

2. Study figures A, B, C, and D. Select the letter in which all triangles are similar.

A.

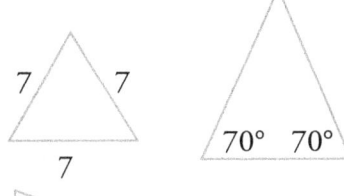

B.

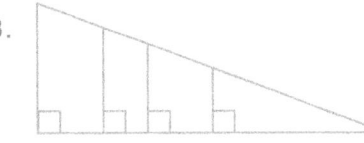

C.

D.

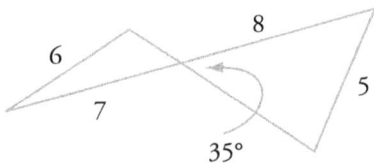

Answer is B.

Choice A is not correct because one triangle is equilateral and the other is isosceles. Choice C is not correct because the two smaller triangles are similar, but the large triangle is not. Choice D is not correct because the lengths and angles are not proportional to each other. Therefore, the correct answer is B because all the triangles have the same angles.

MATHEMATICS

SKILL 4.4 Perform computations related to area, volume, and perimeter for basic shapes

Formulas

Figure	Area Formula	Perimeter Formula
Rectangle	LW	2(L + W)
Triangle	$\frac{1}{2}bh$	a + b + c
Parallelogram	bh	sum of lengths of sides
Trapezoid	$\frac{1}{2}h(a + b)$	sum of lengths of sides

Perimeter

PERIMETER: the sum of the lengths of the sides of any polygon

The PERIMETER of any polygon is the sum of the lengths of the sides.

Example: A farmer has a piece of land shaped as shown below. He wishes to fence this land at an estimated cost of $25 per linear foot. What is the total cost of fencing this property to the nearest foot?

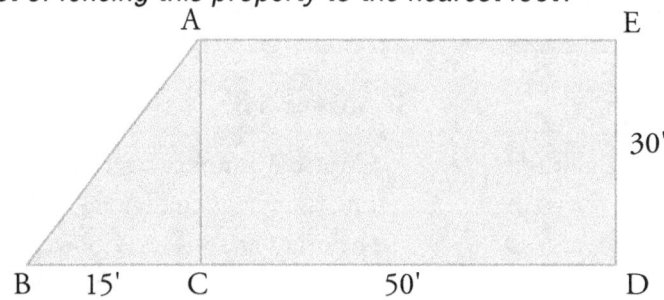

From the right triangle ABC, AC = 30 and BC = 15.

Since $(AB) = (AC)^2 + (BC)^2$
$(AB) = (30)^2 + (15)^2$

So $\sqrt{(AB)^2} = AB = \sqrt{1125} = 33.5410$ feet

To the nearest foot, AB = 34 feet.

Perimeter of the piece of land is = AB + BC + CD + DE + EA
= 34 + 15 + 50 + 30 + 50 = 179 feet
Cost of fencing = $25 × 179 = $4,475.00

GEOMETRY AND MEASUREMENT

Area

The AREA of a polygon is the number of square units covered by the figure.

AREA: the number of square units covered by a polygon

Example: What will be the cost of carpeting a rectangular office that measures 12 feet by 15 feet if the carpet costs $12.50 per square yard?

12 ft.

15 ft.

The problem is asking you to determine the area of the office. The area of a rectangle is *length × width = A*.

Substitute the given values in the equation $A = lw$.
 $A = (12 \text{ ft.})(15 \text{ ft.})$
 $A = 180 \text{ ft.}$

The problem asked you to determine the cost of carpet at $12.50 per square yard.

First, you need to convert 180 ft.² into yards².
 1 yd. = 3 ft.
 (1 yard)(1 yard) = (3 feet)(3 feet)
 $1 \text{ yd}^2 = 9 \text{ ft}^2$
 Hence, $\frac{180 \text{ ft}^2}{1} = \frac{1 \text{ yd}^2}{9 \text{ ft}^2} = \frac{20}{1} = 20 \text{ yd}^2$
 The carpet cost $12.50 per square yard; thus the cost of carpeting the office described is $12.50 × 20 = $250.00.

Example: Find the area of a parallelogram whose base is 6.5 cm and the height of the altitude to that base is 3.7 cm.

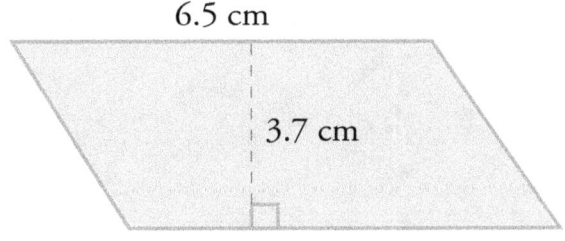

6.5 cm

3.7 cm

$A_{\text{parallelogram}} = bh$
 $= (3.7)(6.5)$
 $= 24.05 \text{ cm}^2$

MATHEMATICS

Example: Find the area of this triangle.

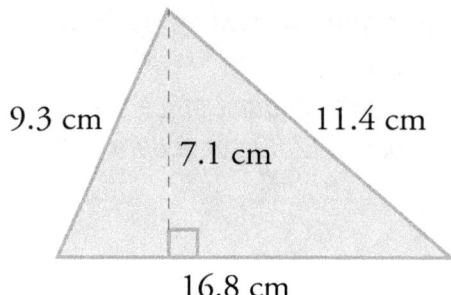

$$A_{triangle} = \tfrac{1}{2}bh$$
$$= 0.5(16.8)(7.1)$$
$$= 59.64 \text{ cm}^2$$

Example: Find the area of this trapezoid.

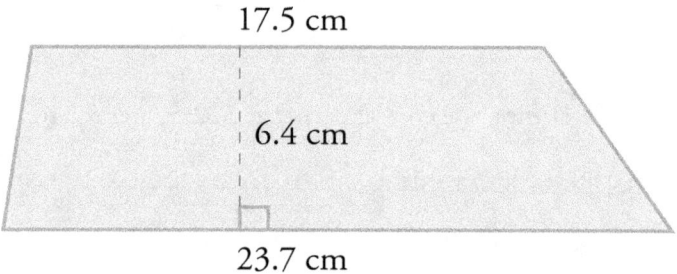

The area of a trapezoid equals one-half the sum of the bases times the altitude.

$$A_{trapezoid} = \tfrac{1}{2}h(b_1 + b_2)$$
$$A_{trapezoid} = 0.5(6.4)(17.5 + 23.7)$$
$$A_{trapezoid} = 131.84 \text{ cm}^2$$

CIRCUMFERENCE: the distance around a circle

The distance around a circle is the CIRCUMFERENCE. The ratio of the circumference to the diameter is represented by the Greek letter pi. $\pi \sim 3.14 \sim \tfrac{22}{7}$.

The circumference of a circle is found by the formula $C = 2\pi r$ or $C = \pi d$ where r is the radius of the circle and d is the diameter.

AREA OF A CIRCLE: found by the formula $A = \pi r^2$

The AREA OF A CIRCLE is found by the formula $A = \pi r^2$.

Example: Find the circumference and area of a circle whose radius is 7 meters.

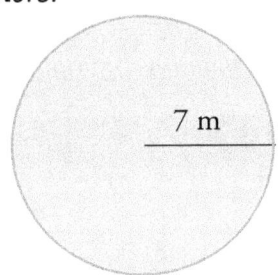

$C = \pi r$
$= 2(3.14)(7)$
$= 43.96$ m

$A = \pi r^2$
$= 3.14(7)(7)$
$= 153.86$ m^2

Volume and Surface Area

Volume and Surface area are computed using the following formulas:

Figure	Volume	Total Surface Area
Right Cylinder	$\pi r^2 h$	$2\pi rh + 2\pi r^2$
Right Cone	$\dfrac{\pi r^2 h}{3}$	$\pi r\sqrt{r^2+h^2} + \pi r^2$
Sphere	$\dfrac{4}{3}\pi r^3$	$4\pi r^2$
Rectangular Solid	LWH	$2LW + 2WH + 2LH$

Figure	Lateral Area	Total Area	Volume
Regular Pyramid	1/2Pl	1/2Pl+B	1/3Bh

P = Perimeter, h = height, B = Area of Base, l = slant height

Example: What is the volume of a shoe box with a length of 35 cm, a width of 20 cm and a height of 15 cm inches?

Volume of a rectangular solid
= Length × Width × Height
= 35 × 20 × 15
= 10500cm^3

Example: A water company is trying to decide whether to use traditional cylindrical paper cups or to offer conical paper cups since both cost the same. The traditional cups are 8 cm wide and 14 cm high. The conical cups are 12 cm wide and 19 cm high. The company will use the cup that holds the most water.

Draw and label a sketch of each.

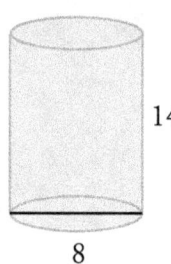
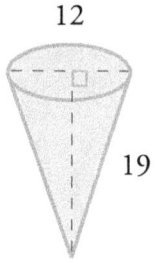

$V = \pi r^2 h$	$V = \dfrac{\pi r^2 h}{3}$	1. Write a formula.
$V = \pi(4)^2(14)$	$V = \dfrac{1}{3}\pi(6)^2(19)$	2. Substitute.
$V = 703.717 \text{ cm}^3$	$V = 716.283 \text{ cm}^3$	3. Solve.

The choice should be the conical cup since its volume is greater.

Example: How much material is needed to make a basketball that has a diameter of 15 inches? How much air is needed to fill the basketball?

Draw and label a sketch:

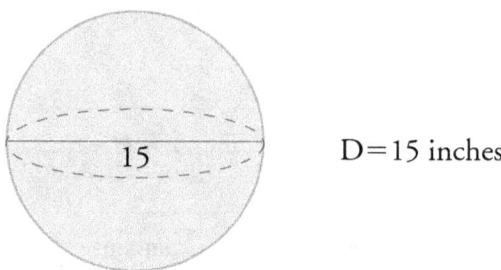

D = 15 inches

Total surface area	Volume	
$TSA = 4\pi r^2$	$V = \dfrac{4}{3}\pi r^3$	1. Write a formula.
$= 4\pi(7.5)^2$	$= \dfrac{4}{3}\pi(7.5)^3$	2. Substitute.
$= 706.858 \text{ in}^2$	$= 1767.1459 \text{ in}^3$	3. Solve.

GEOMETRY AND MEASUREMENT

Sample Test Questions and Rationale

(Easy)

1. What measure could be used to report the distance traveled in walking around a track?

   A. Degrees
   B. Square meters
   C. Kilometers
   D. Cubic feet

   Answer is C.

   Degrees measure angles, square meters measure area, cubic feet measure volume, and kilometers measure length. *Kilometers* is the only reasonable answer, which is C.

(Rigorous)

2. The owner of a rectangular piece of land 40 yards in length and 30 yards in width wants to divide it into two parts. She plans to join two opposite corners with a fence as shown in the diagram below. The cost of the fence will be approximately $25 per linear foot. What is the estimated cost for the fence needed by the owner?

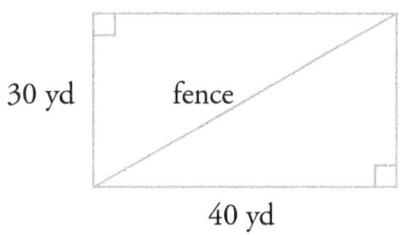

   A. $1,250
   B. $62,500
   C. $5,250
   D. $3,750

   Answer is D.

   Find the length of the diagonal by using the Pythagorean theorem. Let x be the length of the diagonal.
   $30^2 + 40^2 = x^2$
   $900 + 1600 = x^2$
   $2500 = x^2$
   $\sqrt{2500} = \sqrt{x^2}$
   $x = 50$ yards

   Convert to feet.
   $\frac{50 \text{ yards}}{x \text{ feet}} = \frac{1 \text{ yard}}{3 \text{ feet}} \rightarrow 150$ feet
   It cost $25.00 per linear foot, so the cost is (150 ft)($25) = $3,750, which is answer D.

MATHEMATICS

Sample Test Questions and Rationale (cont.)

(Average)

3. What is the area of a square whose side is 13 feet?

   A. 169 feet
   B. 169 square feet
   C. 52 feet
   D. 52 square feet

   Answer is B.

   Area = length times width (lw).
   Length = 13 feet
   Width = 13 feet (square, so length and width are the same)
   Area = $13 \times 13 = 169$ square feet

(Rigorous)

4. The trunk of a tree has a 2.1 meter radius. What is its circumference?

   A. 2.1π square meters
   B. 4.2π meters
   C. 2.1π meters
   D. 4.2π square meters

   Answer is B.

   Area is measured in square feet. The formula for circumference is $2\pi r$, where r is the radius. The circumference is $2\pi 2.1 = 4.2\pi$ meters (not square meters because not measuring area), which is answer B.

SKILL 4.5 Graph data on an xy-coordinate plane

COORDINATE PLANE: a plane with a point selected as an origin, some length selected as a unit of distance, and two perpendicular lines that intersect at the origin, with positive and negative direction selected on each line

A **COORDINATE PLANE** is a plane with a point selected as an origin, some length selected as a unit of distance, and two perpendicular lines that intersect at the origin, with positive and negative direction selected on each line. Traditionally, the lines are called x (drawn from left to right, with positive direction to the right of the origin) and y (drawn from bottom to top, with positive direction upward of the origin). Coordinates of a point are determined by the distance of this point from the lines, and the signs of the coordinates are determined by whether the point is in the positive or in the negative direction from the origin. The standard coordinate plane consists of a plane divided into 4 quadrants by the intersection of two axes: the x-axis (horizontal axis) and the y-axis (vertical axis).

GEOMETRY AND MEASUREMENT

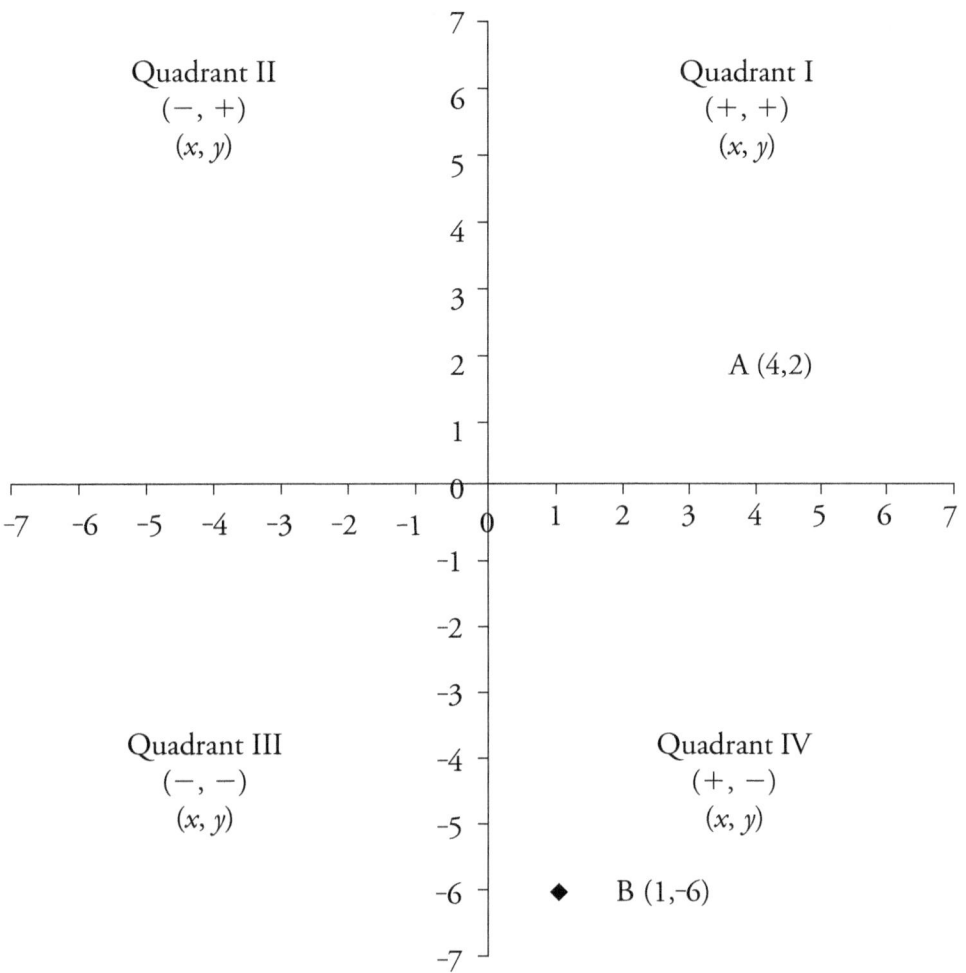

COORDINATES are a unique ordered pair of numbers that identify a point on the coordinate plane. The first number in the ordered pair identifies the position with regard to the x-axis while the second number identifies the position on the y-axis (x, y).

In the coordinate plane shown above, point A has the ordered pair (4,2); point B has the ordered pair (1,-6).

The **SLOPE** of a line is the "slant" of a line. A downward left-to-right slant means a negative slope. An upward slant is a positive slope.

The formula for calculating the slope of a line with coordinates (x^1, y^1) and (x^2, y^2) is:

$$\text{slope} = \frac{y_2 - y_1}{x_2 - x_1}$$

The top of the fraction represents the change in the y coordinates; it is called the **RISE**. The bottom of the fraction represents the change in the x coordinates, it is called the **RUN**.

> **COORDINATES:** a unique ordered pair of numbers that identify a point on the coordinate plane
>
> **SLOPE:** the "slant" of a line
>
> **RISE:** the change in the y coordinates of a line, represented by the top of the fraction in the formula for its slope
>
> **RUN:** the change in the x coordinates of a line, represented by the bottom of the fraction in the formula for its slope

MATHEMATICS

Example: Find the slope of a line with points at (2,2) and (7,8).

$\dfrac{(8)-(2)}{(7)-(2)}$ Plug the values into the formula.

$\dfrac{6}{5}$ Solve the rise over run.

$= 1.2$ Solve for the slope.

The length of a line segment is the DISTANCE between two different points, A and B. The formula for the length of a line is:

$$\text{length} = \sqrt{(x_1 - x_2)^2 + (y_1 - y_2)^2}$$

> **DISTANCE:** the length of a line segment between two different points, A and B

Example: Find the length between the points (2,2) and (7,8).

$= \sqrt{(2-7)^2 + (2-8)^2}$ Plug the values into the formula.

$= \sqrt{(-5)^2 + (-6)^2}$ Calculate the x and y differences.

$= \sqrt{25 + 36}$ Square the values.

$= \sqrt{61}$ Add the two values.

$= 7.81$ Calculate the square root.

COMPETENCY 5
DATA ANALYSIS

SKILL 5.1 Interpret information from tables, charts, and graphs

To make a bar graph or a pictograph, determine the scale to be used for the graph. Then determine the length of each bar on the graph or determine the number of pictures needed to represent each item of information. Be sure to include an explanation of the scale in the legend.

Example: A class had the following grades: 4 A's, 9 B's, 8 C's, 1 D, 3 F's. Graph these on a bar graph and a pictograph.

Pictograph

Grade	Number of Students
A	☺☺☺☺
B	☺☺☺☺☺☺☺☺☺
C	☺☺☺☺☺☺☺☺
D	☺
F	☺☺☺

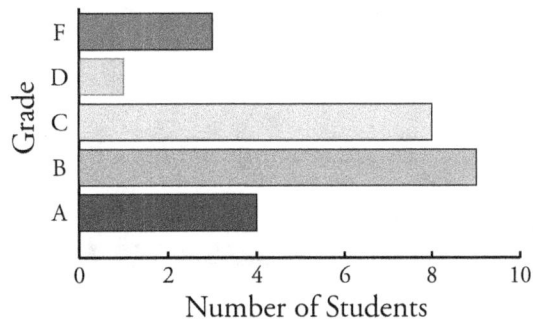

To make a line graph, determine appropriate scales for both the vertical and horizontal axes (based on the information to be graphed). Describe what each axis represents and mark the scale periodically on each axis. Graph the individual points of the graph and connect the points on the graph from left to right.

Example: Graph the following information using a line graph.

The number of National Merit finalists/school year

	90–91	91–92	92–93	93–94	94–95	95–96
Central	3	5	1	4	6	8
Wilson	4	2	3	2	3	2

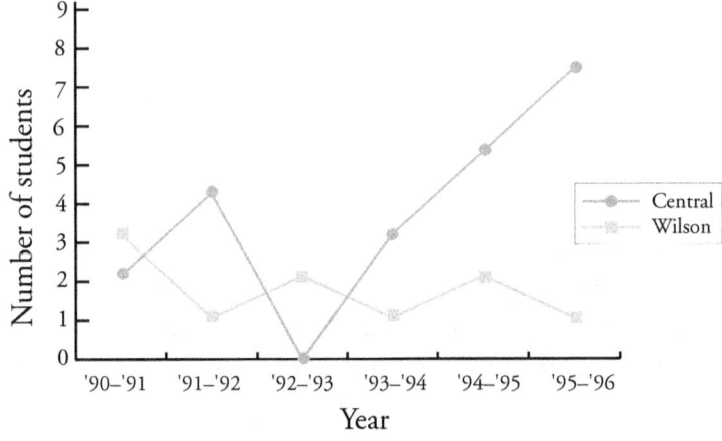

MATHEMATICS

To make a **circle graph**, total all the information that is to be included on the graph. Determine the central angle to be used for each sector of the graph using the following formula:

$$\frac{\text{information}}{\text{total information}} \times 360° = \text{degrees in central} \angle$$

Lay out the central angles to these sizes, label each section, and include its percent.

Example: Graph this information on a circle graph:

MONTHLY EXPENSES	
Rent	$400
Food	$150
Utilities	$75
Clothes	$75
Church	$100
Misc.	$200

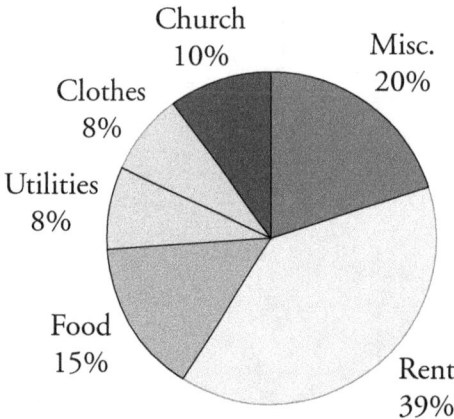

SCATTER PLOTS: compare two characteristics of the same group of things or people and usually consist of a large body of data

CORRELATION: the relationship between two variables

SCATTER PLOTS compare two characteristics of the same group of things or people and usually consist of a large body of data. They show how much one variable is affected by another. The relationship between the two variables is their **CORRELATION**. The closer the data points come to making a straight line when plotted, the closer the correlation.

DATA ANALYSIS

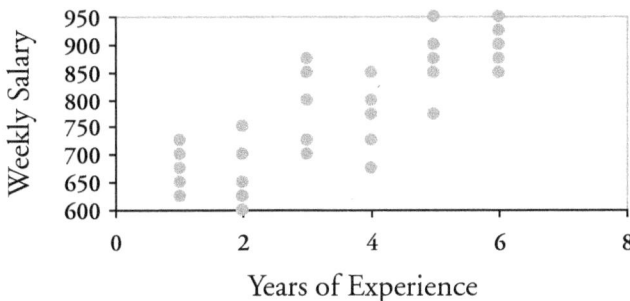

STEM AND LEAF PLOTS are visually similar to line plots. The STEMS are the digits in the greatest place value of the data values, and the LEAVES are the digits in the next greatest place values. Stem and leaf plots are best suited for small sets of data and are especially useful for comparing two sets of data. The following is an example using test scores:

4	9
5	4 9
6	1 2 3 4 6 7 8 8
7	0 3 4 6 6 6 7 7 7 8 8 8 8
8	3 5 5 7 8
9	0 0 3 4 5
10	0 0

HISTOGRAMS are used to summarize information from large sets of data that can be naturally grouped into intervals. The vertical axis indicates FREQUENCY (the number of times any particular data value occurs), and the horizontal axis indicates data values or ranges of data values. The number of data values in any interval is the FREQUENCY OF THE INTERVAL.

STEM AND LEAF PLOTS: best suited for small sets of data and are especially useful for comparing two sets of data

STEMS: the digits in the greatest place value of the data values

LEAVES: the digits in the next greatest place values

HISTOGRAMS: used to summarize information from large sets of data that can be naturally grouped into intervals

FREQUENCY: the number of times any particular data value occurs

FREQUENCY OF THE INTERVAL: the number of data values in any intervalvalue occurs

MATHEMATICS

Sample Test Questions and Rationale

(Rigorous)

1. The following chart shows the yearly average number of international tourists visiting Palm Beach for 1990–1994. How may more international tourists visited Palm Beach in 1994 than in 1991?

   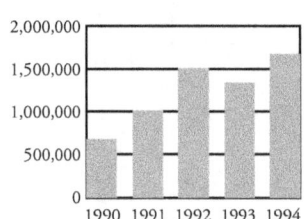

   A. 100,000
   B. 600,000
   C. 1,600,000
   D. 8,000,000

   Answer is B.

   The number of tourists in 1991 was 1,000,000 and the number in 1994 was 1,600,000. Subtract to get a difference of 600,000, which is answer B.

(Average)

2. Consider the graph of the distribution of the length of time it took individuals to complete an employment form.

   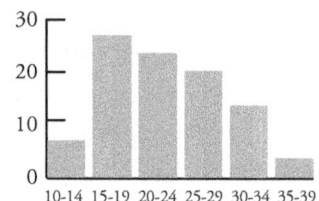

   Approximately how many individuals took less than 15 minutes to complete the employment form?

   A. 35
   B. 28
   C. 7
   D. 4

   Answer is C.

   According to the chart, the number of people who took <u>less than</u> 15 minutes is 7, which is answer C.

SKILL 5.2 Interpret trends over time given a table, chart, or graph with time-related data

TREND: shows the correlation between two sets of data on a line graph

A **TREND** line on a line graph shows the correlation between two sets of data. A trend may show positive correlation (both sets of data get bigger together), negative correlation (one set of data gets bigger while the other gets smaller), or no correlation.

An **INFERENCE** is a statement that is derived from reasoning. When reading a graph, inferences help with interpretation of the data that is being presented. From this information, a conclusion and even predictions about what the data actually means is possible.

> **INFERENCE:** a statement that is derived from reasoning

Example: Katherine and Tom were both doing poorly in math class. Their teacher had a conference with each of them in November. The following graph shows their math test scores during the school year.

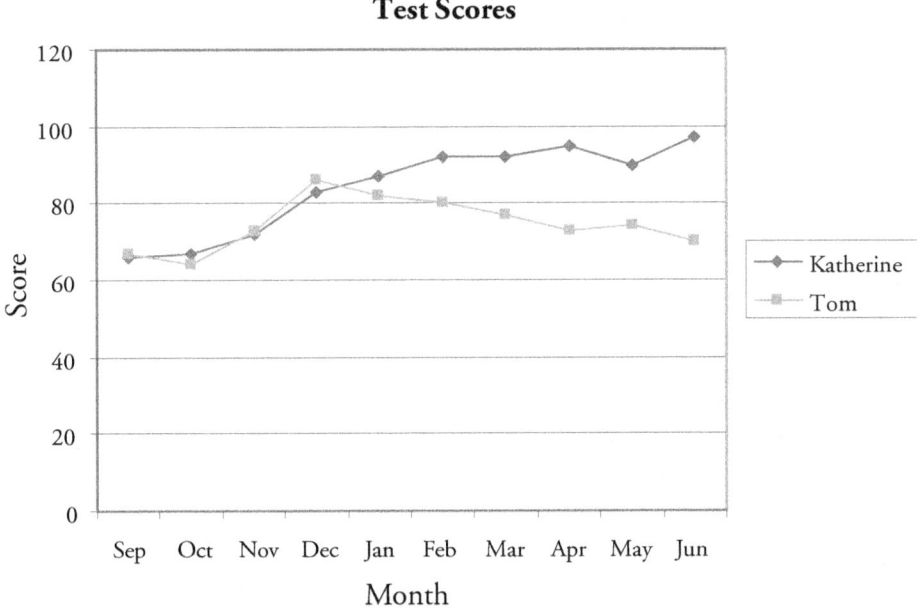

What kind of trend does this graph show?
   This graph shows that there is a positive trend in Katherine's test scores and a negative trend in Tom's test scores.

What inferences can you make from this graph?
   We can infer that Katherine's test scores rose steadily after November. Tom's test scores spiked in December but then began to fall again and became negatively trended.

What conclusion can you draw based upon this graph?
   We can conclude that Katherine took her teacher's meeting seriously and began to study in order to do better on the exams. It seems as though Tom tried harder for a bit, but his test scores eventually slipped back down to the level where he began.

MATHEMATICS

SKILL 5.3 Create basic tables, charts, and graphs

See Skill 5.1

SKILL 5.4 Compute means, medians, and modes

MEAN: the *sum* of the numbers given, *divided* by the number of items being averaged

The arithmetic MEAN (or average) of a set of numbers is the *sum* of the numbers given, *divided* by the number of items being averaged.

Example: Find the mean. Round to the nearest tenth.
24.6, 57.3, 44.1, 39.8, 64.5
  The sum is 230.3 ~ 5
  = 46.06, rounded to 46.1

MEDIAN: the middle number of a set

The MEDIAN of a set is the middle number. To calculate the median, the terms must be arranged in order. If there is an even number of terms, the median is the mean of the two middle terms.
Example: Find the median.
12, 14, 27, 3, 13, 7, 17, 12, 22, 6, 16
  Rearrange the terms.
  3, 6, 7, 12, 12, 13, 14, 16, 17, 22, 27
  Since there are 11 numbers, the middle would be the sixth number or 13.

MODE: the number that occurs with the greatest frequency in a set of numbers

The MODE of a set of numbers is the number that occurs with the greatest frequency. A set can have no mode if each term appears exactly one time. Similarly, there can be more than one mode.

Example: Find the mode.
26, 15, 37, **26**, 35, **26**, 15
  15 appears twice, but 26 appears 3 times, therefore the mode is 26.

RANGE: the difference between the highest and lowest value of data items

The RANGE is the difference between the highest and lowest value of data items.

Example: Given the ungrouped data below, calculate the mean and range.

15	22	28	25	34	38
18	25	30	33	19	23

Mean $(\bar{X}) = 25.8333333$

Range: $38 - 15 = 23$

Sample Test Question and Rationale

(Rigorous)

1. What is the mode of the data in the following sample?

   9, 10, 11, 9, 10, 11, 9, 13

   A. 9
   B. 9.5
   C. 10
   D. 11

Answer is A.

The mode is the number that appears most frequently. 9 appears 3 times, which is more than the other numbers. Therefore the answer is A.

COMPETENCY 6
APPLICATION OF MATHEMATICS SKILLS AND KNOWLEDGE TO CLASSROOM INSTRUCTION

The Math Application questions assess the examinee's ability to apply the three categories of math skills listed in Section III (Math Skills and Knowledge) in a classroom setting or in support of classroom instruction. The questions focus on testing mathematical competencies needed to assist the teacher with instruction. The test questions do not require knowledge of advanced-level mathematics vocabulary. Examinees may not use calculators.

See Competencies 3.0-5.0.

SAMPLE TEST
MATHEMATICS

(Average) (Skill 3.1)
1. $\frac{-4}{9} + \frac{-7}{10} =$
   A. $\frac{23}{90}$
   B. $\frac{-23}{90}$
   C. $\frac{103}{90}$
   D. $\frac{-103}{90}$

(Average) (Skill 3.1)
2. $5.6 \times -0.11 =$
   A. -0.616
   B. 0.616
   C. 6.110
   D. -6.110

(Average) (Skill 3.1)
3. $4\frac{2}{9} \times \frac{7}{10} =$
   A. $4\frac{9}{10}$
   B. $\frac{266}{90}$
   C. $2\frac{43}{45}$
   D. $2\frac{6}{20}$

(Rigorous) (Skill 3.1)
4. The price of gas was $3.27 per gallon. Your tank holds 15 gallons of fuel. You are using two tanks a week. How much will you save weekly if the price of gas goes down to $2.30 per gallon?
   A. $26.00
   B. $29.00
   C. $15.00
   D. $17.00

(Easy) (Skill 3.3)
5. $-9\frac{1}{4} \square -8\frac{2}{3}$
   A. $=$
   B. $<$
   C. $>$
   D. $\leq$

(Easy) (Skill 3.5)
6. $0.74 =$
   A. $\frac{74}{100}$
   B. 7.4%
   C. $\frac{33}{50}$
   D. $\frac{74}{10}$

(Average) (Skill 3.6)
7. 303 is what percent of 600?
   A. 0.505%
   B. 5.05%
   C. 505%
   D. 50.5%

(Rigorous) (Skill 3.6)
8. An item that sells for $375 is put on sale at $120. What is the percent of decrease?
   A. 25%
   B. 28%
   C. 68%
   D. 34%

(Average) (Skill 3.6)

9. A restaurant employs 465 people. There are 280 waiters and 185 cooks. If 168 waiters and 85 cooks receive pay raises, what percent of the waiters will receive a pay raise?

   A. 36.13%
   B. 60%
   C. 60.22%
   D. 40%

(Average) (Skill 3.7)

10. $(3 \times 9)^4 =$

    A. $(3 \times 9)(3 \times 9)(27 \times 27)$
    B. $(3 \times 9)(3 \times 9)$
    C. (12×36)
    D. $(3 \times 9) + (3 \times 9) + (3 \times 9) + (3 \times 9)$

(Easy) (Skill 3.8)

11. Choose the expression that is not equivalent to $5x + 3y + 15z$:

    A. $5(x + 3z) + 3y$
    B. $3(x + y + 5z)$
    C. $3y + 5(x + 3z)$
    D. $5x + 3(y + 5z)$

(Average) (Skill 3.8)

12. $\frac{7}{9} + \frac{1}{3} \div \frac{2}{3} =$

    A. $\frac{5}{3}$
    B. $\frac{3}{2}$
    C. 2
    D. $\frac{23}{18}$

(Rigorous) (Skill 3.8)

13. Choose the statement that is true for all real numbers.

    A. $a = 0, b \neq 0$, then $\frac{b}{a}$ = undefined.
    B. $-(a+(-a)) = 2a$
    C. $2(ab) = -(2a)b$
    D. $-a(b = 1) = ab - a$

(Average) (Skill 3.11)

14. Given the formula $d = rt$, (where d = distance, r = rate, and t = time), calculate the time required for a vehicle to travel 585 miles at a rate of 65 miles per hour.

    A. 8.5 hours
    B. 6.5 hours
    C. 9.5 hours
    D. 9 hours

(Rigorous) (Skill 3.11)

15. Given $f(x) = (x)^3 - 3(x)^2 + 5$, find $x = (-2)$.

    A. 15
    B. -15
    C. 25
    D. -25

(Rigorous) (Skill 3.11)

16. For each of the statements below, determine whether $x = \frac{1}{6}$ is a solution.

    i. $6x \leq 4x^2 + 2$
    ii. $10x + 1 = 3(4x - 3)$
    iii. $|x - 1| = x$

    A. i, ii, and iii

    B. i and iii

    C. i only

    D. iii only

(Easy) (Skill 3.11)

17. Choose the equation that is equivalent to the following: $\frac{3x}{5} - 5 = 5x$

    A. $3x - 25 = 25x$

    B. $x - \frac{25}{3} = 25x$

    C. $6x - 50 = 75x$

    D. $x + 25 = 25x$

(Rigorous) (Skill 3.11)

18. If, $4x - (3 - x) = 7(x - 3) + 10$, then

    A. $x = 8$

    B. $x = -8$

    C. $x = 4$

    D. $x = -4$

(Easy) (Skill 3.12)

19. Identify the missing term in the following harmonic sequence: $\frac{1}{3}, \frac{1}{6}, \frac{1}{9}, \frac{1}{12}, \frac{1}{15}$?

    A. $\frac{1}{16}$

    B. $\frac{1}{17}$

    C. $\frac{1}{18}$

    D. 18

(Rigorous) (Skill 4.1)

20. It takes 5 equally skilled people 9 hours to shingle Mr. Joe's roof. Let t be the time required for only 3 of these men to do the same job. Select the correct statement of the given condition.

    A. $\frac{3}{5} = \frac{9}{t}$

    B. $\frac{9}{5} = \frac{3}{t}$

    C. $\frac{5}{9} = \frac{3}{t}$

    D. $\frac{14}{9} = \frac{t}{5}$

(Average) (Skill 4.2)

21. Round $1\frac{13}{16}$ of an inch to the nearest quarter of an inch.

    A. $1\frac{1}{4}$ inch

    B. $1\frac{5}{8}$ inch

    C. $1\frac{3}{4}$ inch

    D. 2 inches

(Easy) (Skill 4.3)

22. What type of triangle is △ABC?

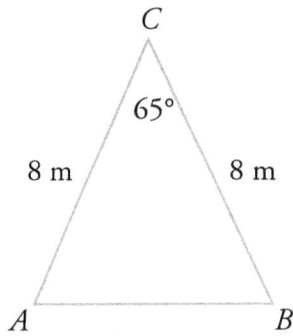

A. Right
B. Equilateral
C. Scalene
D. Isosceles

(Rigorous) (Skill 4.3)

23. Study figures A, B, C, and D. Select the letter in which all triangles are similar.

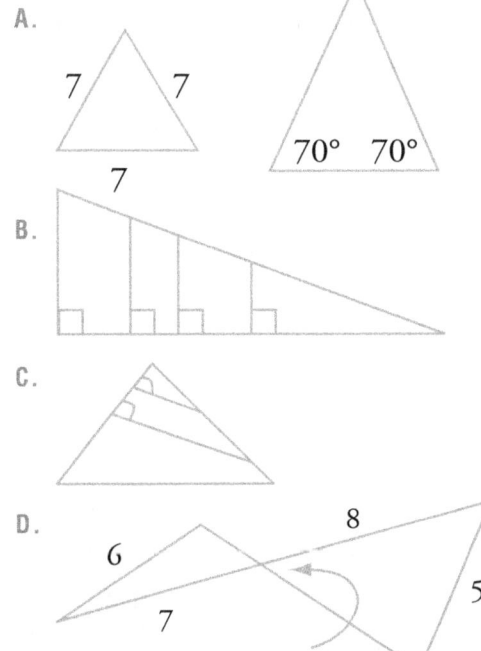

(Easy) (Skill 4.4)

24. What measure could be used to report the distance traveled in walking around a track?

A. Degrees
B. Square meters
C. Kilometers
D. Cubic feet

(Rigorous) (Skill 4.4)

25. The owner of a rectangular piece of land 40 yards in length and 30 yards in width wants to divide it into two parts. She plans to join two opposite corners with a fence as shown in the diagram below. The cost of the fence will be approximately $25 per linear foot. What is the estimated cost for the fence needed by the owner?

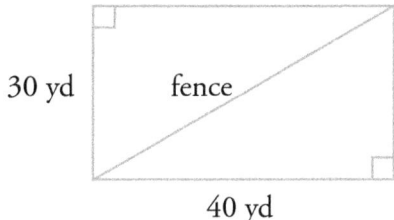

A. $1,250
B. $62,500
C. $5,250
D. $3,750

(Average) (Skill 4.4)

26. What is the area of a square whose side is 13 feet?

A. 169 feet
B. 169 square feet
C. 52 feet
D. 52 square feet

(Rigorous) (Skill 4.4)

27. The trunk of a tree has a 2.1 meter radius. What is its circumference?

    A. 2.1 π square meters

    B. 4.2 π meters

    C. 2.1 π meters

    D. 4.2 π square meters

(Rigorous) (Skill 5.1)

28. The following chart shows the yearly average number of international tourists visiting Palm Beach for 1990–1994. How may more international tourists visited Palm Beach in 1994 than in 1991?

    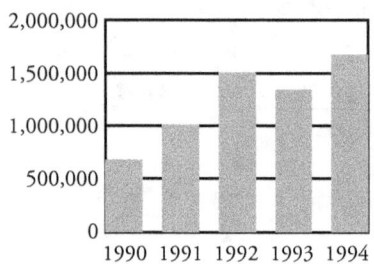

    A. 100,000

    B. 600,000

    C. 1,600,000

    D. 8,000,000

(Average) (Skill 5.1)

29. Consider the graph of the distribution of the length of time it took individuals to complete an employment form.

    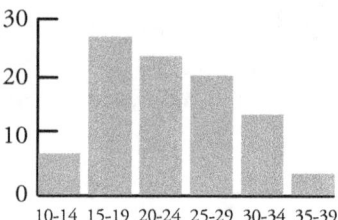

    Approximately how many individuals took less than 15 minutes to complete the employment form?

    A. 35

    B. 28

    C. 7

    D. 4

(Rigorous) (Skill 5.4)

30. What is the mode of the data in the following sample?

    9, 10, 11, 9, 10, 11, 9, 13

    A. 9

    B. 9.5

    C. 10

    D. 11

Answer Key

1. D	11. B	21. C
2. A	12. D	22. D
3. C	13. A	23. B
4. B	14. D	24. C
5. B	15. B	25. D
6. A	16. C	26. B
7. D	17. A	27. B
8. C	18. C	28. B
9. B	19. C	29. C
10. A	20. A	30. A

Rigor Table

	Easy 20%	Average Rigor 40%	Rigorous 40%
Question	5, 6, 17, 19, 22, 24	1, 2, 3, 7, 9, 10, 11, 12, 14, 21, 26, 29	4, 8, 13, 15, 16, 18, 20, 23, 25, 27, 28, 30

DOMAIN III
WRITING

WRITING

PERSONALIZED STUDY PLAN

PAGE	COMPETENCY AND SKILL	KNOWN MATERIAL/ SKIP IT
153	**7: Writing Skills and Knowledge**	☐
	7.1: Basic grammatical errors in standard written English	☐
	7.2: Errors in word usage	☐
	1.3: Errors in punctuation	☐
	7.4: Parts of a sentence	☐
	7.5: Parts of speech s	☐
	7.6: Errors in spelling	☐
198	**8: Application of Writing Skills and Knowledge to Classroom Instruction**	☐
	8.1: Use prewriting to generate and organize ideas	☐
	8.2: Identify and use appropriate reference materials	☐
	8.3: Draft and revise	☐
	8.4: Edit written documents for clarity, grammar, sentence integrity, word usage, punctuation, and spelling	☐
	8.5: Write for different purposes and audiences	☐
	8.6: Recognize and write in different modes and forms	☐

COMPETENCY 7
WRITING SKILLS AND KNOWLEDGE

SKILL 7.1 Basic grammatical errors in standard written English

See Skills 7.3 – 7.6

> **Sample Test Questions and Rationale**
>
> For sample test questions and rationales requiring a reading passage, see page 217.

SKILL 7.2 Errors in word usage (e.g., their/they're/there, then/than)

Commonly Misused Words

Accept is a verb meaning to receive or to tolerate. **Except** is usually a preposition meaning excluding. Except is also a verb meaning to exclude.

Advice is a noun meaning recommendation. **Advise** is a verb meaning to recommend.

Affect is usually a verb meaning to influence. **Effect** is usually a noun meaning result. Effect can also be a verb meaning to bring about.

An **allusion** is an indirect reference. An **illusion** is a misconception or false impression.

Add is a verb to mean to put together. **Ad** is a noun that is the abbreviation for the word advertisement.

Ain't is a common nonstandard contraction for the contraction aren't.

Allot is a verb meaning to distribute. **A lot** can be an adverb that means often, or to a great degree. It can also mean a large quantity.

Allowed is used here as an adjective that means permitted. **Aloud** is an adverb that means audibly.

Bare is an adjective that means naked or exposed. It can also indicate a minimum. As a noun, **bear** is a large mammal. As a verb, bear means to carry a heavy burden.

Capitol refers to a city or a building where lawmakers meet. **Capital** refers to wealth or resources.

A **chord** is a noun that refers to a group of musical notes. **Cord** is a noun meaning rope or a long electrical line.

Compliment is a noun meaning a praising or flattering remark. **Complement** is a noun that means something that completes or makes perfect.

Climactic is derived from climax, the point of greatest intensity in a series or progression of events. **Climatic** is derived from climate; it refers to meteorological conditions.

Discreet is an adjective that means tactful or diplomatic; **discrete** is an adjective that means separate or distinct.

Dye is a noun or verb used to indicate artificially coloring something. **Die** is a verb that means to pass away. Die is also a noun that means a cube-shaped game piece.

Effect is a noun that means outcome. **Affect** is a verb that means to act or produce an effect on.

Elicit is a verb meaning to bring out or to evoke. **Illicit** is an adjective meaning unlawful.

Emigrate means to leave one country or region to settle in another. **Immigrate** means to enter another country and reside there.

Gorilla is a noun meaning a large great ape. **Guerrilla** is a member of a band of irregular soldiers.

Hoard is a verb that means to accumulate or store up. **Horde** is a large group.

Lead is a verb that means to guide or serve as the head of. It is also a noun that is a type of metal.

Medal is a noun that means an award that is strung round the neck. **Meddle** is a verb that means to involve oneself in a matter without right or invitation. **Metal** is an element such as silver or gold. **Mettle** is a noun meaning toughness or guts.

Morning is a noun indicating the time between midnight and midday. **Mourning** is a verb or noun pertaining to the period of grieving after a death.

Past is a noun meaning a time before now (past, present, and future). **Passed** is past tense of the verb "to pass."

Piece is a noun meaning portion. **Peace** is a noun meaning the opposite of war.

Peak is a noun meaning the tip or height to reach the highest point. **Peek** is a verb that means to take a brief look. **Pique** is a verb meaning to incite or raise interest.

Principal is a noun meaning the head of a school or an organization or a sum of money. **Principle** is a noun meaning a basic truth or law.

Rite is a noun meaning a special ceremony. **Right** is an adjective meaning correct or direction. **Write** is a verb meaning to compose in writing.

Than is a conjunction used in comparisons; **then** is an adverb denoting time. That pizza is more *than* I can eat. Tom laughed, and *then* we recognized him.

There is an adverb specifying place; it is also an expletive. Adverb: Sylvia is lying *there* unconscious. Expletive: *There* are two plums left. **Their** is a possessive pronoun. **They're** is a contraction of they are. Fred and Jane finally washed *their* car. *They're* later than usual today.

To is a preposition; **too** is an adverb; **two** is a number.

Your is a possessive pronoun; **you're** is a contraction of you are.

Strategies to Help Students Conquer These Demons

Practice using them in sentences. Context is useful in understanding the difference. Drill is necessary to overcome the misuses.

To effectively teach language, it is necessary to understand that, as human beings acquire language, they realize that words have denotative and connotative meanings. Generally, denotative words point to things and connotative words deal with mental suggestions that the words convey. The word *skunk* has a denotative meaning if the speaker can point to the actual animal as he speaks the word and intends the word to identify the animal. *Skunk* has connotative meaning depending upon the tone of delivery, the socially acceptable attitudes about the animal, and the speaker's personal feelings about the animal.

WRITING

PROBLEM PHRASES	
Correct	**Incorrect**
Supposed to	Suppose to
Used to	Use to
Toward	Towards
Anyway	Anyways
Couldn't care less	Could care less
For all intents and purposes	For all intensive purposes
Come to see me	Come and see me
En route	In route
Regardless	Irregardless
Second, third	Secondly, thirdly

Other Confusing Words

Lie is an intransitive verb meaning to recline or rest on a surface. Its principal parts are lie, lay, lain. **Lay** is a transitive verb meaning to put or place. Its principal parts are lay, laid.

> *Birds lay eggs.*
> *I lie down for bed around 10 pm.*

Set is a transitive verb meaning to put or to place. Its principal parts are set, set, set. **Sit** is an intransitive verb meaning to be seated. Its principal parts are sit, sat, sat.

> *I set my backpack down near the front door.*
> *They sat in the park until the sun went down.*

Among is a preposition to be used with three or more items. **Between** is to be used with two items.

> *Between you and me, I cannot tell the difference among those three Johnson sisters.*

As is a subordinating conjunction used to introduce a subordinating clause. **Like** is a preposition and is followed by a noun or a noun phrase.

> *As I walked to the lab, I realized that the recent experiment findings were much like those we found last year.*

Can is a verb that means to be able. **May** is a verb that means to have permission. They are only interchangeable in cases of possibility.

> *I can lift 250 pounds.*
> *May I go to Alex's house?*

SKILL 7.3 Errors in punctuation

Commas

COMMAS indicate a brief pause. They are used to set off dependent clauses and long introductory word groups, to separate words in a series, to set off unimportant material that interrupts the flow of the sentence, and to separate independent clauses joined by conjunctions.

> **COMMAS:** indicate a brief pause

Error:	*After I finish my master's thesis I plan to work in Chicago.*
Problem:	A comma is needed after an introductory dependent word-group containing a subject and verb.
Correction:	*After I finish my master's thesis, I plan to work in Chicago.*
Error:	*I washed waxed and vacuumed my car today.*
Problem:	Nouns, phrases, or clauses in a list, as well as two or more coordinate adjectives that modify one word, should be separated by commas. Although the word *and* is sometimes considered optional, it is often necessary to clarify the meaning.
Correction:	*I washed, waxed, and vacuumed my car today.*

WRITING

Error:	*She was a talented dancer but she is mostly remembered for her singing ability.*
Problem:	A comma is needed before a conjunction that joins two independent clauses (complete sentences).
Correction:	*She was a talented dancer, but she is mostly remembered for her singing ability.*

Error:	*This incident is I think typical of what can happen when the community remains so divided.*
Problem:	Commas are needed between nonessential words or words that interrupt the main clause.
Correction:	*This incident is, I think, typical of what can happen when the community remains so divided.*

Semicolons and Colons

SEMICOLONS are needed to separate two or more closely related independent clauses when the second clause is introduced by a transitional adverb. (These clauses may also be written as separate sentences, preferably by placing the adverb within the second sentence.) COLONS are used to introduce lists and to emphasize what follows.

> **SEMICOLONS:** needed to separate two or more closely related independent clauses when the second clause is introduced by a transitional adverb

> **COLONS:** used to introduce lists and to emphasize what follows

Error:	*I climbed to the top of the mountain, it took me three hours.*
Problem:	A comma alone cannot separate two independent clauses. Instead a semicolon is needed to separate two related sentences.
Correction:	*I climbed to the top of the mountain; it took me three hours.*

Error:	*In the movie, asteroids destroyed Dallas, Texas, Kansas City, Missouri, and Boston, Massachusetts.*
Problem:	Semicolons are needed to separate items in a series that already contains internal punctuation.
Correction:	*In the movie, asteroids destroyed Dallas, Texas; Kansas City, Missouri; and Boston, Massachusetts.*

Error:	*Essays will receive the following grades, A for excellent, B for good, C for average, and D for unsatisfactory.*
Problem:	A colon is needed to emphasize the information or list that follows.
Correction:	*Essays will receive the following grades: A for excellent, B for good, C for average, and D for unsatisfactory.*
Error:	*The school carnival included: amusement rides, clowns, food booths, and a variety of games.*
Problem:	The material preceding the colon and the list that follows is not a complete sentence. Do not separate a verb (or preposition) from the object.
Correction:	*The school carnival included amusement rides, clowns, food booths, and a variety of games.*

Apostrophes

APOSTROPHES are used to show either contractions or possession.

> **APOSTROPHES:** used to show either contractions or possession

Error:	*She shouldnt be permitted to smoke cigarettes in the building.*
Problem:	An apostrophe is needed in a contraction in place of the missing letter.
Correction:	*She shouldn't be permitted to smoke cigarettes in the building.*
Error:	*My cousins motorcycle was stolen from his driveway. (one cousin)*
Problem:	An apostrophe is needed to show possession.
Correction:	*My cousin's motorcycle was stolen from the driveway. (Note: If two cousins owned the motorcycle, the sentence would read: My cousins' motorcycle was stolen from the driveway.)*
Error:	*The childs new kindergarten teacher was also a singer.*
Problem:	An apostrophe is needed to show possession.
Correction:	*The child's new kindergarten teacher was also a singer. (Note: The apostrophe must be added to show ownership.)*

Error: *Children laughter could be heard in the other room.*

Problem: *An apostrophe and the letter s are needed in the sentence to show whose laughter it is.*

Correction: *Children's laughter could be heard in the other room. (Note: Because the word children is already plural, the apostrophe and s must be added afterward to show ownership.)*

Quotation Marks

In a quoted statement that is either declarative or imperative, place the period inside the closing quotation marks.

> "The airplane crashed on the runway during takeoff."

If the quotation is followed by other words in the sentence, place a comma inside the closing quotations marks and a period at the end of the sentence.

> "The airplane crashed on the runway during takeoff," said the announcer.

In most instances in which a quoted title or expression occurs at the end of a sentence, the period is placed before either the single or double quotation marks.

> "The middle school readers were unprepared to understand Bryant's poem 'Thanatopsis.'"
>
> Early book-length adventure stories like Don Quixote and The Three Musketeers were known as "picaresque novels."

There is an instance in which the final quotation mark would precede the period—if the content of the sentence were about a speech or quote so that the understanding of the meaning would be confused by the placement of the period.

> The first thing out of his mouth was "Hi, I'm home."

but

> The first line of his speech began, "I arrived home to an empty house."

In sentences that are interrogatory or exclamatory, the question mark or exclamation point should be positioned outside the closing quotation marks if the quote itself is a statement or command or cited title.

> Who decided to lead us in the recitation of the "Pledge of Allegiance"?
>
> Why was Tillie shaking as she began her recitation, "Once upon a midnight dreary..."?
>
> I was embarrassed when Mrs. White said, "Your slip is showing"!

In sentences that are declarative but the quotation is a question or an exclamation, place the question mark or exclamation point inside the quotation marks.

> The hall monitor yelled, "Fire! Fire!"
>
> "Fire! Fire!" yelled the hall monitor.
>
> Cory shrieked, "Is there a mouse in the room?" (In this instance, the question supersedes the exclamation.)

Quotations—whether words, phrases, or clauses—should be punctuated according to the rules of the grammatical function they serve in the sentence.

> The works of Shakespeare, "the bard of Avon," have been contested as originating with other authors.
>
> "You'll get my money," the old man warned, "when 'Hell freezes over.'"
>
> Sheila cited the passage that began "Four score and seven years ago...." (Note the ellipsis followed by an enclosed period.)
>
> "Old Ironsides" inspired the preservation of the U.S.S. Constitution.

Use quotation marks to enclose the titles of shorter works: songs, short poems, short stories, essays, and chapters of books. (See "Using Italics" for punctuating longer titles.)

> "The Tell-Tale Heart"   "Casey at the Bat"   "America the Beautiful"

Dashes and Italics

Use DASHES to denote sudden breaks in thought.

> Some periods in literature—the Romantic Age, for example—spanned different time periods in different countries.

DASHES: used to denote sudden breaks in thought

Use dashes instead of commas if commas are already used elsewhere in the sentence for amplification or explanation.

> The Fireside Poets included three Brahmans—James Russell Lowell, Henry David Wadsworth, Oliver Wendell Holmes—and John Greenleaf Whittier.

Use ITALICS to punctuate the titles of long works of literature, names of periodical publications, musical scores, works of art and motion picture television, and radio programs. (When unable to write in italics, students should be instructed to underline in their own writing where italics would be appropriate.)

ITALICS: used to punctuate the titles of long works of literature, names of periodical publications, musical scores, works of art and motion picture television, and radio programs

> The Idylls of the King   Hiawatha   The Sound and the Fury
> Mary Poppins   Newsweek   The Nutcracker Suite

SKILL 7.4 Parts of a sentence (e.g., subject and verb/predicate)

Sentence Structure

Recognize simple, compound, complex, and compound-complex sentences. Use dependent (subordinate) and independent clauses correctly to create these sentence structures.

Simple

A simple sentence consists of one independent clause.

> *Joyce wrote a letter.*

Compound

A compound sentence consists of two or more independent clauses. The two clauses are usually connected by a coordinating conjunction (and, but, or, nor, for, so, yet). Compound sentences are sometimes connected by semicolons.

> *Joyce wrote a letter, and Dot drew a picture.*

Complex

A complex sentence consists of an independent clause plus one or more dependent clauses. The dependent clause may precede the independent clause or follow it.

> *While Joyce wrote a letter, Dot drew a picture.*

Compound-Complex

A compound-complex sentence consists of one or more dependent clauses plus two or more independent clauses.

> *When Mother asked the girls to demonstrate their new-found skills, Joyce wrote a letter, and Dot drew a picture.*

Note: Do **not** confuse compound sentence elements with compound sentences.

Simple sentence with compound subject

> *Joyce and Dot wrote letters.*
> *The girl in row three and the boy next to her were passing notes across the aisle.*

Simple sentence with compound predicate

> Joyce wrote letters and drew pictures.
> The captain of the high school debate team graduated with honors and studied broadcast journalism in college.

Simple sentence with compound object of preposition

> Colleen graded the students' essays for style and mechanical accuracy.

Types of Clauses

CLAUSES are connected word groups that are composed of at least one subject and one verb. (A subject is the doer of an action or the element that is being joined. A verb conveys either the action or the link.)

> Students are waiting for the start of the assembly.
> SUBJECT   VERB

> At the end of the play, students wait for the curtain to come down.
>   SUBJECT   VERB

CLAUSES: connected word groups that are composed of at least one subject and one verb

Clauses can be independent or dependent.

Independent clauses can stand alone or can be joined to other clauses.

Independent clause	for and nor	
Independent clause,	but or yet so	Independent clause
Independent clause	;	Independent clause
Dependent clause	,	Independent clause
Independent clause		Dependent clause

Dependent clauses, by definition, contain at least one subject and one verb. However, they cannot stand alone as a complete sentence. They are structurally dependent on the main clause.

There are two types of dependent clauses:

1. Those with a subordinating conjunction
2. Those with a relative pronoun

Sample coordinating conjunctions: Although, When, If, Unless, Because

> *Unless a cure is discovered, many more people will die of the disease.*
> DEPENDENT CLAUSE + INDEPENDENT CLAUSE

Sample relative pronouns: Who, Whom, Which, That

> *The White House has an official website, which contains press releases, news updates, and biographies of the President and Vice-President.*
> INDEPENDENT CLAUSE + RELATIVE PRONOUN + RELATIVE DEPENDENT CLAUSE

Fragments

Fragments occur:

1. If word groups standing alone are missing either a subject or a verb
2. If word groups containing a subject and verb and standing alone are actually made dependent because of the use of subordinating conjunctions or relative pronouns

Error: *The teacher waiting for the class to complete the assignment.*

Problem: This sentence is not complete because an ing word alone does not function as a verb. When a helping verb is added (for example, was waiting), it will become a sentence.

Correction: *The teacher was waiting for the class to complete the assignment.*

Error: *Until the last toy was removed from the floor.*

Problem: Words such as until, because, although, when, and if make a clause dependent and thus incapable of standing alone. An independent clause must be added to make the sentence complete.

Correction: *Until the last toy was removed from the floor, the kids could not go outside to play.*

Error: *The city will close the public library. Because of a shortage of funds.*

Problem: The problem is the same as above. The dependent clause must be joined to the independent clause.

Correction: *The city will close the public library because of a shortage of funds.*

Practice Exercise

Choose the option that corrects the underlined portion(s) of the sentence. If no error exists, choose "D. No change is necessary."

1. Despite the lack of funds in the <u>budget the city</u> found it necessary to rebuild roads that were damaged from the recent floods.
   A. budget: the city
   B. budget, the city
   C. budget; the city
   D. No change is necessary

2. After determining that the fire was caused by faulty <u>wiring, the</u> building inspector said the construction company should be fined.
   A. wiring. The
   B. wiring the
   C. wiring; the
   D. No change is necessary

3. Many years after buying a grand <u>piano Henry</u> decided he'd rather play the violin instead.
   A. piano: Henry
   B. piano, Henry
   C. piano; Henry
   D. No change is necessary

4. Computers are being used more and more <u>frequently. because</u> of their capacity to store information.
   A. frequently because
   B. frequently, because
   C. frequently; because
   D. No change is necessary

5. Doug washed the floors <u>every day. to</u> keep them clean for the guests.
   A. every day to
   B. every day,
   C. every day;
   D. No change is necessary

Answer Key

1. **B.**

   The clause that begins with *despite* is independent and must be separated with the clause that follows by a comma. Option A is incorrect because a colon is used to set off a list or to emphasize what follows. In Option B, a comma incorrectly suggests that the two clauses are dependent.

2. **D.**

   In the test item, a comma correctly separates the dependent clause *After...wiring* at the beginning of the sentence from the independent clause that follows. Option A incorrectly breaks the two clauses into separate sentences, while Options B omits the comma, and Option C incorrectly suggests that the phrase is an independent clause.

3. **B.**

   The phrase *Henry decided...instead* must be joined to the independent clause. Option A incorrectly puts a colon before *Henry decided*, and Option C incorrectly separates the phrase as if it were an independent clause.

4. **A.**

   The second clause *because...information* is dependent and must be joined to the first independent clause. Option B is incorrect because as the dependent clause comes at the end of the sentence, rather than at the beginning, a comma is not necessary. In Option C, a semicolon incorrectly suggests that the two clauses are independent.

5. **A.**

   The second clause *to keep...guests* is dependent and must be joined to the first independent clause. Option B is incorrect because as the dependent clause comes at the end of the sentence, rather than at the beginning, a comma is not necessary. In Option C, a semicolon incorrectly suggests that the two clauses are independent.

Run-on Sentences and Comma Splices

Comma splices appear when two sentences are joined by only a comma. Fused sentences appear when two sentences are run together with no punctuation at all.

WRITING SKILLS AND KNOWLEDGE

Error: *Dr. Sanders is a brilliant scientist, his research on genetic disorders won him a Nobel Prize.*

Problem: A comma alone cannot join two independent clauses (complete sentences). The two clauses can be joined by a semicolon, or they can be separated by a period.

Correction: *Dr. Sanders is a brilliant scientist; his research on genetic disorders won him a Nobel Prize.*
OR
Dr. Sanders is a brilliant scientist. His research on genetic disorders won him a Nobel Prize.

Error: *California is noted for its beaches they are long, sandy, and beautiful.*

Problem: The first sentence ends with the word beaches, and the second sentence cannot be joined with the first. The fused sentence error can be corrected in several ways: (1) one clause may be made dependent on another with a subordinating conjunction or a relative pronoun; (2) a semicolon may be used to combine two equally important ideas; (3) the two independent clauses may be separated by a period.

Correction: *California is noted for its beaches, which are long, sandy, and beautiful.*
OR
California is noted for its beaches; they are long, sandy, and beautiful.
OR
California is noted for its beaches. They are long, sandy, and beautiful.

Error: *The number of hotels has increased, however, the number of visitors has grown also.*

Problem: The first sentence ends with the word increased, and a comma is not strong enough to connect it to the second sentence. The adverbial transition however does not function the same way as a coordinating conjunction and cannot be used with commas to link two sentences. Several different corrections are available.

Correction: *The number of hotels has increased; however, the number of visitors has grown also.*
[Two separate but closely related sentences are created with the use of the semicolon.]
OR
The number of hotels has increased. However, the number of visitors has grown also.

[Two separate sentences are created.]
OR
Although the number of hotels have increased, the number of visitors has grown also.
[One idea is made subordinate to the other and separated with a comma.]
OR
The number of hotels have increased, but the number of visitors has grown also.
[The comma before the coordinating conjunction *but* is appropriate. The adverbial transition *however* does not function the same way as the coordinating conjunction *but* does.]

Practice Exercise

Choose the option that corrects an error in the underlined portion(s). If no error exists, choose "D. No change is necessary."

1. Scientists are excited at the ability to clone a <u>sheep, however</u>, it is not yet known if the same can be done to humans.

   A. sheep, however
   B. sheep. However,
   C. sheep, however;
   D. No change is necessary

2. Because of the rising cost of college <u>tuition the</u> federal government now offers special financial assistance, <u>such as loans</u>, to students.

   A. tuition, the
   B. tuition; the
   C. such as loans
   D. No change is necessary

3. As the number of homeless people continues to <u>rise, major cities</u> like <u>New York and Chicago</u>, are now investing millions of dollars in low-income housing.

   A. rise. Major cities
   B. rise; major cities
   C. New York and Chicago
   D. No change is necessary

4. Unlike <u>the 1950s, in 2008 most</u> households find the husband and wife working full-time to make <u>ends meet in many</u> different career fields.

   A. the 1950s; in 2008 most
   B. the 1950s in 2008 most
   C. ends meet, in many
   D. No change is necessary

WRITING SKILLS AND KNOWLEDGE

Answer Key

1. **B.**

   Option B correctly separates two independent clauses. The comma in Option A after the word *sheep* creates a run-on sentence. The semicolon in Option C does not separate the two clauses but occurs at an inappropriate point.

2. **A.**

   The comma in Option A correctly separates the independent clause and the dependent clause. The semicolon in Option B is incorrect because one of the clauses is independent. Option C requires a comma to prevent a run-on sentence.

3. **C.**

   Option C is correct because a comma creates a run-on. Option A is incorrect because the first clause is dependent. The semicolon in Option B incorrectly divides the dependent clause from the independent clause.

4. **D.**

   Option D correctly separates the two clauses with a comma. Option A incorrectly uses a semicolon to divide the clauses. The lack of a comma in Option B creates a run-on sentence. Option C puts a comma in an inappropriate place.

SKILL 7.5 **Parts of speech** *(nouns, verbs, pronouns, adjectives, adverbs, and prepositions)*

Standard Verb Forms

Past tense and past participles

Both regular and irregular verbs must appear in their standard forms for each tense. Note: the -ed or -d ending is added to regular verbs in the past tense and for past participles.

REGULAR VERB FORMS		
Infinitive	**Past Tense**	**Past Participle**
Bake	Baked	Baked

Table continued on next page

WRITING

Infinitive	Past Tense	Past Participle
Be	Was, were	Been
Become	Became	Become
Break	Broke	Broken
Bring	Brought	Brought
Choose	Chose	Chosen
Come	Came	Come
Do	Did	Done
Draw	Drew	Drawn
Eat	Ate	Eaten
Fall	Fell	Fallen
Forget	Forgot	Forgotten
Freeze	Froze	Frozen
Give	Gave	Given
Go	Went	Gone
Grow	Grew	Grown
Have/has	Had	Had
Hide	Hid	Hidden
Know	Knew	Known
Lay	Laid	Laid
Lie	Lay	Lain
Ride	Rode	Ridden

Table continued on next page

WRITING SKILLS AND KNOWLEDGE

Infinitive	Past Tense	Past Participle
Rise	Rose	Risen
Run	Ran	Run
See	Saw	Seen
Steal	Stole	Stolen
Take	Took	Taken
Tell	Told	Told
Throw	Threw	Thrown
Wear	Wore	Worn
Write	Wrote	Written

Error: *She should have went to her doctor's appointment at the scheduled time.*

Problem: The past participle of the verb *to go* is *gone*. *Went* expresses the simple past tense.

Correction: *She should have gone to her doctor's appointment at the scheduled time.*

Error: *My train is suppose to arrive before two o'clock.*

Problem: The verb following *train* is a present tense passive construction, which requires the present tense verb *to be* and the past participle.

Correction: *My train is supposed to arrive before two o'clock.*

Error: *Linda should of known that the car wouldn't start after leaving it out in the cold all night.*

Problem: *Should of* is a nonstandard expression. *Of* is not a verb.

Correction: *Linda should have known that the car wouldn't start after leaving it out in the cold all night.*

WRITING

Practice Exercise

Choose the option that corrects an error in the underlined portion(s). If no error exists, choose "D. No change is necessary."

1. My professor **had knew** all along that we would pass his course.
   A. know
   B. had known
   C. knowing
   D. No change is necessary

2. Kevin was asked to erase the vulgar words he **had wrote**.
   A. writes
   B. has write
   C. had written
   D. No change is necessary

3. Melanie **had forget** to tell her parents that she left the cat in the closet.
   A. had forgotten
   B. forgot
   C. forget
   D. No change is necessary

4. Craig always **leave** the house a mess when his parents aren't there.
   A. left
   B. leaves
   C. leaving
   D. No change is necessary

5. The store manager accused Kathy of **having stole** more than five hundred dollars from the safe.
   A. has stolen
   B. having stolen
   C. stole
   D. No change is necessary

Answer Key

1. **B.**

   Option B is correct because the past participle needs the helping verb *had*. Option A is incorrect because it is in the infinitive tense. Option C incorrectly uses the present participle.

2. **C.**

   Option C is correct because the past participle follows the helping verb *had*. Option A uses the verb in the present tense. Option B is an incorrect use of the verb.

3. **A.**

   Option A is correct because the past participle uses the helping verb *had*. Option B uses the wrong form of the verb. Option C uses the wrong form of the verb.

4. **B.**

   Option B correctly uses the past tense of the verb. Option A uses the verb in an incorrect way. Option C uses the verb without a helping verb like *is*.

5. **B.**

   Option B is correct because it is the present participle. Option A and C use the verb incorrectly.

Inappropriate shifts in verb tense

Verb tenses must refer to the same time period consistently, unless a change in time is required.

Error: *Despite the increased amount of students in the school this year, overall attendance is higher last year at the sporting events.*

Problem: The verb is represents an inconsistent shift to the present tense when the action refers to a past occurrence.

Correction: *Despite the increased amount of students in the school this year, overall attendance was higher last year at sporting events.*

WRITING

Error: *My friend Lou, who just competed in the marathon, ran since he was twelve years old.*

Problem: Because Lou continues to run, the present perfect tense is needed.

Correction: *My friend Lou, who just competed in the marathon, has run since he was twelve years old.*

Error: *The Mayor congratulated Wallace Mangham, who renovates the city hall last year.*

Problem: Although the speaker is talking in the present, the action of renovating the city hall was in the past.

Correction: *The Mayor congratulated Wallace Mangham, who renovated the city hall last year.*

WRITING SKILLS AND KNOWLEDGE

Practice Exercise

Choose the option that corrects an error in the underlined portion(s). If no error exists, choose "D. No change is necessary."

1. After we <u>washed</u> the fruit that had <u>growing</u> in the garden, we knew there <u>was</u> a store that would buy it.

   A. washing
   B. grown
   C. is
   D. No change is necessary

2. The tourists <u>used</u> to visit the Atlantic City boardwalk whenever they <u>vacationed</u> during the summer. Unfortunately, their numbers have <u>diminished</u> every year.

   A. use
   B. vacation
   C. diminish
   D. No change is necessary

3. When the temperature <u>drops</u> to below thirty-two degrees Fahrenheit, the water on the lake <u>freezes</u>, which <u>allowed</u> children to skate across it.

   A. dropped
   B. froze
   C. allows
   D. No change is necessary

4. The artists were <u>hired</u> to <u>create</u> a monument that would pay tribute to the men who were <u>killed</u> in World War II.

   A. hiring
   B. created
   C. killing
   D. No change is necessary

5. Emergency medical personnel rushed to the scene of the shooting, where many injured people <u>waiting</u> for treatment.

   A. wait
   B. waited
   C. waits
   D. No change is necessary

Answer Key

1. **B.**

    The past participle *grown* is needed instead of *growing*, which is the progressive tense. Option A is incorrect because the past participle *washed* takes the *ed*. Option C incorrectly replaces the past participle *was* with the present tense *is*.

2. **D.**

    Option A is incorrect because *use* is the present tense. Option B incorrectly uses the noun *vacation*. Option C incorrectly uses the present tense *diminish* instead of the past tense *diminished*.

3. **C.**

    The present tense *allows* is necessary in the context of the sentence. Option A is incorrect because *dropped* is a past participle. Option B is incorrect because *froze* is also a past participle.

4. **D.**

    Option A is incorrect because *hiring* is the present tense. Option B is incorrect because *created* is a past participle. In Option C, *killing* doesn't fit into the context of the sentence.

5. **B.**

    In Option B, *waited* corresponds with the past tense *rushed*. In Option A, *wait* is incorrect because it is present tense. In Option C, *waits* is incorrect because the noun *people* is plural and requires the singular form of the verb.

Agreement between Subject and Verb

A verb must correspond in the singular or plural form with the simple subject; it is not affected by any interfering elements. Note: A simple subject is never found in a prepositional phrase (a phrase beginning with a word such as *of, by, over, through, until*).

WRITING SKILLS AND KNOWLEDGE

PRESENT TENSE VERB FORM		
	Singular	**Plural**
1st person (talking about oneself)	I do	We do
2nd person (talking to another)	You do	You do
3rd person (talking about someone or something)	He She does It	They do

Error: *Sally, as well as her sister, plan to go into nursing.*

Problem: The subject in the sentence is Sally alone, not the word sister. Therefore, the verb must be singular.

Correction: *Sally, as well as her sister, plans to go into nursing.*

Error: *There has been many car accidents lately on that street.*

Problem: The subject *accidents* in this sentence is plural; the verb must be plural also—even though it comes before the subject.

Correction: *There have been many car accidents lately on that street.*

Error: *Every one of us have a reason to attend the school musical.*

Problem: The simple subject is the *one*, not the *us* in the prepositional phrase. Therefore, the verb must be singular also.

Correction: *Every one of us has a reason to attend the school musical.*

Error: *Either the police captain or his officers is going to the convention.*

Problem: In either/or and neither/nor constructions, the verb agrees with the subject closer to it.

Correction: *Either the police captain or his officers are going to the convention.*

WRITING

Practice Exercise

Choose the option that corrects an error in the underlined portion(s). If no error exists, choose "No change is necessary."

1. Every year, the store <u>stays</u> open late while shoppers desperately <u>try</u> to purchase Christmas presents as they <u>prepare</u> for the holiday.
   - A. stay
   - B. tries
   - C. prepared
   - D. No change is necessary

2. Paul McCartney, joined by George Harrison and Ringo Starr, <u>sing</u> classic Beatles songs on a special greatest-hits CD.
   - A. singing
   - B. sings
   - C. sung
   - D. No change is necessary

3. My friend's cocker spaniel always <u>manages</u> to <u>knock</u> over the trash cans while <u>chasing</u> cats across the street.
   - A. chased
   - B. manage
   - C. knocks
   - D. No change is necessary

4. Some of the ice on the driveway <u>have melted</u>.
   - A. having melted.
   - B. has melted.
   - C. has melt.
   - D. No change is necessary

5. Neither the criminal forensics experts nor the DNA blood evidence <u>provide</u> enough support for that verdict.
   - A. provides
   - B. were providing
   - C. are providing
   - D. No change is necessary

Answer Key

1. **D.**

   Option D is correct because *store* is third person singular and requires the third person singular verbs *stays*. Option B is incorrect because the plural noun *shoppers* requires a plural verb *try*. In Option C, there is no reason to shift to the past tense *prepared*.

2. **B.**

   Option B is correct because the subject, *Paul McCartney*, is singular and requires the singular verb *sings*. Option A is incorrect because the present participle *singing* does not stand alone as a verb. Option C is incorrect because the past participle *sung* alone cannot function as the verb in this sentence.

3. **D.**

   Option D is the correct answer because the subject *cocker spaniel* is singular and requires the singular verb *manages*. Options A, B, and C do not work structurally with the sentence.

4. **B.**

   The subject of the sentence is *some*, which requires a third person singular verb, *has melted*. Option A incorrectly uses the present participle *having*, which does not act as a helping verb. Option C does not work structurally with the sentence.

5. **A.**

   In Option A, the singular subject *evidence* is closer to the verb and thus requires the singular in the neither/nor construction. Both Options B and C are plural forms with the helping verb and the present participle.

Plural Nouns

A good dictionary is an invaluable resource that can replace the need to learn complex spelling rules based on phonics or letter doubling, especially when the exceptions to these rules have not been mastered by adulthood. Learning to use a dictionary and a thesaurus will be a rewarding use of time.

Most plurals of nouns that end in hard consonants or in hard consonant sounds followed by a silent *e* are made by adding -*s*. Plurals of some words ending in vowels are formed by adding only -*s*.

> *fingers, numerals, banks, bugs, riots, homes, gates, radios, bananas*

For nouns that end in soft consonant sounds—*s, j, x, z, ch*, and *sh*—the plurals are formed by adding -*es*. Plurals of some nouns ending in *o* are formed by adding -*es*.

> *dresses, waxes, churches, brushes, tomatoes*

For nouns ending in *y* preceded by a vowel, just add -*s*.

> *boys, alleys*

For nouns ending in *y* preceded by a consonant, change the *y* to *i* and add -*es*.

> *babies, corollaries, frugalities, poppies*

Some nouns' plurals are formed irregularly or remain the same.

> *sheep, deer, children, leaves, oxen*

Some nouns derived from foreign words, especially Latin words, are made plural in two different ways. Sometimes the meanings are the same; other times the two plural forms are used in slightly different contexts. It is always wise to consult the dictionary.

> *appendices, appendixes*   *criterion, criteria*
> *indexes, indices*   *crisis, crises*

Make the plurals of closed (solid) compound words in the usual way.

> *timelines, hairpins*
> *cupfuls, handfuls*

Make the plurals of open or hyphenated compounds by adding the change in inflection to the word that changes in number.

> *fathers-in-law, courts-martial, masters of art, doctors of medicine*

Make the plurals of letters, numbers, and abbreviations by adding *-s*.

fives and tens, IBMs, 1990s, ps and qs (Note that letters are italicized.)

Possessive Nouns

Make the possessives of singular nouns by adding an apostrophe followed by the letter *s* (*'s*).

baby's bottle, mother's job, elephant's eye, teacher's desk, sympathizer's protests, week's postponement

Make the possessives of singular nouns ending in *s* by adding either an apostrophe or an apostrophe followed by the letter *s*, depending upon common usage or sound. When the possessive sounds awkward, use a prepositional phrase instead. Even with the sibilant ending, with a few exceptions, it is advisable to use the *'s* construction.

dress's color, species' characteristics (or characteristics of the species), James' hat (or James's hat), Dolores's shirt

Make the possessives of plural nouns ending in *s* by adding an apostrophe after the *s*.

horses' coats, jockeys' times, four days' time

Make the possessives of plural nouns that do not end in s by adding *'s*, just as with singular nouns.

children's shoes, deer's antlers, cattle's horns

Make the possessives of compound nouns by adding the inflection at the end of the word or phrase.

the mayor of Los Angeles' campaign, the mailman's new truck, the mailmen's new trucks, my father-in-law's first wife, the keepsakes' values, several daughters-in-law's husbands

Agreements between Pronoun and Antecedent

A pronoun must correspond to its antecedent in number (singular or plural), person (first, second, or third person) and gender (male, female, or neutral). A pronoun must refer clearly to a single word, not to a complete idea.

A **PRONOUN SHIFT** is a grammatical error in which the author starts a sentence, paragraph, or section of a paper using one particular type of pronoun and then suddenly shifts to another. This often confuses the reader.

> **PRONOUN SHIFT:** a grammatical error in which the author starts a sentence, paragraph, or section of a paper using one particular type of pronoun and then suddenly shifts to another

Error: *A teacher should treat all their students fairly.*

Problem: Since *A teacher* is singular, the pronoun referring to it must also be singular. Otherwise, the noun has to be made plural.

Correction: *A teacher should treat all his [or her] students fairly.*
OR
Teachers should treat all their students fairly.

Error: *When an actor is rehearsing for a play, it often helps if you can memorize the lines in advance.*

Problem: *Actor* is a third-person word; that is, the writer is talking about the subject. The pronoun *you* is in the second person, which means the writer is talking to the subject.

Correction: *When actors are rehearsing for plays, it helps if they can memorize the lines in advance.*

Error: *The workers in the factory were upset when his or her paychecks didn't arrive on time.*

Problem: *Workers* is a plural form, while *his or her* refers to one person.

Correction: *The workers in the factory were upset when their paychecks didn't arrive on time.*

Error: *The charity auction was highly successful, which pleased everyone.*

Problem: In this sentence the pronoun *which* refers to the idea of the auction's success. In fact, *which* has no antecedent in the sentence; the word *success* is not stated.

Correction: *Everyone was pleased at the success of the auction.*

Error: *Lana told Melanie that she would like aerobics.*

Problem: The person that *she* refers to is unclear; *she* could be either Lana or Melanie.

Correction: *Lana said that Melanie would like aerobics.*
OR
Lana told Melanie that she, Melanie, would like aerobics.

Error: *I dislike accounting, even though my brother is one.*

Problem: A person's occupation is not the same as a field, and the pronoun *one* is thus incorrect. Note that the word *accountant* is not used in the sentence, so *one* has no antecedent.

Correction: *I dislike accounting, even though my brother is an accountant.*

WRITING

Practice Exercise

Choose the option that corrects an error in the underlined portion(s). If no error exists, choose "D. No change is necessary."

1. <u>You</u> can get to Martha's Vineyard by driving from Boston to Woods Hole. Once there, you can travel over on a boat, but <u>you</u> may find traveling by <u>airplane</u> to be an exciting experience.

   A. They
   B. visitors
   C. it
   D. No change is necessary

2. Both the city leader and the <u>journalist</u> are worried about the new interstate; <u>she fears the new roadway</u> will destroy precious farmland.

   A. journalist herself
   B. they fear
   C. it
   D. No change is necessary

3. When <u>hunters</u> are looking for deer in <u>the woods</u>, <u>you</u> must remain quiet for long periods of time.

   A. they
   B. it
   C. we
   D. No change is necessary

4. Florida's strong economy is based on the citrus industry. <u>Producing</u> orange juice for most of the country.

   A. They produce
   B. Who produce
   C. Farmers there produce
   D. No change is necessary

5. Dr. Kennedy told Paul, <u>his</u> assistant, that <u>he</u> would have to finish grading the tests before going home, no matter how long <u>it</u> took.

   A. their
   B. Paul
   C. they
   D. No change is necessary

WRITING SKILLS AND KNOWLEDGE

Answer Key

1. **D.**

   Pronouns must be consistent. As *you* is used throughout the sentence, the shift to *visitors* is incorrect. Option A, *They*, is vague and unclear. Option C, *it*, is also unclear.

2. **B.**

   The plural pronoun *they* is necessary to agree with the two nouns *leader* and *journalist*. There is no need for the reflexive pronoun *herself* in Option A. Option C, *it*, is vague.

3. **A.**

   The shift to *you* is unnecessary. The plural pronoun *they* is necessary to agree with the noun *hunters*. The word *we* in Option C is vague; the reader does not know who the word *we* might refer to. Option B, *it*, has no antecedent.

4. **C.**

   The noun *farmers* is needed for clarification because *producing* is vague. Option A is incorrect because *they produce* is vague. Option B is incorrect because *who* has no antecedent and creates a fragment.

5. **B.**

   The repetition of the name *Paul* is necessary to clarify who the pronoun *he* is referring to. (It could be Dr. Kennedy.) Option A is incorrect because the singular pronoun *his* is needed, not the plural pronoun *their*. Option C is incorrect because the pronoun *it* refers to the plural noun *tests*.

Rules for Clear Pronoun References

Make sure that the antecedent reference is clear and cannot refer to something else
A "distant relative" is a relative pronoun or a relative clause that has been placed too far away from the antecedent to which it refers. It is a common error to place a verb between the relative pronoun and its antecedent.

Error: *Return the books to the library that are overdue.*

Problem: The relative clause "that are overdue" refers to the "books" and should be placed immediately after the antecedent.

Correction: *Return the books that are overdue to the library.*
OR
Return the overdue books to the library.

A pronoun should not refer to adjectives or possessive nouns

Adjectives, nouns, and possessive pronouns should not be used as antecedents. This will create ambiguity in sentences.

Error: *In Todd's letter, he told his mom he'd broken the priceless vase.*

Problem: In this sentence the pronoun *he* seems to refer to the noun phrase *Todd's letter*, though it was probably meant to refer to the possessive noun *Todd's*.

Correction: *In his letter, Todd told his mom that he had broken the priceless vase.*

A pronoun should not refer to an implied idea

A pronoun must refer to a specific antecedent rather than an implied antecedent. When an antecedent is not stated specifically, the reader has to guess or assume the meaning of a sentence. Pronouns that do not have antecedents are called expletives. "It" and "there" are the most common expletives, though other pronouns can also become expletives as well. In informal conversation, expletive allow for casual presentation of ideas without supporting evidence. However, in more formal writing, it is best to be more precise.

Error: *She said that it is important to floss every day.*

Problem: The pronoun *it* refers to an implied idea.

Correction: *She said that flossing every day is important.*

Error: *They returned the book because there were missing pages.*

Problem: The pronouns *they* and *there* do not refer to the antecedent.

Correction: *The customer returned the book with missing pages.*

Using who, that, and which

Who, **whom**, and **whose** refer to human beings and can either introduce essential or nonessential clauses. **That** refers to things other than humans and is used to introduce essential clauses. **Which** refers to things other than humans and is used to introduce nonessential clauses.

Error: *The doctor that performed the surgery said the man would recover fully.*

Problem: Since the relative pronoun is referring to a human, *who* should be used.

Correction: *The doctor who performed the surgery said the man would fully recover.*

Error: *That ice cream cone that you just ate looked really delicious.*

Problem: *That* has already been used, so you must use *which* to introduce the next clause, whether it is essential or nonessential.

Correction: *That ice cream cone which you just ate looked really delicious.*

Proper Case Forms

Pronouns, unlike nouns, change case forms. Pronouns must be in the subjective, objective, or possessive form according to their function in the sentence.

Personal Pronouns

	SUBJECTIVE (NOMINATIVE)		POSSESSIVE		OBJECTIVE	
	Singular	Plural	Singular	Plural	Singular	Plural
1st person	I	We	My	Our	Me	Us
2nd person	You	You	Your	Your	You	You
3rd person	He She It	They	His Her Its	Their	Him Her It	them

WRITING

Relative Pronouns

Who	Subjective/Nominative
Whom	Objective
Whose	Possessive

Error: *Tom and me have reserved seats for next week's baseball game.*

Problem: The pronoun *me* is the subject of the verb *have reserved* and should be in the subjective form.

Correction: *Tom and I have reserved seats for next week's baseball game.*

Error: *Mr. Green showed all of we students how to make paper hats.*

Problem: The pronoun *we* is the object of the preposition *of*. It should be in the objective form, *us*.

Correction: *Mr. Green showed all of us students how to make paper hats.*

Error: *Who's coat is this?*

Problem: The interrogative possessive pronoun is *whose*; *who's* is the contraction for *who is*.

Correction: *Whose coat is this?*

Error: *The voters will choose the candidate whom has the best qualifications for the job.*

Problem: The case of the relative pronoun *who* or *whom* is determined by the pronoun's function in the clause in which it appears. The word *who* is in the subjective case, and *whom* is in the objective. Analyze how the pronoun is being used within the sentence.

Correction: *The voters will choose the candidate who has the best qualifications for the job.*

Practice Exercise

Choose the option that corrects an error in the underlined portion(s). If no error exists, choose "D. No change is necessary."

1. Even though Sheila and <u>he</u> had planned to be alone at the diner, <u>they</u> were joined by three friends of <u>their's</u> instead.

   A. him

   B. him and her

   C. theirs

   D. No change is necessary

2. Uncle Walter promised to give his car to <u>whomever</u> will guarantee to drive it safely.

   A. whom

   B. whoever

   C. them

   D. No change is necessary

3. Eddie and <u>him</u> gently laid <u>the body</u> on the ground next to the sign.

   A. he

   B. them

   C. it

   D. No change is necessary

4. Mary, <u>who</u> is competing in the chess tournament, is a better player than <u>me</u>.

   A. whose

   B. whom

   C. I

   D. No change is necessary

5. <u>We, ourselves,</u> have decided not to buy property in that development; however, our friends have already bought <u>themselves</u> some land.

   A. We, ourself,

   B. their selves

   C. their self

   D. No change is necessary

WRITING

> ## Answer Key
>
> 1. **C.**
>
>   The possessive pronoun *theirs* doesn't need an apostrophe. Option A is incorrect because the subjective pronoun *he* is needed in this sentence. Option B is incorrect because the subjective pronoun *they*, not the objective pronouns *him* and *her*, is needed.
>
> 2. **B.**
>
>   The subjective case *whoever*—not the objective case *whomever*—is the subject of the relative clause *whoever will guarantee to drive it safely*. Option A is incorrect because *whom* is an objective pronoun. Option C is incorrect because *car* is singular and takes the pronoun *it*.
>
> 3. **A.**
>
>   The subjective pronoun *he* is needed as the subject of the verb *laid*. Option B is incorrect because *them* is vague; the noun *body* is needed to clarify *it*. Option C is incorrect because *it* is vague, and the noun *sign* is necessary for clarification.
>
> 4. **C.**
>
>   The subjective pronoun *I* is needed because the comparison is understood. Option A incorrectly uses the possessive *whose*. Option B is incorrect because the subjective pronoun *who*, and not the objective *whom*, is needed.
>
> 5. **B.**
>
>   The reflexive pronoun *themselves* refers to the plural *friends*. Option A is incorrect because the plural *we* requires the reflexive *ourselves*. Option C is incorrect because the possessive pronoun *their* is never joined with either *self* or *selves*.

Correct Use of Adjectives and Adverbs

Adjectives are words that modify or describe nouns or pronouns. Adjectives usually precede the words they modify, but not always; for example, an adjective occurs after a linking verb.

Adverbs are words that modify verbs, adjectives, or other adverbs. They cannot modify nouns. Adverbs answer such questions as how, why, when, where, how much, or how often something is done. Many adverbs are formed by adding -ly.

Error: *The birthday cake tasted sweetly.*

Problem: *Tasted* is a linking verb; the modifier that follows should be an adjective, not an adverb.

Correction: *The birthday cake tasted sweet.*

Error: *You have done good with this project.*

Problem: *Good* is an adjective and cannot be used to modify a verb phrase such as *have done*.

Correction: *You have done well with this project.*

Error: *The coach was positive happy about the team's chance of winning.*

Problem: The adjective *positive* cannot be used to modify another adjective, *happy*. An adverb is needed instead.

Correction: *The coach was positively happy about the team's chance of winning.*

Error: *The fireman acted quick and brave to save the child from the burning building.*

Problem: *Quick* and *brave* are adjectives and cannot be used to describe a verb. Adverbs are needed instead.

Correction: *The fireman acted quickly and bravely to save the child from the burning building.*

WRITING

Practice Exercise

Choose the option that corrects an error in the underlined portion(s). If no error exists, choose "D. No change is necessary."

1. Moving **quick** throughout the house, the burglar **removed** several priceless antiques before **carelessly** dropping his wallet.
   A. quickly
   B. remove
   C. careless
   D. No change is necessary

2. The car **crashed loudly** into the retaining wall before spinning **wildly** on the sidewalk.
   A. crashes
   B. loudly
   C. wild
   D. No change is necessary

3. The airplane **landed safe** on the runway after **nearly** colliding with a helicopter.
   A. land
   B. safely
   C. near
   D. No change is necessary

4. The **horribly bad** special effects in the movie disappointed us **great**.
   A. horrible
   B. badly
   C. greatly
   D. No change is necessary

5. The man promised to **faithfully** obey the rules of the social club.
   A. faithful
   B. faithfulness
   C. faith
   D. No change is necessary

Answer Key

1. **A.**

   The adverb *quickly* is needed to modify *moving*. Option B is incorrect because it uses the wrong form of the verb. Option C is incorrect because the adverb *carelessly* is needed before the verb *dropping*, not the adjective *careless*.

2. **D.**

   The sentence is correct as it is written. Adverbs *loudly* and *wildly* are needed to modify *crashed* and *spinning*. Option A incorrectly uses the verb *crashes* instead of the participle *crashing*, which acts as an adjective.

3. **B.**

   The adverb *safely* is needed to modify the verb *landed*. Option A is incorrect because *land* is a noun. Option C is incorrect because *near* is an adjective, not an adverb.

4. **C.**

   The adverb *greatly* is needed to modify the verb *disappointed*. Option A is incorrect because *horrible* is an adjective, not an adverb. Option B is incorrect because *bad* needs to modify the adverb *horribly*.

5. **D.**

   The adverb *faithfully* is the correct modifier of the verb *promised*. Option A is an adjective used to modify nouns. Neither Option B nor Option C, both of which are nouns, is a modifier.

Appropriate Comparative and Superlative Degree Forms

When comparisons are made, the correct form of the adjective or adverb must be used. The comparative form is used for two items. The superlative form is used for more than two.

WRITING

	Comparative	**Superlative**
slow	slower	slowest
young	younger	youngest
tall	taller	tallest
With some words, more and most are used to make comparisons instead of -er and -est.		
quiet	more quiet	most quiet
energetic	more energetic	most energetic
quick	more quickly	most quickly

Comparisons must be made between similar structures or items. In the sentence "My house is similar in color to Steve's," one house is being compared to another house as understood by the use of the possessive Steve's.

On the other hand, if the sentence reads "My house is similar in color to Steve," the comparison would be faulty because it would be comparing the house to Steve, not to Steve's house.

Error: *Last year's rides at the carnival were bigger than this year.*

Problem: In the sentence as it is worded above, the rides at the carnival are being compared to this year, not to this year's rides.

Correction: *Last year's rides at the carnival were bigger than this year's.*

SKILL 7.6 Errors in spelling

See Skill 7.5

Spelling correctly is not always easy because English not only utilizes an often inconsistent spelling system, but also uses many words derived from other languages. Good spelling is important because incorrect spelling damages the physical appearance of writing and may puzzle your reader.

WRITING SKILLS AND KNOWLEDGE

COMMONLY MISSPELLED WORDS			
commitment	patience	height	guarantee
succeed	obstinate	leisurely	tropical
necessary	achievement	shield	misfortune
connected	responsibility	foreign	particular
opportunity	prejudice	innovative	yield
embarrassed	familiar	similar	possession
occasionally	hindrance	proceed	accumulate
receive	controversial	contemporary	hospitality
their	publicity	beneficial	judgment
accelerate	prescription	attachment	conscious

I before E

i before e	grieve, fiend, niece, friend
except after c	receive, conceive, receipt
or when sounded like "a"	as in reindeer, weight, and reign
Exceptions:	weird, foreign, seize, leisure

WRITING

Practice Exercise

Circle the correct spelling of the word in each parenthesis.

1. The (shield, sheild) protected the gladiator from serious injury.
2. Tony (received, recieved) an award for his science project.
3. Our (neighbors, nieghbors), the Thomsons, are in the Witness Protection Program.
4. Janet's (friend, freind), Olivia, broke her leg while running the marathon.
5. She was unable to (conceive, concieve) a child after her miscarriage.
6. Rudolph the Red-Nosed (Riendeer, Reindeer) is my favorite Christmas song.
7. The farmer spent all day plowing his (feild, field).
8. Kat's (wieght, weight) loss plan failed, and she gained twenty pounds!
9. They couldn't (beleive, believe) how many people showed up for the concert.
10. Ruby's (niece, neice) was disappointed when the movie was sold out.

Answer Key

1. shield
2. received
3. neighbors
4. friend
5. conceive
6. reindeer
7. field
8. weight
9. believe
10. niece

WRITING SKILLS AND KNOWLEDGE

Practice Exercise

Add suffixes to the following words and write the correct spelling form in the blanks.

1. swing + ing = _____
2. use + able = _____
3. choke + ing = _____
4. furnish + ed = _____
5. punish + ment = _____
6. duty + ful = _____
7. bereave + ment = _____
8. shovel + ing = _____
9. argue + ment = _____
10. connect + ed = _____
11. remember + ed = _____
12. treat + able = _____
13. marry + s = _____
14. recycle + able = _____
15. waste + ful = _____
16. pray + ing = _____
17. reconstruct + ing = _____
18. outrage + ous = _____

Answer Key

1. swinging
2. useable
3. choking
4. furnished
5. punishment
6. dutiful
7. bereavement
8. shoveling
9. argument
10. connected
11. remembered
12. treatable
13. marries
14. recyclable
15. wasteful
16. praying
17. reconstructing
18. outrageous

WRITING

COMPETENCY 8
APPLICATION OF WRITING SKILLS AND KNOWLEDGE TO CLASSROOM INSTRUCTION

> **SKILL 8.1** Use prewriting to generate and organize ideas *(including freewriting and using outlines)*

Prewriting

Students gather ideas before writing. PREWRITING may include clustering, listing, brainstorming, mapping, free writing, and charting. Providing many ways for a student to develop ideas on a topic will increase his or her chances for success.

Remind students that as they prewrite they need to consider their audience. Prewriting strategies assist students in a variety of ways. Listed below are the most common prewriting strategies students can use to explore, plan, and write on a topic. It is important to remember when teaching these strategies that not all prewriting must eventually produce a finished piece of writing. In fact, in the initial lesson of teaching prewriting strategies, it might be more effective to have students practice prewriting strategies without the pressure of having to write a finished product.

PREWRITING: may include clustering, listing, brainstorming, mapping, free writing, and charting

- Keep an idea book so that they can jot down ideas that come to mind.
- Write in a daily journal.
- Write down whatever comes to mind; this is called free writing. Students do not stop to make corrections or interrupt the flow of ideas.

A variation of this technique is focused FREE WRITING—writing on a specific topic—to prepare for an essay.

FREE WRITING: writing on a specific topic

- Make a list of all ideas connected with their topic; this is called BRAINSTORMING.

BRAINSTORMING: making a list of all ideas connected with their topic

- Make sure students know that this technique works best when they let their mind work freely. After completing the list, students should analyze the list to see if there is a pattern or way to group the ideas.
- Ask the questions Who? What? When? Where? When? and How? Help the writer approach a topic from several perspectives.
- Create a visual map on paper to gather ideas. Cluster circles and lines to show connections between ideas. Students should try to identify the relationship

that exists between their ideas. If they cannot see the relationships, have them pair up, and exchange papers and have their partners look for some related ideas.

- Observe details of sight, hearing, taste, touch, and smell.
- Visualize by making mental images of something and write down the details in a list.

Creating a Working Outline

A good thesis gives structure to your essay and helps focus your thoughts. When forming your thesis, look at your prewriting strategy—clustering, questioning, or brainstorming. Then decide quickly which two or three major areas you'll discuss. Remember you must limit the scope of the paper because of the time factor.

The OUTLINE lists those main areas or points as topics for each paragraph.

Looking at the prewriting cluster on computers, you might choose several areas in which computers help us—for example, in science and medicine, business, and education. You might also consider people's reliance on this "wonder" and include at least one paragraph about this reliance. A formal outline for this essay might look like this:

I. Introduction and thesis
II. Computers used in science and medicine
III. Computers used in business
IV. Computers used in education
V. People's reliance on computers
VI. Conclusion

> **OUTLINE:** lists those main areas or points as topics for each paragraph

Under time pressure, however, you may use a shorter organizational plan, such as abbreviated key words in a list. For example:

1. intro: wonders of the computer   OR   a. intro: wonders of computers—science
2. science   b. in the space industry
3. med   c. in medical technology
4. schools   d. conclusion
5. business
6. conclusion

After they have practiced with each of these prewriting strategies, ask them to pick out the ones they prefer and ask them to discuss how they might use the techniques to help them with future writing assignments. It is important to remember that they can use more than one prewriting strategy at a time. They may find that different writing situations suggest certain techniques.

WRITING

SKILL 8.2 Identify and use appropriate reference materials

It is necessary for each student to become knowledgeable about, and comfortable with using, all instructional resources. But the primary skill each student must acquire is the ability to identify their assignment's specific problem, issue, or need to be addressed. If this can be understood and verbalized, the student will be able to select the appropriate resource tool from among the available resources once these have been introduced, used, and understood.

As early as possible, we try to instill the skills necessary to make each child an independent researcher. The teaching faculty and library and support staff should work together to ensure that all students know the location of, and have access to, all appropriate learning resources, whether in the classroom, the school library, a lab, or another resource center. The students should be made familiar with the layout of each resource center and understand the operations of available equipment. This could be anything from a card catalogue to a computer terminal or microfilm reader.

Working with each student to associate appropriate resources with identifiable needs is primary. Teaching effective and efficient use of each resource is the next concern. Time and practice (preferably, with prescribed exercises) should be expended on the rudiments of using explicit directives (such as tables of contents, indices, or Web browsers) to make a necessary search expeditious, effective and even fun. Repeated and purposeful practice is the surest method of instilling these skills in young students. Children are sometimes impulsive and impatient. Even after students have been taught proper reference and research procedure and technique, many will choose to just jump right into the text and slog back and forth through the pages, randomly, seeking an answer.

While it can never be by nature instinctive, it should become second nature for the student (through practice) to always reference a table of contents and/or index to expedite the search, avoid frustration, and make the task easier.

SKILL 8.3 Draft and revise *(including composing or refining a thesis statement, writing focused and organized paragraphs, and writing a conclusion)*

Even before you select a topic, determine what each prompt is asking you to discuss. This first decision is crucial. If you pick a topic you don't really understand or about which you have little to say, you'll have difficulty developing your essay. So take a few moments to analyze each topic carefully *before* you begin to write.

Topic A: A modern invention that can be considered a wonder of the world

In general, the topic prompts have two parts:

- The *subject* of the topic
- An *assertion* about the subject

The SUBJECT is a *modern invention*. In this prompt, the word *modern* indicates that you should discuss something invented recently, at least in this century. The word *invention* indicates you're to write about something created by humans (not natural phenomena such as mountains or volcanoes). You may discuss an invention that has potential for harm, such as chemical warfare or the atomic bomb; or you may discuss an invention that has the potential for good: the computer, DNA testing, television, antibiotics, and so on.

> **SUBJECT:** relates directly to the topic but expresses the specific area you have chosen to discuss

The ASSERTION (a statement of point of view) is that *the invention has such powerful or amazing qualities that it should be considered a wonder of the world*. The assertion states your point of view about the subject, and it limits the range for discussion. In other words, you would discuss particular qualities or uses of the invention, not just discuss how it was invented or whether it should have been invented at all.

> **ASSERTION:** a statement of point of view

Note also that this particular topic encourages you to use examples to show the reader that a particular invention is a modern wonder. Some topic prompts lend themselves to essays with an argumentative edge—one in which you take a stand on a particular issue and persuasively prove your point. Here, you undoubtedly could offer examples or illustrations of the many "wonders" and uses of the particular invention you chose.

Be aware that misreading or misinterpreting the topic prompt can lead to serious problems. Papers that do not address the topic occur when one reads too quickly or only half-understands the topic. This may happen if you misread or misinterpret words. Misreading can also lead to a paper that addresses only part of the topic prompt rather than the entire topic.

To develop a complete essay, spend a few minutes planning. Jot down your ideas and quickly sketch an outline. Although you may feel under pressure to begin writing, you will write more effectively if you plan out your major points.

Prewriting

Before actually writing, you'll need to generate content and develop a writing plan. The following are three prewriting techniques that can be helpful.

Brainstorming

When brainstorming, quickly create a list of words and ideas that are connected to the topic. Let your mind roam free to generate as many relevant ideas as possible in a few minutes. For example, on the topic of computers you may write:

- Computer—modern invention
- Types—personal computers, micro-chips in calculators and watches
- Wonder—acts like an electronic brain
- Uses—science, medicine, offices, homes, schools
- Problem—too much reliance; the machines aren't perfect

This list helps you focus on the topic and states the points you could develop in the body paragraphs. The brainstorming list keeps you on track and is well worth the few minutes it takes to jot down the ideas. While you haven't ordered the ideas, seeing them on paper is an important step.

Questioning

Questioning helps you focus as you mentally ask a series of exploratory questions about the topic. You may use the five W's, the five most basic questions: **who**, **what**, **where**, **when**, **why**, and **how**.

"**What** is my subject?"
[computers]

"**What** types of computers are there?"
[personal computers, micro-chip computers]

"**Why** have computers been a positive invention?"
[acts like an electronic brain in machinery and equipment; helps solve complex scientific problems]

"**How** have computers been a positive invention?"
[used to make improvements in:
- science (space exploration, moon landings)
- medicine (MRIs, CAT scans, surgical tools, research models)
- business (PCs, FAX, telephone equipment)
- education (computer programs for math, languages, science, social studies), and
- personal use (family budgets, tax programs, healthy diet plans)]

"**How** can I show that computers are good?"
[citing numerous examples]

APPLICATION OF WRITING SKILLS AND KNOWLEDGE TO CLASSROOM INSTRUCTION

"**What** problems do I see with computers?"
[too much reliance; not yet perfect]

"**What** personal experiences would help me develop examples to respond to this topic?"
[my own experiences using computers]

Of course, you may not have time to write out the questions completely. You might just write the words *who, what, where, why,* and *how* and the major points next to each. An abbreviated list might look as follows:

What—computers/modern wonder/making life better
How—through technological improvements: lasers, calculators, CAT scans, MRIs
Where—in science and space exploration, medicine, schools, offices

In a few moments, your questions should help you to focus on the topic and generate interesting ideas and points to make in the essay. Later in the writing process, you can look back at the list to be sure you've made the key points you intended to make.

Clustering

Some visual thinkers find clustering an effective prewriting method. When clustering, you draw a box in the center of your paper and write your topic within that box. Then you draw lines from the center box and connect it to small satellite boxes that contain related ideas. Note the cluster below on computers:

SAMPLE CLUSTER

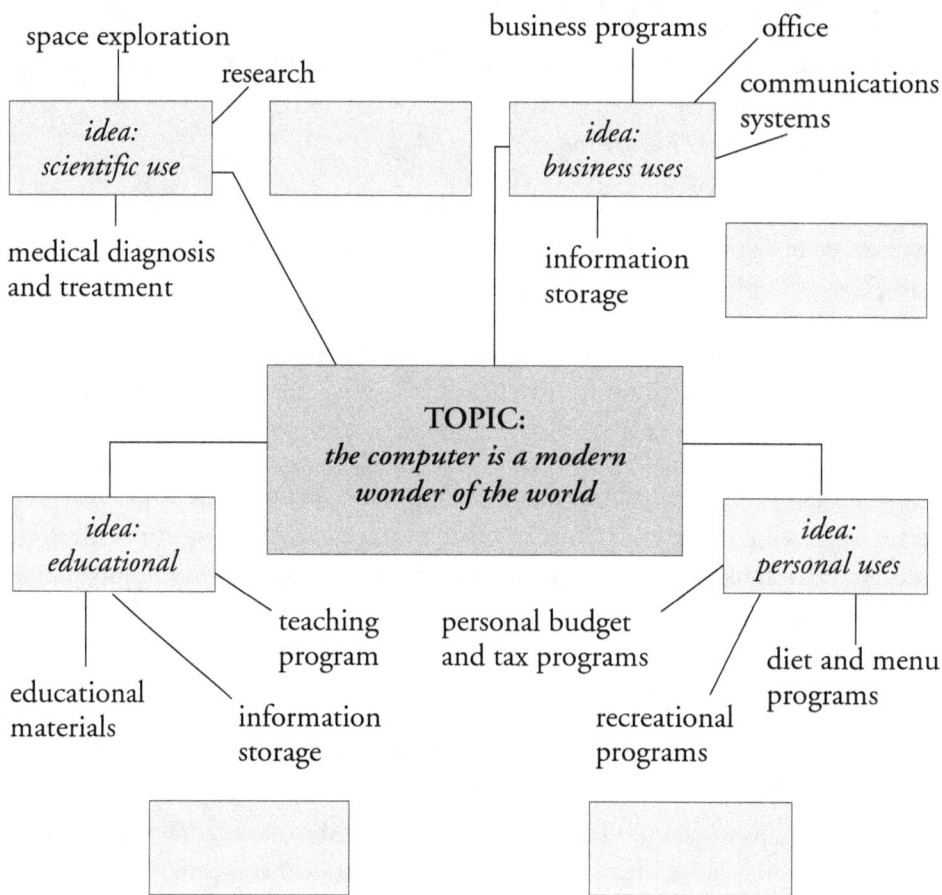

Writing the Thesis

After focusing on the topic and generating your ideas, form your thesis, which is the controlling idea of your essay. The thesis is your general statement to the reader that expresses your point of view and guides your essay's purpose and scope. The thesis should allow you either to explain your subject or to take an arguable position about it. A strong thesis statement is neither too narrow nor too broad.

Subject and assertion of the thesis

From the analysis of the general topic, you saw the topic in terms of its two parts—*subject* and *assertion*. On the exam, your thesis or viewpoint on a particular topic is stated in two important points:

- The *subject* of the paper
- The *assertion* about the subject

The subject of the thesis relates directly to the topic prompt but expresses the specific area you have chosen to discuss. (Remember, the exam topic will be general and will allow you to choose a particular subject related to the topic.) For example, the computer is one modern invention.

The assertion of the thesis is your viewpoint, or opinion, about the subject. The assertion provides the motive or purpose for your essay, and it may be an arguable point or one that explains or illustrates a point of view.

For example, you may present an argument for or against a particular issue. You may contrast two people, objects, or methods to show that one is better than the other. You may analyze a situation in all aspects and make recommendations for improvement. You may assert that a law or policy should be adopted, changed, or abandoned. You may also, as in the computer example, explain to your reader that a situation or condition exists; rather than argue a viewpoint, you would use examples to illustrate your assertion about the essay's subject.

Specifically, the subject of Topic A is *the computer*. The assertion is that *it is a modern wonder that has improved our lives and that we rely on*. Now you have created a workable thesis in a few moments:

The computer is a modern wonder of the world that has improved our lives and that we have come to rely on.

Guidelines for writing thesis statements

The following guidelines are not a formula for writing thesis statements, but rather are general strategies for making your thesis statement clearer and more effective.

1. State a *particular point of view* about the topic with both a *subject* and an *assertion*. The thesis should give the essay purpose and scope and thus provide the reader a guide. If the thesis is vague, your essay may be undeveloped because you do not have an idea to assert or a point to explain. Weak thesis statements are often framed as facts, questions, or announcements:

    A. Avoid a fact statement as a thesis. While a fact statement may provide a subject, it generally does not include a point of view about the subject that provides the basis for an extended discussion.

        Example: *Recycling saved our community over $10,000 last year.* This fact statement provides a detail, not a point of view. Such a detail might be found within an essay, but it does not state a point of view.

    B. Avoid framing the thesis as a vague question. In many cases, rhetorical questions do not provide a clear point of view for an extended essay.

Example: *How do people recycle?* This question neither asserts a point of view nor helpfully guides the reader to understand the essay's purpose and scope.

C. Avoid the "announcer" topic sentence that merely states the topic you will discuss.

Example: *I will discuss ways to recycle.* This sentence states the subject, but the scope of the essay is only suggested. Again, this statement does not assert a viewpoint that guides the essay's purpose. It merely "announces" that the writer will write about the topic.

2. Start with a workable thesis. You might revise your thesis as you begin writing and discover your own point of view.

3. If feasible and appropriate, perhaps state the thesis in multi-point form, expressing the scope of the essay. By stating the points in parallel form, you clearly lay out the essay's plan for the reader.

Example: *To improve the environment, we can recycle our trash, elect politicians who see the environment as a priority, and support lobbying groups who work for environmental protection.*

4. Because of the exam time limit, place your thesis in the first paragraph to key the reader to the essay's main idea.

Creating a working outline
See Skill 8.1

Developing the Essay

With a working thesis and outline, you can begin writing the essay. The essay should be in three main sections:

1. The **introduction** sets up the essay and leads to the thesis statement.

2. The **body paragraphs** are developed with concrete information leading from the topic sentences.

3. The **conclusion** ties the essay together.

Introduction

Put your thesis statement into a clear, coherent opening paragraph. One effective device is to use a funnel approach in which you begin with a brief description of the broader issue and then move to a clearly focused, specific thesis statement.

Consider the following introductions to the essay on computers. The length of each is an obvious difference. Read each and consider the other differences.

- Does each introduce the subject generally?
- Does each lead to a stated thesis?
- Does each relate to the topic prompt?

Introduction 1: *Computers are used every day. They have many uses. Some people who use them are workers, teachers, and doctors.*

Analysis: This introduction does give the general topic—computers used every day—but it does not explain what those uses are. This introduction does not offer a point of view in a clearly stated thesis, nor does it convey the idea that computers are a modem wonder.

Introduction 2: *Computers are used just about everywhere these days. I don't think there's an office around that doesn't use computers, and we use them a lot in all kinds of jobs. Computers are great for making life easier and work better. I don't think we'd get along without the computer.*

Analysis: This introduction gives the general topic about computers and mentions one area that uses computers. The thesis states that people couldn't get along without computers, but it does not state the specific areas the essay discusses. Note, too, the meaning is not helped by vague diction such as a lot or great.

Introduction 3: *Each day we either use computers or see them being used around us. We wake to the sound of a digital alarm operated by a microchip. Our cars run by computerized machinery. We use computers to help us learn. We receive phone calls and letters transferred from computers across continents. Our astronauts walked on the moon, and returned safely, all because of computer technology. The computer is like a wonderful electronic brain that we have come to rely on, and it has changed our world through advances in science, business, and education.*

Analysis: This introduction is the most thorough and fluent because it provides interest in the general topic and offers specific information about computers as a modern wonder. It also leads to a thesis that directs the reader to the scope of the discussion—advances in science, business, and education.

Topic Sentences

Just as the essay must have an overall focus reflected in the thesis statement, each paragraph must have a central idea reflected in the topic sentence. A good topic sentence also provides transition from the previous paragraph and relates to the essay's thesis. Good topic sentences, therefore, provide unity throughout the essay.

Consider the following potential topic sentences. Be sure that each provides transition and clearly states the subject of the paragraph.

Topic Sentence 1: *Computers are used in science.*

Analysis: This sentence simply states the topic—computers used in science. It does not relate to the thesis or provide transition from the introduction. The reader still does not know how computers are used.

Topic Sentence 2: *Now I will talk about computers used in science.*

Analysis: Like the faulty "announcer" thesis statement, this "announcer" topic sentence is vague and merely names the topic.

Topic Sentence 3: *First, computers used in science have improved our lives.*

Analysis: The transition word *First* helps link the introduction and this paragraph. It adds unity to the essay. It does not, however, give specifics about the improvement computers have made in our lives.

Topic Sentence 4: *First used in scientific research and spaceflights, computers are now used extensively in the diagnosis and treatment of disease.*

Analysis: This sentence is the most thorough and fluent. It provides specific areas that will be discussed in the paragraph and offers more than an announcement of the topic. The writer gives concrete information about the content of the paragraph that will follow.

SUMMARY GUIDELINES FOR WRITING TOPIC SENTENCES
Specifically relate the topic to the thesis statement.
State clearly and concretely the subject of the paragraph.
Provide some transition from the previous paragraph.
Avoid topic sentences that are facts, questions, or announcers.

Supporting Details

If you have a good thesis and a good outline, you should be able to construct a complete essay. Your paragraphs should contain concrete, interesting information and supporting details to support your point of view. As often as possible, create images in your reader's mind. Fact statements also add weight to your opinions, especially when you are trying to convince the reader of your viewpoint. Because every good thesis has an assertion, you should offer specifics, facts, data, anecdotes, expert opinion, and other details to *show* or *prove* that assertion. While *you* know what you mean, your *reader* does not. On the exam, you must explain and develop ideas as fully as possible in the time allowed.

In the following paragraph, the sentences in **bold print** provide a skeleton of a paragraph on the benefits of recycling. The sentences in bold are generalizations that by themselves do not explain the need to recycle. The sentences in *italics* add details to SHOW the general points in bold. Notice how the supporting details help you understand the necessity for recycling.

> **While one day recycling may become mandatory in all states, right now it is voluntary in many communities.** *Those of us who participate in recycling are amazed by how much material is recycled.* **For many communities, the blue-box recycling program has had an immediate effect.** *By just recycling glass, aluminum cans, and plastic bottles, we have reduced the volume of disposable trash by one third, thus extending the useful life of local landfills by over a decade. Imagine the difference if those dramatic results were achieved nationwide.* **The amount of reusable items we thoughtlessly dispose of is staggering.** *For example, Americans dispose of enough steel everyday to supply Detroit car manufacturers for three months. Additionally, we dispose of enough aluminum annually to rebuild the nation's air fleet. These statistics, available from the Environmental Protection Agency (EPA), should encourage all of us to watch what we throw away.* **Clearly, recycling in our homes and in our communities directly improves the environment.**

Notice how the author's supporting examples enhance the message of the paragraph and relate to the author's thesis noted above. If you only read the bold-face sentences, you have a glimpse at the topic. This paragraph of illustration, however, is developed through numerous details creating specific images: *reduced the volume of disposable trash by one-third; extended the useful life of local landfills by more than a decade; enough steel everyday to supply Detroit car manufacturers for three months; enough aluminum to rebuild the nation's air fleet.* If the writer had merely written a few general sentences, as those shown in bold face, you would not fully understand the vast amount of trash involved in recycling or the positive results of current recycling efforts.

Concluding paragraph

End your essay with a brief, straightforward **concluding paragraph** that ties together the essay's content and leaves the reader with a sense of its completion. The conclusion should reinforce the main points and offer some insight into the topic, provide a sense of unity for the essay by relating it to the thesis, and signal clear closure of the essay.

WRITING

> **SKILL 8.4** Edit written documents for clarity, grammar, sentence integrity *(run-ons and sentence fragments)*, **word usage, punctuation, and spelling**

Techniques for Revising Written Texts to Achieve Clarity and Economy of Expression

Enhancing interest

- Start out with an attention-grabbing introduction. This sets an engaging tone for the entire piece and will be more likely to pull the reader in.

- Use dynamic vocabulary and varied sentence beginnings. Keep the readers on their toes. If they can predict what you are going to say next, switch it up.

- Avoid using clichés (as cold as ice, the best thing since sliced bread, nip it in the bud). These are easy shortcuts, but they are not interesting, memorable, or convincing.

Ensuring understanding

- Avoid using the words "clearly," "obviously," and "undoubtedly." Often, things that are clear or obvious to the author are not as apparent to the reader. Instead of using these words, make your point so strongly that it is clear on its own.

- Use the word that best fits the meaning you intend, even if it is longer or a little less common. Try to find a balance, and go with a familiar yet precise word.

- When in doubt, explain further.

Revision of sentences to eliminate wordiness, ambiguity, and redundancy

Sometimes this exercise is seen by students as simply catching errors in spelling or word use. Students need to reframe their thinking about revising and editing. Some questions that need to be asked are:

- Is the reasoning coherent?
- Is the point established?
- Does the introduction make the reader want to read this discourse?
- What is the thesis? Is it proven?
- What is the purpose? Is it clear? Is it useful, valuable, interesting?

- Is the style of writing so wordy that it exhausts the reader and interferes with engagement?
- Is the writing so spare that it is boring?
- Are the sentences too uniform in structure?
- Are there too many simple sentences?
- Are too many of the complex sentences the same structure?
- Are the compounds truly compounds or are they unbalanced?
- Are parallel structures truly parallel?
- If there are characters, are they believable?
- If there is dialogue, is it natural or stilted?
- Is the title appropriate?
- Does the writing show creativity or is it boring?
- Is the language appropriate? Is it too formal? Too informal? If jargon is used, is it appropriate?

Studies have clearly demonstrated that the most fertile area in teaching writing is this one. If students can learn to revise their own work effectively, they are well on their way to becoming effective, mature writers. Word processing is an important tool for teaching this stage in the writing process. Microsoft Word has tracking features that make the revision exchanges between teachers and students more effective than ever before.

Techniques to maintain focus

- **Focus on a main point:** The point should be clear to readers, and all sentences in the paragraph should relate to it.
- **Start the paragraph with a topic sentence:** This should be a general, one-sentence summary of the paragraph's main point, relating both back toward the thesis and toward the content of the paragraph. (A topic sentence is sometimes unnecessary if the paragraph continues a developing idea clearly introduced in a preceding paragraph, or if the paragraph appears in a narrative of events where generalizations might interrupt the flow of the story.)
- **Stick to the point:** Eliminate sentences that do not support the topic sentence.
- **Be flexible:** If there is not enough evidence to support the claim your topic sentence is making, do not fall into the trap of wandering or introducing new ideas within the paragraph. Either find more evidence or adjust the topic sentence to collaborate with the evidence that is available.

WRITING

Sample Test Questions and Rationale

DIRECTIONS: Choose the option that best expresses the meaning of the underlined sentence. If it should not be changed, choose Option A, "No change."

(Rigorous)

1. Selecting members of a President's cabinet can often be an aggravating process. <u>Either there are too many or too few qualified candidates for a certain position, and then they have to be confirmed by the Senate, where there is the possibility of rejection.</u>

   A. No change
   B. Qualified candidates for certain positions face the possibility of rejection, when they have to be confirmed by the Senate
   C. The Senate has to confirm qualified candidates, who face the possibility of rejection
   D. Because the Senate has to confirm qualified candidates; they face the possibility of rejection

   Answer is C.

   Option C is the most straightforward and concise sentence. Option A is too unwieldy with the wordy *Either ... or phrase* at the beginning. Option B doesn't make clear the fact that candidates face rejection by the Senate. Option D illogically implies that candidates face rejection because they have to be confirmed by the Senate.

(Rigorous)

2. Treating patients for drug and/or alcohol abuse is a difficult process. <u>Even though there are a number of different methods for helping the patient overcome a dependency, there is no way of knowing which is best in the long run.</u>

   A. No change
   B. Even though different methods can help a patient overcome a dependency, there is no way to know which is best in the long run
   C. Even though there is no way to know which way is best in the long run, patients can overcome their dependencies when they are helped
   D. There is no way to know which method will help the patient overcome a dependency in the long run, even though there are many different ones

   Answer is B.

   Option B is concise and logical. Option A tends to ramble with the use of there are and the verbs *helping* and *knowing*. Option C is awkwardly worded and repetitive in the first part of the sentence and vague in the second because it never indicates how the patients can be helped. Option D contains the unnecessary phrase *even though there are many different ones.*

Sample Test Questions and Rationale (cont.)

(Rigorous)

3. Many factors account for the decline in quality of public education. <u>Overcrowding, budget cutbacks, and societal deterioration which have greatly affected student learning.</u>

    A. No change

    B. Student learning has been greatly affected by overcrowding, budget cutbacks, and societal deterioration

    C. Due to overcrowding, budget cutbacks, and societal deterioration, student learning has been greatly affected

    D. Overcrowding, budget cutbacks, and societal deterioration have affected student learning greatly

Answer is B.

Option B is concise and best explains the causes of the decline in student education. The unnecessary use of *which* in Option A makes the sentence feel incomplete. Option C has weak coordination between the reasons for the decline in public education and the fact that student learning has been affected. Option D incorrectly places the adverb *greatly* after *learning*, instead of before affected.

DIRECTIONS: Choose the sentence that logically and correctly expresses the comparison.

(Average)

4. A. The Empire State Building in New York is taller than buildings in the city

    B. The Empire State Building in New York is taller than any other building in the city

    C. The Empire State Building in New York is tallest than other buildings in the city

Answer is B.

Because the Empire State Building is a building in New York City, the phrase any other must be included. Option A is incorrect because the Empire State Building is implicitly compared to itself since it is one of the buildings. Option C is incorrect because *tallest* is the incorrect form of the adjective.

(Average)

5. Many of the clubs in Boca Raton are noted for their _____ elegance.

    A. vulgar

    B. tasteful

    C. ordinary

Answer is B.

Tasteful means beautiful or charming, which would correspond to an elegant club. The words *vulgar* and *ordinary* have negative connotations.

WRITING

Sample Test Questions and Rationale

(Average)

6. When a student is expelled from school, the parents are usually _____ in advance.

   A. rewarded
   B. congratulated
   C. notified

Answer is C.

Notified means informed or told, which fits the sentence. The words *rewarded* and *congratulated* have positive connotations and don't make sense regarding someone being expelled from school.

SKILL 8.5 **Write for different purposes and audiences** *(including using appropriate language and taking a position for or against something)*

Tailoring language for a particular audience is an important skill. Writing to be read by a business associate will surely sound different from writing to be read by a younger sibling. Not only are the vocabularies different, but the formality/informality of the discourse will need to be adjusted.

Determining what the language should be for a particular audience, then, hinges on two things: word choice and formality/informality. The most formal language does not use contractions or slang. The most informal language will probably feature a more casual use of common sayings and anecdotes. Formal language will use longer sentences and will not sound like a conversation. The most informal language will use shorter sentences—not necessarily simple sentences, but shorter constructions—and may sound like a conversation.

> **TONE:** the writer's attitude toward the material and/or readers
>
> **CONNOTATIONS:** attach affective meanings to words

TONE exists in both formal and informal writing. Tone is the writer's attitude toward the material and/or readers. Tone may be playful, formal, intimate, angry, serious, ironic, outraged, baffled, tender, serene, depressed, and so on. The overall tone of a piece of writing is dictated by both the subject matter and the audience. Tone is also related to the actual words that make up the document as we attach affective meanings to words, called CONNOTATIONS. Gaining this conscious control over language makes it possible to use language appropriately in various situations and to evaluate its uses in literature and other forms of communication. By evoking the proper responses from readers/listeners, we can prompt them to take action.

APPLICATION OF WRITING SKILLS AND KNOWLEDGE TO CLASSROOM INSTRUCTION

The following questions are an excellent way to assess the audience and tone of a given piece of writing.

1. Who is your audience? (friend, teacher, business person, someone else)

2. How much does this person know about you and/or your topic?

3. What is your purpose? (to prove an argument, to persuade, to amuse, to register a complaint, to ask for a raise)

4. What emotions do you have about the topic? (nervous, happy, confident, angry, sad, no feelings at all)

5. What emotions do you want to register with your audience? (anger, nervousness, happiness, boredom, interest)

6. What persona do you need to create in order to achieve your purpose?

7. What choice of language is best suited to achieving your purpose with your particular subject? (slang, friendly but respectful, formal)

8. What emotional quality do you want to transmit to achieve your purpose (matter of fact, informative, authoritative, inquisitive, sympathetic, angry) and to what degree do you want to express this tone?

Persuasive writing features facts and opinions that are used to get the reader to agree with something the author believes. Persuasive writing may have as its purpose getting you to change your mind, take a position on an issue, perform an action, or judge an event. Of course, there are many different ways to accomplish this goal. Authors may be straightforward and objective, in which case they will marshal a number of facts to support a position. Alternatively, authors may use emotional words, and in so doing, reveal their personal preferences, biases, or strongly held opinions. While news articles aim to inform, other commonly read material such as editorials, reviews, and letters generally contain an element of persuasion.

SKILL 8.6 Recognize and write in different modes and forms (e.g., descriptive essays, persuasive essays, narratives, letters)

An essay is an extended discussion of a writer's point of view about a particular topic. This point of view may be supported by using such writing modes as examples, argument and persuasion, analysis, or comparison/contrast. In any case, a good essay is clear, coherent, well organized, and fully developed.

WRITING

> **BASIC EXPOSITORY WRITING:** gives information not previously known about a topic, or explains or defines a topic

> **DESCRIPTIVE WRITING:** centers on a person, place, or object, using concrete and sensory words to create a mood or impression and arranges details in a chronological or spatial sequence

> **NARRATIVE WRITING:** developed using an incident or anecdote or a related series of events

> **PERSUASIVE WRITING:** implies the writer's ability to select vocabulary and arrange facts and opinions to direct the actions of the reader

> **JOURNALISTIC WRITING:** theoretically free of writer bias

When authors set out to write a passage, they usually have a purpose for doing so. That purpose may be to give information that might be interesting or useful to a reader; it may be to persuade the reader to a point of view or to move the reader to act in a particular way; it may be to tell a story; or it may be to describe something in such a way that an experience becomes available to the reader through one of the five senses. There are five primary devices for expressing a particular purpose in a piece of writing:

BASIC EXPOSITORY WRITING gives information not previously known about a topic, or explains or defines a topic. Facts, examples, statistics, statements of cause and effect, direct tone, objective rather than subjective delivery, and non-emotional information are presented in a formal manner.

DESCRIPTIVE WRITING centers on a person, place, or object, using concrete and sensory words to create a mood or impression and arranging details in a chronological or spatial sequence.

NARRATIVE WRITING is developed using an incident or anecdote or a related series of events. Chronology, answers to the five W's (who, what, when, where, why), a topic sentence, and a conclusion are essential ingredients.

PERSUASIVE WRITING implies the writer's ability to select vocabulary and arrange facts and opinions in such a way as to direct the actions of the listener or reader. Persuasive writing may incorporate exposition and narration when they illustrate the main idea.

JOURNALISTIC WRITING is theoretically free of writer bias. When relaying information about an event, a person, or a thing, facts and objectivity are essential in journalistic writing.

Sample Test Questions and Rationale

DIRECTIONS: The passage below contains many errors. Read the passage. Then answer each test item by choosing the option that corrects an error in the underlined portion(s). One of the underlined choices will be an error or there will be no errors. If no errors exist, choose "D. No change is necessary."

Climbing to the top of Mount Everest is an adventure. One which everyone—whether physically fit or not—seems eager to try. The trail stretches for miles, the cold temperatures are usually frigid and brutal.

Climbers must endure severel barriers on the way, including other hikers, steep jagged rocks, and lots of snow. Plus, climbers often find the most grueling part of the trip is their climb back down, just when they are feeling exhausted.

Climbers who take precautions are likely to find the ascent less arduous than the unprepared. By donning heavy flannel shirts, gloves, and hats, climbers prevented hypothermia, as well as simple frostbite. A pair of rugged boots is also one of the necesities. If climbers are to avoid becoming dehydrated, there is beverages available for them to transport as well.

Once climbers are completely ready to begin their lengthy journey, they can comfortable enjoy the wonderful scenery. Wide rock formations dazzle the observers eyes with shades of gray and white, while the peak forms a triangle that seems to touch the sky. Each of the climbers are reminded of the splendor and magnificence of God's great Earth.

(Rigorous) (Skill 7.1)

1. Plus, climbers often find the most grueling part of the trip is <u>their</u> climb back <u>down,</u> just when they <u>are</u> feeling exhausted.

   A. his
   B. down; just
   C. were
   D. No change is necessary

   Answer is D.

   The present tense must be used consistently throughout, therefore Option C is incorrect. Option A is incorrect because the singular pronoun *his* does not agree with the plural antecedent *climbers*. Option B is incorrect because a comma, not a semicolon, is needed to separate the dependent clause from the main clause.

(Average) (Skill 7.1)

2. By donning heavy flannel shirts, gloves, and <u>hats, climbers prevented</u> hypothermia, as well as simple frostbite.

   A. hats climbers
   B. can prevent
   C. hypothermia;
   D. No change is necessary

   Answer is B.

   The verb *prevented* is in the past tense and must be changed to the present *can prevent* to be consistent. Option A is incorrect because a comma is needed after a long introductory phrase. Option C is incorrect because the semicolon creates a fragment of the phrase *as well as simple frostbite*.

WRITING

Sample Test Questions and Rationale (cont.)

(Easy) (Skill 7.1)

3. If climbers are to avoid <u>becoming</u> dehydrated, there <u>is</u> beverages available for <u>them</u> to transport as well.

   A. becomming
   B. are
   C. him
   D. No change is necessary

   Answer is B.

   The plural verb *are* must be used with the plural subject *beverages*. Option A is incorrect because *becoming* has only one *m*. Option C is incorrect because the plural pronoun *them* is needed to agree with the referent *climbers*.

(Easy) (Skill 7.1)

4. Once climbers are completely ready to begin <u>their</u> lengthy <u>journey, they</u> can <u>comfortable</u> enjoy the wonderful scenery.

   A. they're
   B. journey; they
   C. comfortably
   D. No change is necessary

   Answer C.

   The adverb form *comfortably* is needed to modify the verb phrase *can enjoy*. Option A is incorrect because the possessive plural pronoun is spelled *their*. Option B is incorrect because a semicolon would make the first half of the item seem like an independent clause when the subordinating conjunction *once* makes that clause dependent.

(Rigorous) (Skill 7.1)

5. Wide rock formations dazzle the <u>observers eyes</u> with shades of gray and <u>white, while</u> the peak <u>forms</u> a triangle that seems to touch the sky.

   A. observers' eyes
   B. white; while
   C. formed
   D. No change is necessary

   Answer is A.

   An apostrophe is needed to show the plural possessive form *observers' eyes*. Option B is incorrect because the semicolon would make the second half of the item seem like an independent clause when the subordinating conjunction *while* makes that clause dependent. Option C is incorrect because *formed* is in the wrong tense.

(Average) (Skill 7.1)

6. Each of the climbers <u>are</u> reminded of the splendor and <u>magnificence</u> of <u>God's</u> great Earth.

   A. is
   B. magnifisence
   C. Gods
   D. No change is necessary

   Answer is A.

   The singular verb *is* agrees with the singular subject *each*. Option B is incorrect because *magnificence* is misspelled. Option C is incorrect because an apostrophe is needed to show possession.

Sample Test Questions and Rationale (cont.)

(Easy) (Skill 7.2)

7. <u>Climbers who</u> take precautions are likely to find the ascent <u>less difficult than</u> the unprepared.

   A. Climbers, who
   B. least difficult
   C. then
   D. No change is necessary

Answer is D.

No change is needed. Option A is incorrect because a comma would make the phrase *who take precautions* seem less restrictive or less essential to the sentence. Option B is incorrect because *less* is appropriate when two items—the prepared and the unprepared—are compared. Option C is incorrect because the comparative adverb *than*, not *then*, is needed.

(Rigorous) (Skill 7.3)

8. Climbing to the top of Mount Everest is an <u>adventure. One</u> which everyone<u>—whether</u> physically fit or not—<u>seems</u> eager to try.

   A. adventure, one
   B. people, whether
   C. seem
   D. No change is necessary

Answer is A.

A comma is needed between *adventure* and *one* to avoid creating a fragment of the second part. In Option B, a comma after *everyone* would not be appropriate when the dash is used on the other side of *not*. In Option C, the singular verb seems is needed to agree with the singular subject *everyone*.

(Average) (Skill 7.3)

9. The <u>trail</u> stretches for <u>miles</u>, the cold temperatures are <u>usually</u> frigid and brutal.

   A. trails
   B. miles;
   C. usual
   D. No change is necessary

Answer is B.

A semicolon, not a comma, is needed to separate the first independent clause from the second independent clause. Option A is incorrect because the plural subject *trails* needs the singular verb *stretch*. Option C is incorrect because the adverb form *usually* is needed to modify the adjective *frigid*.

(Average) (Skill 7.6)

10. Climbers must endure <u>severel</u> barriers <u>on the way, including</u> other <u>hikers</u>, steep jagged rocks, and lots of snow.

    A. several
    B. on the way: including
    C. hikers'
    D. No change is necessary

Answer is A.

The word *several* is misspelled in the text. Option B is incorrect because a comma, not a colon, is needed to set off the modifying phrase. Option C is incorrect because no apostrophe is needed after *hikers* since possession is not involved.

Sample Test Questions and Rationale (cont.)

(Easy) (Skill 7.6)

11. A pair of rugged boots <u>is also one</u> of the <u>necesities</u>.

    A. are

    B. also, one

    C. necessities

    D. No change is necessary

Answer is C.

The word *necessities* is misspelled in the text. Option A is incorrect because the singular verb *is* must agree with the singular noun *pair* (a collective singular). Option B is incorrect because if *also* is set off with commas (potential correction), it should be set off on both sides.

DIRECTIONS: The passage below contains several errors. Read the passage. Then answer each test item by choosing the option that corrects an error in the underlined portion(s). No more than one underlined error will appear in each item. If no error exists, choose "D. No change is necessary."

Every job places different kinds of demands on their employees. For example, whereas such jobs as accounting and bookkeeping require mathematical ability; graphic design requires creative/artistic ability.

Doing good at one job does not usually guarantee success at another. However, one of the elements crucial to all jobs are especially notable: the chance to accomplish a goal.

The accomplishment of the employees varies according to the job. In many jobs the employees become accustom to the accomplishment provided by the work they do every day.

In medicine, for example, doctors tests them selves by treating badly injured or critically ill people. In the operating room, a team of Surgeons, is responsible for operating on many of these patients. In addition to the feeling of accomplishment that the workers achieve, some jobs also give a sense of identity to the employees'. Profesions like law, education, and sales offer huge financial and emotional rewards. Politicians are public servants: who work for the federal and state governments. President bush is basically employed by the American people to make laws and run the country.

Finally; the contributions that employees make to their companies and to the world cannot be taken for granted.

Sample Test Questions and Rationale (cont.)

(Average) (Skill 7.1)

12. Every job places different kinds of demands on their employees.

    A. place
    B. its
    C. employes
    D. No change is necessary

Answer is B.

The singular possessive pronoun *its* must agree with its antecedent *job*, which is singular also. Option A is incorrect because *place* is a plural form and the subject, *job*, is singular. Option C is incorrect because the correct spelling of *employees* is given in the sentence.

(Average) (Skill 7.1)

13. However, one of the elements crucial to all jobs are especially notable: the chance to accomplish of a goal.

    A. However
    B. is
    C. notable;
    D. No change is necessary

Answer is B.

The singular verb *is* is needed to agree with the singular subject *one*. Option A is incorrect because a comma is needed to set off the transitional word *however*. Option C is incorrect because a colon, not a semicolon, is needed to set off an item.

(Average) (Skill 7.1)

14. The accomplishment of the employees varies according to the job.

    A. accomplishment,
    B. employee's
    C. vary
    D. No change is necessary

Answer is C.

The singular verb *vary* is needed to agree with the singular subject *accomplishment*. Option A is incorrect because a comma after *accomplishment* would suggest that the modifying phrase of the employees is additional instead of essential. Option B is incorrect because *employees* is not possessive.

(Easy) (Skill 7.1)

15. In many jobs the employees become accustom to the accomplishment provided by the work they do every day.

    A. became
    B. accustomed
    C. provides
    D. No change is necessary

Answer is B.

The past participle *accustomed* is needed with the verb *become*. Option A is incorrect because the verb tense does not need to change to the past *became*. Option C is incorrect because *provides* is the wrong tense.

WRITING

Sample Test Questions and Rationale (cont.)

(Rigorous) (Skill 7.1)

16. In medicine, for example, doctors <u>test</u> <u>them selves</u> by treating badly injured or <u>critical</u>ly ill people.

    A. tests
    B. themselves
    C. critical
    D. No change is necessary

    Answer is B.

    The reflexive pronoun *themselves* is needed. (Themselves is nonstandard and never correct.) Option A is incorrect because the plural verb *test* is needed to agree with the plural subject *doctors*. Option C is incorrect because the adverb *critically* is needed to modify the verb *ill*.

(Average) (Skill 7.3)

17. <u>For example</u>, <u>whereas</u> such jobs as accounting and bookkeeping require mathematical <u>ability</u>; graphic design requires creative/artistic ability.

    A. For example
    B. whereas,
    C. ability,
    D. No change is necessary

    Answer is C.

    An introductory dependent clause is set off with a comma, not a semicolon. Option A is incorrect because the transitional phrase *for example* should be set off with a comma. Option B is incorrect because the adverb *whereas* functions like *while* and does not take a comma after it.

(Rigorous) (Skill 7.3)

18. In the <u>operating room</u>, a team of <u>Surgeons, is</u> responsible for operating on many of <u>these</u> patients.

    A. operating room:
    B. surgeons is
    C. those
    D. No change is necessary

    Answer is B.

    Surgeons is not a proper name so it does not need to be capitalized. A comma is not needed to break up *a team of surgeons* from the rest of the sentence. Option A is incorrect because a comma, not a colon, is needed to set off an item. Option C is incorrect because *those* is an incorrect pronoun.

(Average) (Skill 7.3)

19. Politicians <u>are</u> public <u>servants: who</u> <u>work</u> for the federal and state governments.

    A. were
    B. servants who
    C. worked
    D. No change is necessary

    Answer is B.

    A colon is not needed to set off the introduction of the sentence. In Option A, *were* is the incorrect tense of the verb. In Option C, *worked* is in the wrong tense.

Sample Test Questions and Rationale (cont.)

(Easy) (Skill 7.3)

20. President <u>bush</u> is basically employed <u>by</u> the American people to <u>make</u> laws and run the country.

    A. Bush
    B. to
    C. made
    D. No change is necessary

Answer is A.

Bush is a proper name and should be capitalized. Option B, *to*, does not fit with the verb *employed*. Option C uses the wrong form of the verb *make*.

(Rigorous) (Skill 7.3)

21. <u>Finally;</u> the contributions that employees make to <u>their</u> companies and to the world cannot be <u>taken</u> for granted.

    A. Finally,
    B. their
    C. took
    D. No change is necessary

Answer is A.

A comma is needed to separate *Finally* from the rest of the sentence. *Finally* is a preposition which usually heads a dependent sentence, hence a comma is needed. Option B is incorrect because *their* is misspelled. Option C is incorrect because *took* is the wrong form of the verb.

(Rigorous) (Skill 7.5)

22. Doing <u>good</u> at one job does not <u>usually</u> guarantee <u>success</u> at another.

    A. well
    B. usualy
    C. succeeding
    D. No change is necessary

Answer is A.

The adverb *well* modifies the word *doing*. Option B is incorrect because *usually* is spelled correctly in the sentence. Option C is incorrect because *succeeding* is in the wrong tense.

(Rigorous) (Skill 7.6)

23. In addition to the feeling of accomplishment that the workers <u>achieve</u>, some jobs also <u>give</u> a sense of identity to the <u>employees'</u>.

    A. acheive
    B. gave
    C. employees
    D. No change is necessary

Answer is C.

Option C is correct because *employees* is not possessive. Option A is incorrect because *achieve* is spelled correctly in the sentence. Option B is incorrect because *gave* is the wrong tense.

WRITING

Sample Test Questions and Rationale

(Rigorous) (Skill 7.6)

24. <u>Profesions</u> like law, <u>education</u>, and sales <u>offer</u> huge financial and emotional rewards.

    A. Professions
    B. education;
    C. offered
    D. No change is necessary

Answer is A.

Option A is correct because *professions* is misspelled in the sentence. Option B is incorrect because a comma, not a semicolon, is needed after *education*. In Option C, *offered* is in the wrong tense.

SAMPLE TEST
WRITING

DIRECTIONS: The passage below contains many errors. Read the passage. Then answer each test item by choosing the option that corrects an error in the underlined portion(s). One of the underlined choices will be an error or there will be no errors. If no errors exist, choose "D. No change is necessary."

Climbing to the top of Mount Everest is an adventure. One which everyone—whether physically fit or not—seems eager to try. The trail stretches for miles, the cold temperatures are usually frigid and brutal.

Climbers must endure severel barriers on the way, including other hikers, steep jagged rocks, and lots of snow. Plus, climbers often find the most grueling part of the trip is their climb back down, just when they are feeling exhausted.

Climbers who take precautions are likely to find the ascent less arduous than the unprepared. By donning heavy flannel shirts, gloves, and hats, climbers prevented hypothermia, as well as simple frostbite. A pair of rugged boots is also one of the necesities. If climbers are to avoid becoming dehydrated, there is beverages available for them to transport as well.

Once climbers are completely ready to begin their lengthy journey, they can comfortable enjoy the wonderful scenery. Wide rock formations dazzle the observers eyes with shades of gray and white, while the peak forms a triangle that seems to touch the sky. Each of the climbers are reminded of the splendor and magnificence of God's great Earth.

(Rigorous) (Skill 7.1)
1. Plus, climbers often find the most grueling part of the trip is <u>their</u> climb back <u>down</u>, just when they <u>are</u> feeling exhausted.
   A. his
   B. down; just
   C. were
   D. No change is necessary

(Average) (Skill 7.1)
2. By donning heavy flannel shirts, gloves, and <u>hats, climbers prevented</u> hypothermia, as well as simple frostbite.
   A. hats climbers
   B. can prevent
   C. hypothermia;
   D. No change is necessary

(Easy) (Skill 7.1)
3. If climbers are to avoid <u>becoming</u> dehydrated, there <u>is</u> beverages available for <u>them</u> to transport as well.
   A. becomming
   B. are
   C. him
   D. No change is necessary

(Easy) (Skill 7.1)

4. Once climbers are completely ready to begin their lengthy journey, they can comfortable enjoy the wonderful scenery.

    A. they're
    B. journey; they
    C. comfortably
    D. No change is necessary

(Rigorous) (Skill 7.1)

5. Wide rock formations dazzle the observers eyes with shades of gray and white, while the peak forms a triangle that seems to touch the sky.

    A. observers' eyes
    B. white; while
    C. formed
    D. No change is necessary

(Average) (Skill 7.1)

6. Each of the climbers are reminded of the splendor and magnificence of God's great Earth.

    A. is
    B. magnifisence
    C. Gods
    D. No change is necessary

(Easy) (Skill 7.2)

7. Climbers who take precautions are likely to find the ascent less difficult than the unprepared.

    A. Climbers, who
    B. least difficult
    C. then
    D. No change is necessary

(Rigorous) (Skill 7.3)

8. Climbing to the top of Mount Everest is an adventure. One which everyone—whether physically fit or not—seems eager to try.

    A. adventure, one
    B. people, whether
    C. seem
    D. No change is necessary

(Average) (Skill 7.3)

9. The trail stretches for miles, the cold temperatures are usually frigid and brutal.

    A. trails
    B. miles;
    C. usual
    D. No change is necessary

(Average) (Skill 7.6)

10. Climbers must endure severel barriers on the way, including other hikers, steep jagged rocks, and lots of snow.

    A. several
    B. on the way: including
    C. hikers'
    D. No change is necessary

(Easy) (Skill 7.6)

11. A pair of rugged boots is also one of the necesities.

    A. are
    B. also, one
    C. necessities
    D. No change is necessary

DIRECTIONS: The passage below contains several errors. Read the passage. Then answer each test item by choosing the option that corrects an error in the underlined portion(s). No more than one underlined error will appear in each item. If no error exists, choose "D. No change is necessary."

Every job places different kinds of demands on their employees. For example, whereas such jobs as accounting and bookkeeping require mathematical ability; graphic design requires creative/artistic ability.

Doing good at one job does not usually guarantee success at another. However, one of the elements crucial to all jobs are especially notable: the chance to accomplish a goal.

The accomplishment of the employees varies according to the job. In many jobs the employees become accustom to the accomplishment provided by the work they do every day.

In medicine, for example, doctors tests them selves by treating badly injured or critically ill people. In the operating room, a team of Surgeons, is responsible for operating on many of these patients. In addition to the feeling of accomplishment that the workers achieve, some jobs also give a sense of identity to the employees'. Profesions like law, education, and sales offer huge financial and emotional rewards. Politicians are public servants: who work for the federal and state governments. President bush is basically employed by the American people to make laws and run the country.

Finally; the contributions that employees make to their companies and to the world cannot be taken for granted.

(Average) (Skill 7.1)
12. Every job <u>places</u> different kinds of demands on <u>their employees</u>.
    A. place
    B. its
    C. employes
    D. No change is necessary

(Average) (Skill 7.1)
13. <u>However, one of the elements crucial to all jobs</u> <u>are</u> especially <u>notable</u>: the chance to accomplish of a goal.
    A. However
    B. is
    C. notable;
    D. No change is necessary

(Average) (Skill 7.1)
14. The <u>accomplishment</u> of the <u>employees</u> <u>varies</u> according to the job.
    A. accomplishment,
    B. employee's
    C. vary
    D. No change is necessary

(Easy) (Skill 7.1)
15. In many jobs the employees <u>become accustom</u> to the accomplishment <u>provided</u> by the work they do every day.
    A. became
    B. accustomed
    C. provides
    D. No change is necessary

(Rigorous) (Skill 7.1)
16. In medicine, for example, doctors <u>test them selves</u> by treating badly injured or <u>critically</u> ill people.

    A. tests
    B. themselves
    C. critical
    D. No change is necessary

(Average) (Skill 7.3)
17. <u>For example</u>, <u>whereas</u> such jobs as accounting and bookkeeping require mathematical <u>ability</u>; graphic design requires creative/artistic ability.

    A. For example
    B. whereas,
    C. ability,
    D. No change is necessary

(Rigorous) (Skill 7.3)
18. In the <u>operating room</u>, a team of <u>Surgeons, is</u> responsible for operating on many of <u>these</u> patients.

    A. operating room:
    B. surgeons is
    C. those
    D. No change is necessary

(Average) (Skill 7.3)
19. Politicians <u>are</u> public <u>servants: who</u> <u>work</u> for the federal and state governments.

    A. were
    B. servants who
    C. worked
    D. No change is necessary

(Easy) (Skill 7.3)
20. President bush is basically employed <u>by</u> the American people to <u>make</u> laws and run the country.

    A. Bush
    B. to
    C. made
    D. No change is necessary

(Rigorous) (Skill 7.3)
21. <u>Finally;</u> the contributions that employees make to <u>their</u> companies and to the world cannot be <u>taken</u> for granted.

    A. Finally,
    B. their
    C. took
    D. No change is necessary

(Rigorous) (Skill 7.5)
22. Doing <u>good</u> at one job does not <u>usually</u> guarantee <u>success</u> at another.

    A. well
    B. usualy
    C. succeeding
    D. No change is necessary

(Rigorous) (Skill 7.6)
23. In addition to the feeling of accomplishment that the workers <u>achieve</u>, some jobs also <u>give</u> a sense of identity to the <u>employees'</u>.

    A. acheive
    B. gave
    C. employees
    D. No change is necessary

(Rigorous) (Skill 7.6)

24. <u>Profesions</u> like law, <u>education</u>, and sales <u>offer</u> huge financial and emotional rewards.

    A. Professions
    B. education;
    C. offered
    D. No change is necessary

DIRECTIONS: For the underlined sentence(s), choose the option that expresses the meaning with the most fluency and the clearest logic within the context. If the underlined sentence should not be changed, choose Option A.

(Rigorous) (Skill 8.4)

25. Selecting members of a President's cabinet can often be an aggravating process. <u>Either there are too many or too few qualified candidates for a certain position, and then they have to be confirmed by the Senate, where there is the possibility of rejection.</u>

    A. No change
    B. Qualified candidates for certain positions face the possibility of rejection, when they have to be confirmed by the Senate
    C. The Senate has to confirm qualified candidates, who face the possibility of rejection
    D. Because the Senate has to confirm qualified candidates; they face the possibility of rejection

(Rigorous) (Skill 8.4)

26. Treating patients for drug and/or alcohol abuse is a difficult process. <u>Even though there are a number of different methods for helping the patient overcome a dependency, there is no way of knowing which is best in the long-run.</u>

    A. No change
    B. Even though different methods can help a patient overcome a dependency, there is no way to know which is best in the long-run
    C. Even though there is no way to know which way is best in the long run, patients can overcome their dependencies when they are helped
    D. There is no way to know which method will help the patient overcome a dependency in the long run, even though there are many different ones.

(Rigorous) (Skill 8.4)

27. Many factors account for the decline in quality of public education. <u>Overcrowding, budget cutbacks, and societal deterioration which have greatly affected student learning.</u>

    A. No change
    B. Student learning has been greatly affected by overcrowding, budget cutbacks, and societal deterioration
    C. Due to overcrowding, budget cutbacks, and societal deterioration, student learning has been greatly affected
    D. Overcrowding, budget cutbacks, and societal deterioration have affected student learning greatly

DIRECTIONS: Choose the sentence that logically and correctly expresses the comparison.

(Average) (Skill 8.4)

28. A. The Empire State Building in New York is taller than buildings in the city

    B. The Empire State Building in New York is taller than any other building in the city

    C. The Empire State Building in New York is tallest than other buildings in the city

(Average) (Skill 8.4)

29. Many of the clubs in Boca Raton are noted for their _____ elegance.

    A. vulgar

    B. tasteful

    C. ordinary

(Average) (Skill 8.4)

30. When a student is expelled from school, the parents are usually _____ in advance.

    A. rewarded

    B. congratulated

    C. notified

Answer Key

1. D	11. C	21. A
2. B	12. B	22. A
3. B	13. B	23. C
4. C	14. C	24. A
5. A	15. B	25. C
6. A	16. B	26. B
7. D	17. C	27. B
8. A	18. B	28. B
9. B	19. B	29. B
10. A	20. A	30. C

Rigor Table

	Easy %20	Average Rigor %40	Rigorous %40
Question	3, 4, 7, 11, 15, 20	2, 6, 9, 10, 12, 13, 14, 17, 19, 28, 29, 30	1, 5, 8, 16, 18, 21, 22, 23, 24, 25, 26, 27

PRAXIS

XAMonline publishes study guides for the PRAXIS I & II teacher certification examinations.

Titles Include:
- PRAXIS Art Sample Test
- PRAXIS Biology
- PRAXIS Chemistry
- PRAXIS Earth and Space Sciences
- PRAXIS Special Education Knowledge-Based Core Principles
- PRAXIS Special Education Teaching Students with Behavioral Disorders/Emotional Disturbance
- PRAXIS Early Childhood/Education of Young Children
- PRAXIS Educational Leadership
- PRAXIS Elementary Education
- PRAXIS English Language, Literature and Composition
- PRAXIS Sample Test
- PRAXIS Fundamental Subjects
- PRAXIS School Guidance and Counseling
- PRAXIS General Science
- PRAXIS Library Media Specialist
- PRAXIS Mathematics
- PRAXIS Middle School English Language Arts
- PRAXIS Middle School Mathematics
- PRAXIS Middle School Social Studies
- PRAXIS Physical Education
- PRAXIS Physics
- PRAXIS Para-Professional Assessment
- PRAXIS PPST-1 Basic Skills
- PRAXIS Government/Political Science
- PRAXIS Principles of Learning and Teaching
- PRAXIS Reading
- PRAXIS Social Studies
- PRAXIS Spanish

PASS the FIRST TIME with an XAMonline study guide!

Call or visit us online!
1.800.301.4647
www.XAMonline.com

Thinking of becoming a teacher?

XAMonline.com can help

PASS THE FIRST TIME with an XAMonline study guide!

- Over 15 years' publishing experience
- 300+ study guides
- eBooks
- Praxis I & II
- All state-specific study guides
- Content aligned and focused
- Up-to-date content
- Print-on-Demand technology
- Additional resources: test dates, study & test-taking tips!

www.XAMonline.com

FREE sample test e-mail: freetest@XAMonline.com

XAMonline.com

Teacher Certification Study Guides
1-800-301-4647

PASS THE FIRST TIME

with over 300 titles!

- PRAXIS
- NYSTCE
- TExES
- MTEL
- FTCE
- PLACE
- CEOE
- ICTS
- GACE
- MTTC
- AEPA
- WEST
- ORELA
- VCLA
- CSET
- NMTA

Call or visit us online!
1.800.301.4647
www.XAMonline.com

www.ingramcontent.com/pod-product-compliance
Lightning Source LLC
Chambersburg PA
CBHW081214230426
43666CB00015B/2723